About The Author

Beatrice P. Patt holds the B.A. degree from Hunter College and the M.A. and Ph.D. degrees from Bryn Mawr College. She has taught at the latter institution and at Smith College, and is presently Professor of Romance Languages at Queens College of the City University of New York, where she teaches courses in contemporary Spanish Literature. Professor Patt has co-authored *The Generation of 1898 and After, Spanish Literature: 1700-1900, Retratos de Hispanoamérica,* and has contributed to *European Authors 1000–1900.* She has also contributed to the *Hispanic Review* and some of her translations have appeared in *Great Spanish Stories* and *Anthology of Medieval Lyrics.* Professor Patt's fields of interest include the medieval Spanish theatre as well as modern non–Spanish literature, and she has delivered a series of lectures on European literature from Dante to Camus over New York City's radio station WNYC.

PÍO BAROJA

By

BEATRICE P. PATT

Despite a spate of studies on various aspects of Baroja and his works, none so far has been designed primarily for the English-speaking reader interested in grasping the essentials of his thought and art. As the dean of twentieth—century Spanish novelists, Baroja has inevitably attracted wide attention, both favorable and unfavorable, and the labels that have gradually adhered to him have become increasingly difficult to put aside. A fresh look, totally unaffected by all that has been said and written about Baroja is not entirely possible for a critic who lives in the world, but this study is an attempt in the direction of a relatively objective appraisal of the novelist as he is in the process of weaving a dense web of plots and characters and at the same time issuing judgments on an impressive array of subjects, human and divine. A misanthropic humorist, Baroja was a master of sleight of hand, professing to espouse theories which he then frequently contradicted in practise. The signposts erected by the author mislead and confound, and while one of the purposes of this study has been to determine the nature of the quintessential "Barojian" novel, another has been to surprise the novelist in the act of often disagreeing with himself. By means of a predominantly chronological scheme, Baroja's art is traced from innovation to self-imitation, from an attitude of strident criticism to one of melancholy near-acceptance, with emphasis on the gap that separated his pronouncements on sincerity and morality from his intimate practise of a philosophy of convenience.

ERIES

re

y

y

Pío Baroja

By BEATRICE P. PATT

Collection Viollet

PÍO BAROJA

For my husband and daughters, who have enriched
my life immeasurably.

Preface

The enormous and protean literary production of Pío Baroja has been far from neglected in Spain and in other Spanish-speaking countries, but, with the exception of doctoral theses, there have been no critical studies in English. The ideal study, a complete analysis of all the novels and all the essays, still lies in the future, however, for this work has no such pretensions. Within the limits of the allowable space an attempt has been made to take into account the major novels and some of the important essays, but omissions have been unavoidable. Then too the veritable tangle of Baroja's themes and ideas makes it difficult to pick one's way, and at times the writer is tempted into despair at the seeming impossibility of finding the thread that will lead out of the labyrinth. The question of selection and emphasis is inevitably open to debate, and the ultimate choice is up to the critic who must make his decisions with some diffidence.

The method that informs this study is both synthetic and analytical, with the aim of providing first an overview, then a dissection of the most significant works. The order of Chapters 5 and 6 is predominantly although not strictly chronological, for the purpose of giving some indication of Baroja's development over a period of the more than half-century that constituted his literary life. This step-by-step analysis is not of the sort customarily encountered in studies of Baroja, but it has seemed to this author a worthwhile procedure; whether or not it is ultimately justified by the conclusions is another matter.

Although the *Obras Completas* have been utilized as the most convenient and accessible source of the bulk of Baroja's works, the reader must be warned at the outset that the order of the eight volumes that comprise the complete works is capricious to the point of irrationality; the Chronology which precedes the first chapter of this study will help to counteract the possible effects of a perusal of the table of contents of the *Obras*. The customary grouping of many of the novels into trilogies has been followed only when logic dictated such a procedure; in the case of seemingly arbitrary grouping, the designation has been abandoned. The underlying purpose of this study is not so much to classify as to clarify.

For the most part quotations from Baroja have been rendered only in English, and the translations are my own. With the titles of novels and major essays, however, the method has been somewhat different: where a work is known in English through an existing translation, the title by which it has become familiar is used. In the case of works which have not been translated into English, a rather close and literal, though not necessarily literary, translation is supplied. Deviations from this practice occur only when a literal translation would fail to convey the true meaning of the title.

The numerous and indispensable works of reference that were consulted have not been quoted extensively, not because it would not have been worthwhile to do so, but because the length of this work would have been greatly increased thereby; such debts are acknowledged in the Notes and in the Bibliography. The greatest debt of all is to Pío Baroja himself, for it is almost exclusively on his works that this study is based. The hazards of such reliance on the essays, lectures, and novels are of course inestimable; in a thick forest it is not always possible to distinguish between the living shoots and the dead branches.

A near-myth toward the end of his life, Baroja inspired both openly adulatory studies as well as bitterly hostile criticism. Idolators and detractors continue to come forth, each one grounded by intent on the author's written and spoken word. Baroja did not win the Nobel Prize for literature, a slight lamented by many, but his figure still retains its capacity to intrigue, to puzzle, to infuriate and to entertain; to speak of the twentieth-century Spanish novel is to speak, inevitably, of the Basque Pío Baroja.

Queens College of the　　　　　　BEATRICE P. PATT
City University of New York

Contents

Chronology

Chronology

1912   Purchases house "Itzea" in Vera del Bidasoa. Death of father Don Serafín. Publishes *El mundo es ansí* (*The Way of the World*).

1913–   Publishes first volumes of *Las memorias de un hombre de*
1916   *acción* (*Memoirs of a Man of Action*): *El aprendiz de conspirador* (*The Apprentice Conspirator*), *El escuadrón del Brigante* (*The Brigand's Squadron*) in 1913; *Con la pluma y con el sable* (*With Pen and Sword*), *Los recursos de la astucia* (*The Resources of Cunning*) in 1915; *La ruta del aventurero* (*The Route of the Adventurer*), 1916.

1917   Publishes collections of essays *Nuevo tablado de Arlequín* (*New Harlequinade*), *Juventud, egolatría* (*Youth, Egolatry*).

1918   Runs for Congress. *Páginas escogidas* (*Selected Pages*) published. Two more volumes in Aviraneta series appear: *La veleta de Gastizar* (*The Weathervane of Gastizar*), *Los caudillos de 1830* (*The Chieftains of 1830*). Publishes essays *Las horas solitarias* (*Solitary Hours*).

1919   Publishes essays *Momentum catastrophicum* (*Time of Crisis*), *La caverna del humorismo* (*The Grotto of Humor*).

1920   *Los contrastes de la vida* (*The Contrasts of Fortune*) and *La sensualidad pervertida* (*Sublimated Sensuality*) appear.

1921   Publishes *El sabor de la venganza* (*The Taste of Vengeance*), *Las furias* (*The Furies*).

1922   *La leyenda de Jaun de Alzate* (*The Legend of Jaun de Alzate*), *El amor, el dandismo y la intriga* (*Love, Dandyism and Intrigue*) appear.

1923   *El laberinto de las sirenas* (*The Labyrinth of the Sirens*) published.

1924   Publishes *Las figuras de cera* (*The Wax Figures*), essays *Divagaciones apasionadas* (*Passionate Divagations*).

1925   *La nave de los locos* (*The Ship of Fools*) published.

1926   Travels to Germany, Holland, Denmark, England, France. Publishes first two volumes of *Agonías de nuestro tiempo* (*Agonies of our Time*) trilogy: *El gran torbellino del mundo* (*The Great Whirlwind of Life*), *Las veleidades de la fortuna* (*The Caprices of Fortune*).

1927   Publishes *El nocturno del hermano Beltrán* (*Friar Beltrán's Nocturne*), *Los amores tardíos* (*Late Loves*), *Las mascaradas sangrientas* (*Blood-Stained Masquerades*).

1928   *Humano enigma* (*A Human Enigma*), *La senda dolorosa* (*The Thorny Path*) published.

1929   Publishes *Los pilotos de altura* (*The Celestial Navigators*).

1930   *La estrella del Capitán Chimista* (*Captain Chimista's Star*), *Los confidentes audaces* (*The Daring Secret Agents*) appear.

1931   Publishes essays *Intermedios* (*Intermezzi*) and biography *Aviraneta, o la vida de un conspirador* (*Aviraneta, or the Life of a Conspirator*). Second Republic proclaimed.

1932   *La selva oscura* (*The Dark Wood*) trilogy appears: *La familia de Errotacho* (*The Family of Errotacho*), *El cabo de las tormentas* (*The Cape of Storms*), *Los visionarios* (*The Visionaries*).

1934   *Las noches del Buen Retiro* (*Nights in the Gardens of the Retiro*) published. June 7: Baroja elected to the Real Academia española.

1935   May 12: Reads acceptance address "La formación psicológica de un escritor" ("The psychological background of a writer"). Publishes essays *Vitrina pintoresca* (*Picturesque Showcase*) and last volumes of Aviraneta series.

1936   Civil War breaks out. Baroja leaves Spain, establishes residence in the Cité Universitaire in Paris. Publishes *El cura de Monleón* (*The Curate of Monleón*), essays *Rapsodias* (*Rhapsodies*).

1937-   In Paris. Visits Paul Schmitz in Basle, returns to Vera during
1939   1937. Publishes *Laura*, essays *Ayer y hoy* (*Yesterday and Today*), 1939.

1940   June 24: Returns to Spain, establishes residence in Madrid.

1941   Begins *Memorias* (*Memoirs*) entitled *Desde la última vuelta del camino* (*From the Last Bend in the Road*).

1943   Publishes *El caballero de Erlaiz* (*D. Adrián de Erlaiz*).

1944-   Publishes collection of poems *Canciones del suburbio* (*Songs*
1949   *from the Outskirts*), 1944, and *El hotel del Cisne* (*Swan Hotel*), 1946. Completes memoirs.

1950   *El cantor vagabundo* (*The Wandering Singer*) published.

1952   *Las veladas del Chalet Gris* (*Evenings in the Hotel Gris*) appears.

1953   Publishes guide to Basque region, *El país vasco* (*The Basque Country*), and *Los amores de Antonio y Cristina* (*The Loves of Antonio and Christina*).

1955   Essays *Paseos de un solitario* (*Strolls of a Solitary Man*) published. *Memorias* appears in single-volume edition.

1956   October 30: Pío Baroja dies in Madrid, and is buried in the Civil Cemetery.

CHAPTER 1

The Making of a Writer

I *The Generation of 1898*

THE defeat of Spain by the United States in 1898 marked the destruction of the last vestiges of what once had been a mighty Empire, but it marked as well the emergence of a group of writers possessed of a highly critical spirit, acutely aware of the Spanish situation, and passionately eager to reveal and to analyze the spiritual ailments and national weaknesses responsible for the defeat. The disaster of the Spanish-American war represented much more than a loss of colonies and a crushing blow to national vanity; it brought to the surface and held up for scrutiny the outmoded institutions, the corrupt political life, the deficient system of education, the hollowness of decades of complacency. Looking beyond the Pyrenees for enlightened European models to imitate, and within the confines of the Iberian penisula for lost threads of the authentic national tradition, the young writers of the so-called Generation of 1898 faced Janus-like into the future and into the past. Sensitive and thoughtful, such figures as Ganivet, Maeztu, Unamuno, Azorín, Antonio Machado, and Baroja brought to the height of refinement and intensity the critical attitudes already manifested by the Romantic essayist Larra, the regenerationist Costa, the scientist Ramón y Cajal, the novelist Galdós.

The upheavals of the nineteenth century—the War of Independence from 1808 to 1814, the Carlist Wars, the Revolution of 1868, the establishment and dissolution of the First Republic —culminated in the restoration of the Bourbon Monarchy in 1874, a restoration that brought in its wake a wave of groundless optimism and frivolity. If corruption was the guiding force in the nation's politics, grandiloquence and triviality characterized a significant portion of its literature. The men of the Generation of 1898 shared a desire to awaken and to renovate their country, to shake it from its torpor. Antidogmatic, ethical, intellectual, individualistic, they examined the problems of Spain and then, irresistibly subjective, looked inside themselves for a reflection of these problems.

11

The work of the Institución Libre de Enseñanza, founded by Francisco Giner de los Ríos and continued by Manuel Bartolomé Cossío, exerted a strong ethical and moral influence on the young writers who were considered part of the Generation. The Institución, which concerned itself primarily with pedagogical reform, was particularly sensitive to the intellectual and spiritual stagnation that was so lamentably evident in the Spain of the latter part of the nineteenth century. Highly critical of the present but full of hope for the future, the Institución derived its austere flavor in some part from the immediately preceding generation of *krausistas,* followers of the relatively obscure German philosopher Karl Christian Friedrich Krause. Julián Sanz del Río was the guiding spirit of these Spanish postkantians, all of whom had in common their belief in progress and their desire to take life seriously.[1] The *krausistas* left their mark on the disciples of Giner de los Ríos, who adopted as their ethic moral purity, freedom of thought, sincerity, dedication to speculation; the ascetic rather than the aesthetic ideal. That this spirit influenced Baroja to some extent is beyond doubt, despite his pejorative references to the *señoritos* (well brought-up young gentlemen) of the Institución.

The role of the new writers was to fulminate, to criticize, to shatter the foundations of an already crumbling edifice; it was left to subsequent generations to be compromised in an ideological struggle. With the mordant wit and irony that had served so many earlier Spanish writers as a powerful weapon, these philosophically-oriented essayists, novelists, and poets spared no institution, no national foible, no accepted convention. Hypocrisy and complacency were unceremoniously led down from the stage, and nothing was considered too sacred for examination. The invigorating breeze that swept over the Generation of 1898, sweeping with it the débris of nineteenth-century positivistic and materialistic thinking, stemmed in part from previous Spanish regenerationists, but also owed more than a little to Nietzsche, some of whose work, at first available in Spain only through French versions, became known in Spanish translation in 1900.[2]

At the turn of the century, Baroja, Azorín, and Maeztu uncharacteristically constituted themselves as a social action group designated as *los tres* (the three), the purpose of which was to bring about the regeneration of Spain by means of agrarian reform, reforestation, education, economic improvements, etc. They even went so far as to issue a manifesto in 1901, a proclamation so unmemorable to Azorín, at least, that when he was asked to provide details years later he admitted that he did not remember any.[3] That this association was short-lived and, ultimately, of no real consequence, is not surprising in light of the tendency of the members of the Generation of 1898 to substitute ratiocination and feeling for concrete action. Reformers in theory, introspection was their practice; instead of treatises, there are confessions. Speculation becomes an end in itself and the link between thought and action is placed in serious jeopardy. It is not in vain that the eponymous hero of *Antonio Azorín* suffers from *aboulia* or paralysis of the will, a paralysis brought about by the predominance of the critical spirit.

In *La Voluntad,* published in 1902, Azorín paints an early portrait of Pío Baroja in the person of Enrique Olaiz.[4] The latter, in a tone that owes more to Baroja than to Azorín, expresses on the one hand his disapproval of the hegemony of the masses, whether under the sign of socialism, dogmatic anarchism, or democracy, and on the other, his admiration for Larra who symbolized for him the romantic aspiration toward an ideal, so completely out of place in the century in which Olaiz, and by analogy Azorín, were obliged to live. Baroja-Olaiz is speaking here not only for himself but for his colleagues; an olympian scorn for the herd and a corresponding exaltation of the select man is as much the distinguishing mark of the intellectual of the twentieth century as it was the emblem of the early nineteenth-century Romantic. The sensibility of the Generation of 1898, often delicate and moved to lyricism, is also deeply aristocratic. The interest displayed in the *pueblo* (common people), essentially an historical one, constitutes the foundation for the search into the authentic Spanish tradition, its *intrahistoria* (infra-history). These *menudos hechos* or insignificant but infinitely repeated everyday occurrences become an object of investigation and interest, but the true subject is the author himself.

II *The Formative Years*

When presented with the problem of writing a succinct life of Baroja, the would-be biographer is immediately faced with an embarrassment of riches; rarely has an author written so insistently and so frequently of his personal experience. If a novel is indeed, as Lucien Goldmann states, both biography and social chronicle, Baroja is admirably qualified as a novelist on both counts. Baroja's novels, essays, short stories, memoirs, and even his poetry are of a piece, all forming part of a long confession extending over a period of more than fifty years, approximately coinciding with the first half of the twentieth century.

Pío Baroja was born in San Sebastián in 1872, on the Day of the Innocents, December 28. As the future author is careful to explain, he is seven-eighths Basque and one-eighth Lombard, the Italian portion having been contributed by the family of his mother, Doña Carmen Nessi y Goñi. Baroja, who was always very much aware of his ethnic background, notes in a letter written in 1905 that his Cantabrian names (Baroja, Zornoza, Alzate, Eizaguirre) have the ring of old iron, while his Italian names (Nessi, Griggioni) have a soft and sweet sound.[5] This contrast between the hard and the soft, between the intellectual and the sentimental, the realistic and the lyrical, is a characteristic not only of his family names but of his entire literary production. The father of the family, Don Serafín Baroja y Zornoza, a mining engineer with a good deal more fantasy than one ordinarily associates with so stolid a profession, lived on the fringes of bohemianism and counted among his friends such a turn-of-the-century virtuoso as Sarasate. His eldest son Ricardo, dandy, dilettante, painter, occasional writer and inventor, also supplied more than a touch of bohemianism. Don Serafín was a bit of a writer as well as a great reader, and it was in his father's library that Pío Baroja first became acquainted with the works of Dumas, Hugo, Balzac, Jules Verne, Captain Marryat, Montepin, and Sue, the last two writers exerting a long-lasting and not particularly beneficent influence on his novels throughout his career.

His father's profession and temperament demanded a certain degree of mobility and so, while the family moved to Madrid in 1879, they appeared two years later in Pamplona only to reappear in the capital in 1886. A year later Pío Baroja enrolled in the School of Medicine of the University of Madrid and finished his studies in Valencia in 1891. Two years later he read his thesis on *Pain, a Psychophysical Study,* and formally qualified for a post as physician, a position he was subsequently granted in Cestona, having been the only candidate to apply. Baroja had pursued his medical studies without enthusiasm and the year of actual practice in a small Basque town definitively removed whatever residual interest he may have had in continuing with a career in medicine. As a student, he had suffered at the hands of incompetent professors, and as a doctor he felt so ill-equipped that whenever he was forced to take specific measures in the treatment of a patient, he customarily attributed whatever success he may have had to good fortune. Despite their negative aspect, however, his medical experiences left a deep impression. An abiding if not wholly unqualified admiration for science and the scientific method persists in his works until his last years; the number of physicians appearing on the pages of his collected works has been estimated at more than two hundred.[6] For Baroja, at any rate, if literature was his wife, medicine was his mistress.

The early years in San Sebastián, Madrid, and Pamplona left their trace in quite a different way. The bombardment of San Sebastián by the Carlists was Baroja's earliest black memory, and he preserved from this experience a vague and confused recollection of soldiers on stretchers and a cemetery strewn with corpses still clothed in rotting uniforms.[7] The next reference, mentioned in *Juventud, egolatría* (*Youth, Egolatry*) is to the young Baroja's custom of watching funerals go by in front of his house on the Calle Real in Madrid.[8] In at least six different works written over a period of some twenty years, the author recreates a scene which had impressed him profoundly: Toribio Eguía, a condemned prisoner on his way to execution, passed in front of the Baroja house in Pamplona. Attracted and repelled, the half-willing witness went to look at the corpse, after which he found himself unable to erase the gruesome memory.[9] Also associated with Pamplona are the wax figures of criminals which were displayed during the Feast of San Fermín, figures which haunted Baroja and reappeared in *Las figuras de cera* (*The Wax Figures*), *Susana,* and *El hotel del Cisne* (*Swan Hotel*), this last published in 1946. A further note of gothicism was supplied in Madrid when the still-impressionable youth witnessed the execution of a woman and two men for a murder committed in the district called la Guindalera; there are no fewer than seven separate references to this execution,[10] the first dating from 1902 and the last from 1952. The crime of Fuencarral Street was equally immediate, for the author states that he spoke to the murderess, Higinia Balaguer, in a hospital corridor some time before witnessing her execution.[11]

If Stendhal, equally interested in shocking crimes, read the accounts of *causes célèbres* and, as in the case of *Le rouge et le noir,* put some of them to excellent use, Baroja's reaction to crime and its attendant retribution was more immediate and less literary. Although the images haunted him throughout his life he does not at any time seem to have been inspired to dedicate an entire novel to an imaginative recreation of any of these celebrated crimes.

In 1896, after a period spent in San Sebastián, Baroja went back to Madrid to take over from his brother Ricardo the management of a bakery belonging to his aunt, Juana Nessi. It was during the years when Baroja tried unsuccessfully to be an accomplished man of business that he had his first brush with the realities of the class struggle. He never understood why his employees regarded him as the enemy, convinced as he was that it was a question of a personal, not a socio-political relationship.[12] During the bakery period Baroja also dabbled in the stock market where he enjoyed a certain amount of luck but little financial profit, a paradox apparently attributable to the methods of accounting peculiar to his broker. Until 1902 when Baroja definitely abandoned the bakery to devote himself to a literary career, he led the life of the bourgeois intellectual of his era, writing for such periodicals as *El País, El Imparcial, Revista Nueva,* taking the obligatory trips to Paris, participating in the café life of his fellow *literati.* During this time Baroja met Azorín, with whom he maintained an enduring if outwardly uneffusive friendship.[13] The former was, of course, acquainted with Valle-Inclán and Unamuno, but neither writer awakened a spark of cordiality in him. He disapproved of Valle-Inclán's theatricality and resented Unamuno's enormous egoism and prominence.[14] Aside from the painter, Darío de Regoyos, and the writer, Ciro Bayo,[15] Baroja's most devoted friend was the Swiss-German, Paul Schmitz. Ricardo Baroja has described Schmitz as a very cultivated man, with a much sounder intellectual background than that possessed by his Spanish counterparts.[16] Insatiably curious to know everything possible about Spain, Schmitz was in the habit of taking notes on some of the more coherent conversations heard about the café table, and it was undoubtedly this custom of Schmitz's that led Baroja to believe that all Germans invariably take notes on everything. On the whole, Baroja took a dim view of most of his contemporaries; his ethical rationalism made him a humanitarian in the abstract, but the concrete living individual rarely engaged his sympathies.

III *Portrait of the Artist*

There are numerous portraits of Baroja, none of which the author considers a proper likeness.[17] Perhaps the reason can be found in what the writer says of himself: he is of nondescript appearance, neither tall nor short, neither fat nor thin, rather bent over and poorly dressed. This last is an understatement to judge by the testimony of his contemporary González-Ruano, who wrote that his illustrious colleague usually resembled a beggar dressed in a suit snatched from a corpse.[18]

Baroja is uncommonly scrupulous about setting down the

correct details of his coloring, and takes his friend Schmitz to task for describing him as *tête de carotte* (red head);[19] his hair and beard, he insists, are reddish-blond and his eyes are brown with a greenish tinge. His near-baldness is evident in the photographs dating from before his thirtieth year. When Baroja was twenty-two or twenty-three he looked forty, and when he was forty he looked sixty, a process of premature aging usually shared by his fictional alter egos. In Spain Baroja was often taken for a foreigner, a mistake that seems to have pleased him; Granjel describes his physical type as *entre nórdico y eslavo* (between Nordic and Slavic).[20] Baroja goes to considerable lengths to indicate his lack of interest in his physical appearance, but the dedication of an entire chapter in the *Memorias* (*Memoirs*) to descriptions of him by others, plus rebuttals by the author when necessary, do not support such an assumption of indifference.[21]

If Baroja's appearance raised few hopes for a career of distinction, his psychological preparation was even more markedly a preparation for failure. A chapter in *Youth, Egolatry,* entitled *Baroja, no serás nunca nada* (Baroja, you will never amount to anything) and humorously subtitled *Canción* (Song), traces the course of this prophecy from his earliest days at school in San Sebastián to the University of Madrid. When Baroja was four, his teacher Don León Sánchez y Calleja stated that he would never amount to anything, and his mathematics teacher, Don Gregorio Pano in Pamplona, and Don Benito Hernando in San Carlos, took up the refrain.[22] "Los profesores de la infancia y de la juventud se levantan ante mis ojos como la sombra de Banquo, y me dicen: Baroja, tú no serás nunca nada" (The teachers I had when I was a child and a youth rise up before me like Banquo's ghost and tell me: Baroja, you will never amount to anything).

Baroja's undistinguished career as a student may have given some substance to the prophecy, but it was neither as a student nor as a doctor that Baroja was required to prove himself an official success.

IV The Middle Years

Dissatisfied with medicine and a failure in business, Baroja turned to literature as a means of earning a living while at the same time entertaining himself; literature was to supply an outlet for his relentless curiosity and a palliative for his restlessness and chronic boredom.[23] Baroja had already started to write during his student days, but it was only with the publication of

Camino de perfección (*The Way to Perfection*) in 1902 that the writer was officially launched in the literary world.[24]

Between 1902, when the Baroja family firmly established itself in number 34 Mendizábal Street, until the outbreak of the Civil War in 1936, novels and essays flowed from Baroja's pen in an unending stream. The trips to Paris, Tangier, London, Rome, Germany, Switzerland, and the Scandinavian countries served less as interruptions to his literary pursuits than as inspiration for further works. The international background of such novels as *El mundo es ansí* (*The Way of the World*) and *César o nada* (*Caesar or Nothing*), for example, clearly illustrates the author's desire to set his fictions within a geographical framework of places he had visited, things he had seen. Baroja purchased a large house in Vera del Bidasoa in 1912, renewing the link to the Basque country which had been broken seventeen years before with the resignation of his post in Cestona. The Basque landscape occupied a favored place in the novels of the author throughout his long career, and the descriptions invariably suggest the immediacy of pleasurable experience.

The novelist has described himself as a rambler *per se* and a writer *per accidens*.[25] The accuracy of this characterization is incontestable, for many of Baroja's seemingly invented characters were derived from chance encounters and casual conversations in the streets. His muse is the *musa pedestris*, and one of his preferred occupations, aside from browsing in second-hand bookstores, was strolling within Madrid and on its outskirts.[26] Salaverría, in his *Retratos*, recalls Baroja walking relentlessly along the Calle de Alcalá, collecting acquaintances on the way and talking tirelessly,[27] while in contrast José Plá mentions that he often used to see Baroja and Azorín strolling together, silent as ghosts.[28] The walks in the city and the excursions to many different regions of Spain sooner or later found their way into the novels, for the author wasted nothing.

The note of eccentricity evident in many of Baroja's secondary characters is both a reflection of his love for the marginal and displaced types he collected in his wanderings and also some indication of the reaction his personality evoked in others. Baroja stated with rueful pride that only eccentrics found him interesting and that he enjoyed his greatest social successes with humble people, cats, and dogs.[29] The latter affirmation should be taken *cum grano salis* since in the later years Baroja's presence in the homes of aristocrats was not an unheard-of phenomenon,[30] but it does serve to illustrate the author's penchant for personal myth-making. His life-long conviction that he was unappreciated and obscure belongs to the same category of near-myth. It cannot with justice be said that Bajora's literary efforts went unnoticed, for in 1934 he was elected to membership in the illustrious Royal Spanish Academy.

Although lectures and articles for periodicals occupied the author's days along with the novels, Baroja was not content with the purely literary life. In an attempt to gain recognition in a manner acceptable to his peers, the novelist tried his hand at politics, running first for municipal councilman and then for Congress in 1909 and 1918 respectively. On both occasions the neophyte politician's failure would have been spectacular had it attracted more notice; a wry report of the abortive campaign is provided in the *Horas Solitarias* (*Solitary Hours*).[31]

Baroja's prodigious literary output might suggest dire economic necessity, but such was not quite the case. Unlike Dostoyevsky or Balzac, the Spaniard did not write under the pressure of mounting debts and threats of insolvency but was, essentially, an egocentric gentleman-writer who wrote constantly out of a need to reveal the workings of his mind to a public he presumed in advance to be indifferent. His fecundity bespeaks a formidable talent for improvisation, but suggests as well that the writer had a considerable amount of free time at his disposal and was happily unencumbered by extraneous responsibilities.[32]

V *The Later Years*

The ménage of Mendizábal Street was noticeably clannish, with, ultimately, different members of the family on all three levels; Pío Baroja and his mother occupied the top floor,[33] his younger sister Carmen and her husband, the publisher Rafael Caro Raggio, the middle floor, Ricardo Baroja and his wife, also named Carmen, the first floor. The writer was by no means a solitary, for there are references to musical soirées, amateur theatricals, and *tertulias* (social gatherings) in the collective household. Baroja's well-publicized dislike for dances, the theatre, café life and all manner of public events corresponded more to his middle and old age than to his youth; his hatred for sports and bullfights, however, accompanied him throughout his life.[34]

By 1936 Baroja was a well-known figure, a member of the Academy, the author of over fifty novels. When the Civil War broke out in the summer of that year, Baroja was living in the seclusion and apparent safety of Itzea, a happy state that was abruptly terminated with his arrest by the *requetés* or Carlist extremists. Released a few hours later, Baroja decided not to tempt fate again by installing himself in his country home, and with a decisiveness that owed as much to pessimism as to clear-headedness, began to walk in the direction of France.[35]

For the next four years Baroja lived in self-imposed exile in Paris, an exile interrupted in 1937 by a trip to Basle to visit Paul Schmitz and by a brief but authorized return to Spain. The novelist supported himself, however inadequately, by contributing articles regularly to La Nación of Buenos Aires and by writing occasional pieces for other periodicals. It goes without saying that he continued to write essays and novels, the latter at a diminishing rate and with increasingly unsatisfactory results.

Still in Paris at the outbreak of the Second World War, Baroja went to Le Havre with the intention of embarking for America. He had hoped to serve as a war correspondent for the double purpose of satisfying his curiosity and of putting his courage to the test, but to his chagrin the offer of his services was not accepted.[36] When the voyage to America failed equally to materialize, Baroja returned to Vera in the summer of 1940. The aging writer acquired a house on Ruiz de Alarcón in Madrid, his former home on Mendizábal having been destroyed during the bombings of the Civil War. Baroja's mother had died in 1935, but the years spent in the capital from 1940 to the time of his death were, externally at least, not exceptionally lonely. There were many visitors and from 1943 on, a regular tertulia; hordes descended on the almost legendary author on the occasion of his birthdays, tributes were paid, an extensive Homenaje (Homage) was published.[37] On the debit side it must be pointed out that Baroja had the misfortune to outlive his immediate family, and his semi-official position as one of the last of the Generation of 1898 could alleviate only in part a profound feeling of isolation. The departure for Mexico in 1952 of his nephew and companion, Pío Caro Baroja, served to augment still further an intimate sense of abandonment.

In his old age Baroja suffered from arteriosclerosis and his frequent lapses of memory, evident in his conversations and in the late writings, may in part be attributable to this disease. Already gravely ill in the spring of 1956, Baroja suffered a fall and underwent a successful operation for a bone fracture, but it soon became evident that the end was not far off. Three weeks before his death Baroja was visited by his admirer, Ernest Hemingway. When the American novelist was subsequently asked to act as pallbearer at Baroja's funeral, he refused on the grounds that he felt unworthy of such an honor. Baroja was buried on October 31, 1956, in the Civil Cemetery of Madrid.

VI *The Sentimental Life*

In common with his much-admired predecessors Heraclitus, Spinoza, Kant, Schopenhauer, and Nietzsche, Baroja was a bachelor. Both Schopenhauer and Nietzsche provide impressive lists of eminent bachelors, no doubt for the glory of adding their own names to the catalogue,[38] but that Baroja was not enthusiastic about joining this distinguished club is extremely clear from his essays and novels alike. In the *Paseos de un solitario* (*Strolls of a Solitary Man*) Baroja remarks wistfully that he has always been better understood by women than by men,[39] a state of affairs that seems to have pleased him well enough despite a general lack of tangible results. The absence of a *grand amour* in Baroja's life coupled with a fairly impressive collection of derogatory remarks about Spanish women produced for a time the myth of the author's misogyny, but even a cursory reading of his works indicates the fanciful nature of such a conclusion. Baroja has denied the oft-repeated charge of misogyny, but in the interest of objectivity it must be admitted that a denial alone proves very little, since the author also denied, in the face of overwhelming evidence to the contrary, charges of anticlericalism and Gallophobia. The only positive key to Baroja's attitude vis-à-vis women is to be found in the semi-autobiographical novels and in the *Memoirs*; the confessional nature of these works removes all hazard from what might otherwise be considered an improper method of deduction. Baroja's sentimental life was a history of checks, indecision, and frustration. The vague paranoia and recurrent conviction of general failure may spring in part from the resounding echoes of "you will never amount to anything," but the too-frequently played role of unsuccessful suitor, unsuccessful for whatever the reason, must also be taken into account.

In the description of a San Sebastián holiday spent while Baroja was a medical student, the first note of disappointment is sounded. When the aunt with whom he is staying receives visits from two or three young girls who had apparently been his childhood playmates, Baroja is full of interest and enthusiasm, an enthusiasm soon dashed by the disdain the ladies made no attempt to conceal. Indignant, the young student concluded that a man with neither wealth nor elegance could not succeed in attracting the attention of those "walled fortresses."[40] The next episode, also recounted in the *Memoirs,* is a brief, bittersweet idyll, the fleeting nature of which is best symbolized by its situation in time and space: the early morning hours on a

train from Madrid to San Sebastián. The newly-graduated doctor,
greatly attracted to a pretty Basque servant girl, invites her to
join him in his compartment; after spending some happy hours
in conversation and, apparently, in song, the young Baroja
restrains his amorous impulses and lets her go with the admonition
to look him up in Cestona. In this case it is not so much a
question of unreciprocated interest as of lack of determination
and energy.[41] Belonging to the same Cestona period are two
more brief episodes of hope and disappointment. The first is
experienced in the course of an afternoon of conversation with
a charming woman at the local bullfight. The village doctor
makes a grand and extravagant gesture with the proceeds of his
first salary, but it is in vain; the nameless lady goes away and
Baroja sadly concludes: "You think you are something, but you
are nothing but a village doctor."[42] The second episode, which
supplied the inspiration for the story "Bondad oculta" ("Hidden
Goodness") is equally evanescent, although this time it is Baroja
who takes his leave after having failed to act.[43]

In his bakery period Baroja fared no better with the servants
and seamstresses with whom he and his friends and employees
associated; he was more successful as a conversationalist than
as a Don Juan. In view of Baroja's obvious incapacity to find
a mate, first his employees and then an actress intervened in
his behalf with a matchmaking project. Both efforts yielded only
negative results,[44] perhaps because the candidates in question
were a native product. References to the ignorance, greed, superficiality, and callousness of Spanish women, particularly in such
works as *The Way to Perfection* and *El árbol de la ciencia*
(*The Tree of Knowledge*), are almost too numerous to mention.
Many years later, in *Solitary Hours*, the embattled author again
takes up the theme of the Spanish woman's opportunism, her
worship of physical rather than spiritual values, a preference
which on more than one occasion consigned Baroja to the circle
reserved for unsuitable candidates. Further, since Spanish women
were traditionalists, they could not be attracted by an individualist
or by a man who was, at least spiritually, a solitary. For Baroja,
the narrowness of the Catholic tradition and the deficient education which was its consequence were responsible for producing
the half-hysterical mystic or the fat, beastly girl, both of whom
filled him with repugnance.[45]

In Rome in 1908, the author was invited by a Venetian lady
to accompany her to Naples, an invitation he refused, after much
private debate, for lack of funds, ignominiously escaping from
the hotel before he could be caught by his eager, would-be

companion.[46] In Paris in 1913, Baroja met a Russian named Ana Lomonosoff, a married woman who obviously impressed him deeply; the "Intermedio sentimental" ("Sentimental Intermezzo") in the *Memoirs* gives a full account of their melancholy friendship, a story already narrated in part in the section titled "Otoñal" ("Autumn Idyll") of the novel *La sensualidad pervertida* (*Sublimated Sensuality*).[47] The air of discouragement that pervades their meetings and conversations clearly strikes the autumnal note which Baroja subsequently attached to the truncated affair; it was too late.

Again in the *Memoirs* the author recounts, uncharacteristically, a short but somehow carefree encounter which took place in Paris after the conclusion of the first World War with a Viennese whom Baroja liked to call his Hedda Gabler. Aided by a large quantity of alcohol and a cheerful dinner, the writer overcame his natural timidity and accompanied his companion to her room. For Baroja, an adventure of this nature appeared wholly alien, and he could not escape the sensation of playacting.[48]

The *Memoirs* also contains a collection of letters written to Baroja by a variety of women,[49] among them a French girl named Gabriela who kept up their correspondence during the Civil War and in the early years of the ensuing World War.[50] Other letters came to him from English, American, and even some Spanish girls, but the one that confirmed him in the conviction that he was unfortunate in love came from a Circassian. Written about 1922 or 1923, the missive was both a fervent expression of admiration and an invitation in the best operatic manner: the author was to meet "S.W." at the Beaux Arts ball. Baroja, however, was clearly destined to remain a bachelor, for the letter unaccountably disappeared, unopened, among his numerous papers and did not reemerge until twenty years had passed. "Of course I was no longer young at that time, but still . . . what rotten luck!"[51]

Laura, a novel published in 1939, reflects the period of exile in France which the author evidently put to good use by widening his circle of acquaintances. The novel fairly overflows with feminine characters, virtually all of whom were known to Baroja socially. According to the account of the author's life in Paris in 1938 supplied by Antonio Azpeitúa, the then mature writer used to visit a lady from Moscow with great frequency, but apparently was in dread of being left alone with her—whether from fear of himself or of her, Azpeitúa does not specify.[52] The so-called Schopenhauerian misogynist ultimately turned out to be more of a social lion than a bear.

Shortly before the exile returned to Spain in 1940, he received an invitation to wait out the war on the estate of a rich Basque who lived in Bayonne; Baroja, then approaching seventy, refused on the grounds that the Basque had a pretty, twenty-year-old daughter who might be too much of a temptation. While such a remark sounds somewhat less than seriously meant, it is nonetheless worthy of note that the elderly writer continued to be preoccupied with the opposite sex even then.[53]

It is somewhat ironical that Baroja began to be of interest to numerous women only in his later years, when he appears to have made few serious efforts to derive any personal advantage from such contacts. He aptly illustrates his own anecdote according to which Diogenes, when asked the best time to marry, solemnly answered that it is too soon when one is young and too late when one is old.

Baroja's amorous history, or what he has chosen to reveal of it, is marked by frustration brought about, in part by perverse fortune, but in the main by the inability to act decisively in a given situation. Azorín has attributed the failure of Baroja's will to the predominance of the critical spirit: the destruction of the instincts by the intellect. This analysis is very much in the mainstream of the thinking characteristic of the Generation of 1898, for the problem of *aboulia* or lack of will is central to Azorín's own early works, and Unamuno, Baroja, and the post-Generation of 1898 writer Pérez de Ayala all rang many changes on the theme. The object of the analysis, however, brought a different light to bear on the problem. Baroja saw himself as a victim of the perverse morality of the society of which he was a product. Prohibited from following his instincts when young, he was alienated from his own sensuality and consequently incapacitated for the vigorous pursuit of life, a process described via his alter ego Luis Murguía in *Sublimated Sensuality*. If, as Schopenhauer has it in *The World as Will and Idea*, the sex impulse is the assertion of the will to live, then the weakness of the one must be reflected in the weakness of the other.

Baroja considers that the restrictions placed by an unaccommodating society on a youth between the ages of fifteen and twenty-five must necessarily produce an emotional imbalance unless the youth in question can somehow "play the game." That Baroja could not do so can be attributed to fastidiousness; he was repelled by the thought of frequenting a squalid brothel[54] and almost equally horrified at the idea of marrying without the means to maintain a decorous standard of living. Then too, marriage means submission, acceptance of the conventions, and the author preferred to believe that he was unwilling to make the sacrifice. Baroja's damaging intransigence, which depended as much on purely material considerations as on pride and dignity, is less than convincing and it is problematical whether a different moral atmosphere would have produced a different man. The author or doctor mentioned more than once that his chronic arthritis produced, among other symptoms, an obsession with sex.[55] To judge from the available evidence, Baroja's timidity and lack of confidence as a young man, combined with an essentially puritanical point of view, left little opportunity to cure this obsession.

This lack of vigor was, certainly, a source of melancholy, whether it was caused by relative ill health (Baroja has described the arthritic as being neither ill nor well), a weakness of the will, or a lack of confidence and consequent fear of failure, and that it contributed to Baroja's often harsh view of men and institutions as well as to his self-pity seems beyond question. In the novels, the Barojian intellectual rarely reacts decisively in a sentimental situation, and is more inclined to cast aside opportunities than to create them. Arcelu languishes at Sacha's side, Larrañaga is more of a brother than a lover to Nelly, Ossorio is incapable of taking Adela despite his violent desires, Hurtado is virtually unhinged after he finally brings himself to commit adultery with Dorotea, Murguía manages to exchange only one kiss with Ana Lomonosoff. Even César Moncada, who is sporadically strong-willed and decisive, emerges from a night spent with the Countess Brenda looking like a corpse, and is reduced to a state of tremulous anxiety once he becomes engaged to Amparito.[56]

Baroja's attachment to his mother, which he himself did not fail to recognize, and his latent hostility towards both his father and his brother, Ricardo, suggest the desirability of a full-scale psychoanalytic study by a competent professional, for despite the confessional nature of the author's work, there still remain dark corners in need of illumination.[57]

CHAPTER 2

The Writer as Professional

I *The Craft of the Writer*

WHILE there are scattered throughout Baroja's numerous works references to what he conceived to be the proper form and function of the novel, the most concentrated sources for an examination of these theories are to be found in the prologues to *La nave de los locos* (*The Ship of Fools*) and *Los amores tardíos* (*Late Loves*), in Chapter XI of *Solitary Hours,* and in a section of the *Memoirs* entitled *La intuición y el estilo* (*Style and Intuition*).[1]

The novel to Baroja is a *speculum consuetudinis,* an image of life, the Stendhalian mirror along the way. Art is not a conglomerate of rules but rather "the spirit of things reflected in the spirit of man."[2] With its freedom and open horizons, the novel should resemble the flow of history in that there is neither beginning nor end, neither alpha nor omega. This porous or invertebrate novel has no clear plan, proves nothing, points no moral, illustrates no aesthetic theory. Henry James had written that the House of Fiction has many windows, and it is Baroja's belief that all these windows should be opened into the countryside beyond, to embrace whatever object comes into view. There is room for everything in fiction, even for the author himself.[3]

The point of departure is reality, for the writer requires ". . . the springboard of reality for his daring leaps."[4] Just as Stendhal sometimes utilized newspaper clippings as a foundation for his fictions, Baroja modelled his secondary characters, his anecdotes, and interpolated stories on friends and acquaintances, stories he had heard, experiences he had had. While it was the method of the eminent novelist Galdós to first plan a novel and then project it into space, Baroja's procedure was the reverse. It is the character or the place that suggests the work of fiction, and it is the author's desire to write about what has intrigued or surprised him that constitutes the *raison d'être* of the novel. Baroja describes the creative process much as one might describe a walk in the country; the stroller stops to examine a tree, to contemplate a brook, to note every detail in his path, without

26

particular regard for his destination. Unity in an extensive work is inconceivable to Baroja, believing as he does that a long novel is simply a succession of short pieces.[5] The haphazard narrative flow of the old Spanish novels, of a work such as *Pickwick Papers* or of Dostoyevsky's *The House of the Dead* are far more stimulating to him than the "simulated unity" of the French novel in general.[6]

If the goal is vague, the steps along the way are not, for Baroja shared with Stendhal the conviction that the originality and interest of any novel lay in the details. It is the detail that is anchored in reality, and it is the detail that endows the work with its quality of individuality. ". . . in the novel the specific, the individualized are sought. That is to say, exactitude and truth."[7] If the author takes exception to Zola, for example, it is precisely on the grounds that the French writer used generic man as the central character in his novels instead of an individualized, specific figure.

The loose structure of the invertebrate novel has room not only for faithfully recorded details but also accommodates a multiplicity of figures; if a book is long despite a minimal number of characters, Baroja maintains that this is accomplished by means of rhetoric or padding. The author was greatly attracted to humble people, to all that was unusual and picturesque among humanity's flora and fauna, and the flexible and protean nature of his art allowed him to include a huge parade of these figures. The Barojian novel often resembles a fairgrounds; there is a succession of brief sideshows, memorable performances before anonymous crowds, constant movement and activity.

Baroja required that literature be amusing and pleasant, that it excite interest and stir the emotions. He sometimes sighed elegiacally for the days when friends huddled together about a blazing fire to hear tales of guerrilla fighters, ghosts, or smugglers, after which they scurried off to bed with the delightful sensation of having been thoroughly frightened.[8] To capture the imagination, the novel must have mystery which, in turn, suggested to Baroja shadows, fog, a gothic atmosphere. The author's oft-expressed preference for fog to bright sunshine perhaps stems as much from this particular association as it does from his love for the misty Basque countryside. Baroja liked to think that he looked like a Northerner and a magician, and the sorcerer sometimes lurks just behind the pages on the Paris of Victor Hugo and the London of Jack-the-Ripper.[9]

In accordance with his views on the recreational function of literature, Baroja aspired to write novels that would entertain, and to this end deliberately made use of the short paragraph and the short chapter. The former he considered the appropriate vehicle for conveying a direct, analytical, and impressionistic vision, and the latter a concrete and visible protest against the oratorical style which had fallen into such disfavor with his generation. According to his own testimony, Baroja started to read many more books than he ever succeeded in finishing; boredom, the mortal enemy, quickly made its appearance and put the offending author to rout. Baroja's ambition is to reflect the truth in an entertaining manner—*deleitar aprovechando*. The slow pace of the Proustian novel, so dear to the heart of Ortega, is anathema to the Basque who considers the *tempo lento* appropriate only to the cooking of codfish.[10]

Baroja was never fully at ease with his clearly and occasionally loudly enunciated artistic credo and often adopted an apologetic air for having put into practice the very theories he professed to espouse. Baroja wrote in the only way that he knew how, and that he was on the defensive about what he considered his limitations is abundantly illustrated in many of his works. In *Sublimated Sensuality*, Luis Murguía announces disingenuously that the unity of his life will make the unity of his story, and that if he does not supply endings to many of the incidents recounted it is because "that is the way it happened."[11] The narrator Leguía in the prologue to *The Wax Figures* criticizes the story to follow for containing too much description, not enough dialogue, and a general lack of color, and the reader is warned at the outset of *Las inquietudes de Shanti Andía* (*The Restlessness of Shanti Andía*) not to expect any great flights of style, for these are the memoirs of a rough sailor.

It is inconceivable that Baroja should have been insensitive to adverse criticism of his style and of his linguistic sense, and the repetition of such anecdotes as the Orteguian *Baroja tropieza en Coria con la grámatica* ("Baroja stumbles over grammar in Coria")[12] did little to sustain his confidence. The anecdote concerns the novelist's hesitations about whether to write *de zapatillas, con zapatillas,* or *a zapatillas* (in slippers, with slippers, with slippers on), and one cannot fail to notice that what is considered ignorance of grammar in Baroja might equally well be considered in another author a positively Flaubertian search for *le mot juste*.

An essay entitled "La objetividad de la historia" ("The Objectivity of History") contains the observation that a good novel is a more faithful reflection of society than a history, and in one of his genuine *aperçus* Baroja suggests that if some of his fictions have no value as works of art, they are at least worth a good deal as documents.[13] The foregoing is not so much a statement designed to disarm the critics as a serious appraisal of the true nature of one important aspect of the Barojian novel. Purely formal stylistic considerations become irrelevant if a novel is, after all, essentially the testimonial of a particular sensibility living in a particular era.

II *The Writer as Reader and Critic*

The ethnographer Julio Caro Baroja, the author's nephew and literary executor, remarks that when he was young his uncle suggested that he read Stevenson, Rider Haggard, Captain Marryat, and Walter Scott. These novelists, along with Jules Verne, Mayne Reid, Eugene Sue, and Dumas, as well as such French and Spanish serial writers as Ponson de Terrail, Montepin, Fernández y González, and Pérez Escrich had already helped shape the tastes of the future novelist.[14] Under the influence of these writers of romances, Baroja's love for adventure, for far-off lands, for the *outré* and the unlikely, periodically submerged his philosophical skepticism and rationalism, transforming the mordant critic of society into a writer of juvenile fiction.

Baroja mentions on several occasions that his entire *fondo sentimental* (emotional background) was formed in childhood and early youth, a period he delimits variously as extending from ten or twelve to twenty-two or twenty-three or from fourteen or fifteen to twenty-five or twenty-six.[15] It is not merely the affective side of the writer that was formed during that time; it was also his taste. He never outgrew his early readings, never forgot his early experiences, never abandoned his early idols. In literature, philosophy, and science his triple gods were Dickens, Kant, and Claude Bernard, and neither historical, social, nor scientific changes could cast these images down from their pedestals. In the *Memoirs* Baroja criticizes the English for admiring Jane Austen, Thackeray, and Galsworthy at the expense of Dickens;[16] in another section of these confessions he once again proclaims Kant as the greatest philosopher of all, expressing little faith in Spengler, Keyserling, Scheler, and Heidegger, the last two of whom, incidentally, he had read only in résumé.[17] More than eighty years after its publication, Bernard's *Introduction to the Study of Experimental Medicine* still impresses him with its greatness.[18] The same consistency applies to Baroja's preferences in music: his tastes ran to Italian opera and he continued to inveigh against the "kolossal" Wagner long after the composer's innovations had ceased to be a subject of acrimonious discussion.[19]

Occupying a place of honor similar to that of Dickens is Stendhal, whose "one must see clearly into reality" is quoted repeatedly by Baroja.[20] The Spanish author shared with Stendhal his anti-Flaubertian attitude, his gift for rapid composition, his preoccupation with will and action;[21] Baroja once described himself as having been in his youth an unsuccessful Julien Sorel.[22] Dostoyevsky, who is classified with Kierkegaard as the last of the Christian apostles, awakens deep admiration mixed with uneasiness; Baroja finds his fantasies brilliant but pathological. In the *Memoirs* he remarks that he had read all of Dostoyevsky several times over but pointedly denies the influence of Gorki with whose works he was scarcely acquainted.[23] Luis Murguía, speaking for his creator, states that he both likes and is repelled by Russian literature, a literature which reveals an extremely interesting but sickly sensibility.[24]

With undue precipitation and inordinate pessimism, Baroja proclaims in the *Memoirs* that Dostoyevsky and Tolstoy are the last great writers in the world, having already declared about a decade before that he saw no possibility for new and inspired works in literature.[25] Unfavorable comments proliferate: Gide is skillful but not universal, while Proust is not only not universal but is dull into the bargain. Two separate references to the dipping of the madeleine into a *café au lait* are scarcely calculated to inspire confidence in Baroja as a Proustian;[26] in the same volume a reference to Victoria Wolf [*sic*] merely confirms a mounting alarm. French writers generally fare ill at the hands of this Gallophobe: *Madame Bovary* and *Salammbô* were too boring to finish, Chateaubriand is a soporific, Anatole France, Prévost, Bourget and Remy de Gourmont completely worthless. Exceptions to this kind of ferocious attack, aside from Stendhal, are Mérimée, Balzac, and Colette. Also saved from interdiction is the poetry of Verlaine, Bayle's *Dictionary*, and some of the characters in Molière's plays.[27]

Baroja had read fairly widely among English-speaking authors and in various places refers to Fielding, Sterne, Defoe, Meredith, Swift, Poe, Hardy, D. H. Lawrence, Huxley, *inter alia*. What Baroja admired most about the English was their humor; what he admired least about the French was their stylistic virtuosity and solemnity. Baroja has supplied his own reading lists in too many places to make it worthwhile to repeat the entire catalogue here,[28] but the salient characteristic of many of his pronouncements is a certain critical frivolity. The indispensable *Memoirs*

contains the following admission: "I have been an assiduous reader, but not a good one; voracious, but not conscientious." The author confesses that he always read in a haphazard way, skipping paragraphs or sometimes whole pages whenever boredom threatened.[29] In *Solitary Hours* Baroja had already stated that there was scarcely a book he had read in its entirety, and that even in the case of those works he had read many times, he invariably skipped something.[30] It is well to bear in mind this revelation of impatience and carelessness, for it sometimes helps to explain Baroja's inaccurate observations on the work of others and his frequently capricious judgments.

Baroja remarks that he never finished any novel by Zola and described *Das Kapital* as a book "almost nobody has read," not so much on the basis of private information, if any, but because he himself found Marx too boring to read. The following anecdote recounted somewhat wryly in the *Memoirs* gives a clue to the nature of some of his critical judgments: the poet Villaespesa had borrowed some money from him many years before and had not only failed to return it but compounded the crime by sending his father a few days later to request a larger sum. On the basis of this disagreeable experience, since, not having read his poetry Baroja had no other, the novelist invariably affirmed that Villaespesa was a very bad poet.[31]

With the exception of Nordau and the more prominent philosophers, Baroja's acquaintanceship with German literature seems to have been limited to Goethe, Heine, whom the Spaniard "imagines" to be great on the basis of the prose translations he had read, and Kafka whom he characterizes despectively as a miniature Dostoyevsky under the noxious influence of the surrealists and Freudian psychoanalysis.[32]

The author's readings in Spanish are less extensive than his combined readings in French, since he read not only the French writers but also English, Russian, and American authors in French translation. The poet Juan Ruiz, the picaresque novel *Lazarillo de Tormes*, the moralists Antonio de Torquemada and Fray Luis de Granada, Baltasar Gracián and Huarte de San Juan are all admired by Baroja, with Huarte's *Examen de ingenios* occupying a prominent position among his preferred readings.[33] Like his cogenerationists, he held most nineteenth-century Spanish writers in low esteem; the poets Espronceda and Bécquer are among the notable exceptions.[34]

For Baroja, as for most of the writers of the Generation of 1898, the truly interesting writers were non-Spanish Europeans of a universal stamp: Schopenhauer, Nietzsche, Tolstoy, Dostoyevsky, Turgenev, Verlaine, and Ibsen. Periodically there are favorable references to newer, not-yet-consecrated figures such as Julian Green, but the unfavorable reaction is more characteristic. Sartre's *Les Mains Sales,* the works of Pirandello and Mauriac, to name but a few, are summarily dismissed with a phrase of disapprobation.[35]

Without commenting further on the manner in which he read, it is already evident that Baroja had some familiarity with the standard European literature of the nineteenth and twentieth centuries and knew something as well of the Spanish literary tradition. His heterogeneous readings embraced philosophy, history and anthropology, demonology, magic, astrology, and crime. According to José Alberich, who has classified many of the volumes in Baroja's library in Itzea, less than half are devoted to works of fiction while the remaining volumes are concerned with philosophy, anthropology, biology, the occult sciences, geography, and history.[36] Both Nallim and Baroja himself state that there were about ten thousand volumes in this private collection.[37] The readings inevitably found their way into the writings, with such secondary characters as Don Miguelito Torralba and Dr. Armendáriz presenting the fictionalized aspect of the author's disquisitions on diviners, astrologers, and magicians.[38] Imposters are honored with a ten-page historical survey while such mountebanks as Mr. Macbeth alternate with the charlatans Baroja fondly recalls in the *Vitrina pintoresca* (*Picturesque Showcase*).[39]

Baroja's interest in criminality, beginning with his first view of an execution, was enduring if not obsessive. Scattered throughout the works are detailed accounts of executioners and executions, and even in such a late collection as the *Canciones del suburbio* (*Songs from the Outskirts*) there is a poem dedicated to the guillotine and some verses on the subject of the executioner Deibler, "Monsieur de Paris."[40] Criminals abound in the author's works, and are by no means limited to such obviously appropriate novels as *La busca* (*The Quest*) and *Mala hierba* (*Weeds*). In *Swan Hotel* the ex-policeman Barbier's collection of chronicles of crime indicates the extent to which Baroja immersed himself in readings of that nature,[41] and several anecdotes in the *Memoirs* suggest that the novelist's fascination with crime in general and execution and murder in particular is less humanitarian than macabre.[42]

Poem XXXIII of the *Songs from the Outskirts,* which reproduces the ballad of "El horroroso crimen de Peñaranda del Campo" ("The terrible crime of Peñaranda del Campo") already included in the farce similarly entitled, is a burlesque account of a murder supposedly committed by one Pedro García who, not content with chopping up his female victim, tastes a morsel and does not like it.[43] There are further strange flowerings of black humor in the novels. In *Los confidentes audaces* (*The Daring Secret Agents*) there is a nameless individual whose unspecified illness produces such astonishing manifestations that a physician purchases his cadaver in advance, thus enabling the patient to live on the proceeds of his future demise.[44] Damián, the coffinmaker of *Los recursos de la astucia* (*The Resources of Cunning*), finds his work both stimulating and thought provoking, and habitually takes naps in one of his constructions. "If anyone separates me from my coffin, I'm dead,"[45] he declares. The appeal to Baroja of the macabre and the bizarre is but a further indication of his latent romanticism; the humor of the gallows and the love for melodrama go hand in hand with rational observation and analysis.

The dual purpose of this section of our book has been to indicate the direction of the author's tastes and to point out as a *caveat* the imprecision of many of his critical pronouncements. It is curious to note that an avowed skeptic whose *que sais-je,* translated in this case as *nadie sabe nada* (nobody knows anything) should have so often assumed an air of omniscience—an omniscience which makes only too appropriate the application to him of the observation that Diogenes Laertius had made of Heraclitus: ". . . for when a youth he used to say he knew nothing, although when he was grown up he claimed that he knew everything."[46]

III   *The Moral Responsibility of the Writer*

Baroja maintained repeatedly that his primary purpose in writing was to convey a truthful image of life in all its diversity. The author saw himself as an observer, a spontaneous "writer of the streets" rather than a cultivated man of letters, a moralist and a clinician rather than a rhetorician. Baroja shared with Unamuno and Machado the conviction that the moral aspects of life far outweighed aesthetic considerations, and that uncompromising honesty and sincerity were of far greater account than beauty and artifice. In the tradition of Montaigne, Schopenhauer, and Nietzsche, Baroja publicly dedicated himself to the cause of truth, abjuring hypocrisy, lies, and all other forms of fraudulence. Having accepted sincerity as the *sine qua non* of all serious literature, it is the task of the artist to discover the technical means by which he is to convey his vision of the truth, without exaggeration, without equivocation. Baroja stated in many different works and at varying periods of his life that to stylize is to falsify; adornment and conscious elegance, a rich and recherché vocabulary, an eloquent tone, defeat what he considered to be the legitimate ends of literary expression. The Barojian ideal, sustained despite occasional sideglances at what he considered his own defective technique, is clarity, precision, and rapidity, achieved by the deliberate utilization of a spare, unmannered style.

The insistence on simplicity is partly generational in that the literary expression of Baroja's most important contemporaries generally reflected an abhorrence of superficial brilliance and bombast. The rolling periods of nineteenth-century prose and the glitter of the much-applauded oratory of Castelar, for example, gave way to a simpler, more natural syntax and, in the case of Unamuno and Baroja, at least, a less elaborate vocabulary. Baroja even went so far as to declare that he never used in his writings words he had not heard in conversation.[47]

It was Baroja's desire to give to his writings a non-Latin flavor, for he associated the Latin (and Semitic) cult of language with insincerity. Rhetoric, after all, serves to conceal rather than to reveal. Further, Baroja recognized that his own style was poor in "Castilian and Latin flavor,"[48] even mentioning, half-humorously, that it had been said that his Spanish sounded like a translation from the Basque.[49] The association of conscious elegance of expression with fraudulence is not the exclusive property of Baroja, for as recently as 1960 the poet Gabriel Celaya, in a poem included in his Rapsodia euskara (Basque Rhapsody), proclaimed: "We Basques are not fond of juggling pretty phrases. / We Basques despise all those who decorate untruths with words" (Los vascos no gustamos de combinar palabras más o menos bonitas. / Los vascos despreciamos a cuantos, charlatanes, adornan la mentira).[50]

If it is as a Basque that Baroja associates rhetoric with insincerity, it is as a moralist that he condemns the cultivation of beauty for its own sake. The author's puritanism led him to view the pursuit of the pure aesthetic ideal as a sin against life, and to condemn the aesthetic experience as base sensuality. When the aesthetic ideal is pursued, art becomes a substitute for life, and the artist, deprived of his vital energies, is content to find in art what he should properly seek in life. There can be no question of the sincerity of Baroja's objections to the cultivation of art at the expense of life, but it is open to question whether or not he fell into the very trap that he criticizes. In a letter quoted by García Sanchiz the author affirms that he is not a writer by vocation but because of the impossibility of living an intense personal life.[51]

Baroja's frequently expressed dislike of Ruskin and the Pre-Raphaelites is understandable in the light of his distrust of artifice and his abhorrence of those tendencies which he considered inimical to life. His anti-aestheticism inevitably calls to mind some of the more negative aspects of Tolstoy's treatise *What Is Art,* for both the Russian and the Spaniard join together in anathematizing such masters of artifice as Remy de Gourmont, Huysmans, and Maeterlinck, with Tolstoy going so far as to consider the poetry of Baudelaire and Verlaine "far from skillful in form and most contemptible and commonplace in subject-matter."[52] This extreme point of view is happily not shared by Baroja who, like his cogenerationists, admired Verlaine and considered Baudelaire a true poet, although he cannot help adding "decadent, perverse, and sick."[53] D'Annunzio, Barbey D'Aurevilly, and Jean Lorrain are less fortunate, eliciting from Baroja such adjectives as "boring," "ridiculous," and "worthless," while Rubén Darío, the Nicaraguan poet, is characterized malevolently as "an unimaginative snob."[54] If, as Gide states, Oscar Wilde could not forgive Dickens for being human, Baroja evidently could not forgive aesthetes for being artists.

The possible influence of Tolstoy's philistine attitude towards aestheticism was further compounded by Max Nordau, whose *Entartung (Degeneration)* Baroja had read by 1899.[55] Even without the intervention of the latter, however, Baroja's attitude would scarcely have been different. Ibsen's strenuous morality was far more appealing to the puritan than the satanic filigrees of Valle-Inclán, for Baroja shared the belief held by Kierkegaard and Dostoyevsky that the aesthetic way of life was the forerunner of moral and cultural decline.[56] Further, Baroja associated aestheticism and, by extension, the entire art world, with the interests and aspirations of the bourgeoisie. Although himself a member of that class and a practitioner of that most bourgeois of all art forms, the novel, Baroja held the commercialism and materialism of the urban middle class in very low esteem. He looked upon the art world as a tainted product of the cities, as an international business with rules and regulations determined by Jewish merchants, journalists, and collectors. In *Youth, Egolatry* the author asserts that "most lovers of painting and sculpture are junk dealers and Jews in disguise . . ."[57]

Throughout his works there are despective references to

musicians, painters, and sculptors. Baroja transforms the sculptor Carlos Mani into the fictional Alex (or Álejo) Monzón, making of the latter a fatuous *poseur* who is convinced that his failure to achieve recognition in the art world will set the progress of European sculpture back at least one hundred years.[58] The Hungarian violinist Kolozsvar of *Caesar or Nothing* may be a minor musical talent, but he is a true virtuoso with the ladies in London, all of whom feel the irresistible urge to reform him. The sinister musician Amati in *The Way of the World* is a seducer as well as a fortune hunter, thus linking the pursuit of art with sensuality and materialism; Alonso de Guzmán in the tale "La enamorada del talento" ("The Girl Who Was in Love with Talent") is given the benefit of similarly acerbic treatment.[59]

It was Baroja's custom to unceremoniously reject any form of art that did not fulfill his ethical requirements. Cubism, Dada, Expressionism, and Surrealism are "ridiculous," "absurd," "stupid"; Gaudi, Joan Gris, and Picasso are fakes.[60] Experimentation in the arts appears worthless to Baroja in any case, for it was his oft-expressed conviction that everything of value in literature and in art had, by the beginning of the twentieth century, already been said and done.

CHAPTER 3

The Patriot as Xenophobe

IN the course of his copious literary production, Baroja inevitably repeated certain ideas, certain themes, with garrulous insistence. Just as the author periodically felt the need to reiterate his theories about art and the artist, he frequently returned to the knotty question of what he loosely considered anthropological and national differences.[1] Dolicho- and brachycephalics, Latins and Semites, the English, the French, the Germans, and the Basques, all come in for scrutiny, comparison, and contrast. Since the author's attitudes toward politics and religion as well as toward art are inextricably bound up with his attitudes toward Northerners and Southerners in general and Semites in particular, a survey of his opinions would not be amiss.

I *Anthropological Divagations*

The unpromising title of Poem XXVIII, "Los Braquicéfalos" ("The Brachycephalics") of the *Songs from the Outskirts*[2] reveals the persistence of Baroja's interest in anthropological typology and his recurrent custom of referring to Vacher de Lapouge, Houstin Stewart Chamberlain, or Count Gobineau as either authorities to distrust or to follow with discretion. Possibly against his better judgment, Baroja was attracted by the study of cephalic indices and while questioning the reliability of Vacher de Lapouge, for example, often drew conclusions from the very premises he professed to reject. In the above-mentioned poem, Baroja rushes uncharacteristically to the defense of the brachycephalics or round heads, to whom Vacher de Lapouge had denied culture and civilization, having already reserved these attributes for dolichocephalics or long heads. Baroja's sometime authority had made two large divisions: the Aryan (*homo europoeus*), who is dolichocephalic, tall, blond, individualistic, brave, and usually Protestant, and the *homo alpinus* who is brachycephalic, dark, bureaucratic, commonplace, and vulgar. He is usually Catholic.[3] It is not without interest that Baroja is careful to point out that he himself is dolichocephalic.[4] Dr. Recalde, who as one of Baroja's numerous Basque physicians

37

serves as his spokesman in scientific or pseudo-scientific questions, fancifully divides the white race into Cains and Abels, or round heads and long heads. Not surprisingly, the long heads are civilized, scientific, peaceful, and progressive.[5] In an essay devoted to Italy, Baroja expresses naive astonishment at the fact that many men of genius were produced by that country, despite the relative infrequency of the dolichocephalic type.[6]

Baroja's scientific formation made it difficult for him to accept as valid the racial theories put forth by Chamberlain and Gobineau, yet he was at the same time unable to dismiss them entirely. Both in the *Momentum catastrophicum* (*Time of Crisis*) and the *Divagaciones apasionadas* (*Passionate Divagations*), the novelist suggests that some of their pronouncements on ethnic differences lie more in the realm of literature than of science and that much of what Chamberlain and Gobineau have written is arbitrary and purely imaginative, but his conclusion, which does not appear to follow from his argument, is that Count Gobineau's theory of the inequality of races is, in spirit if not in detail, correct.[7]

The mathematician Olsen with whom José Larrañaga sustains lengthy conversations in *El gran torbellino del mundo* (*The Great Whirlwind of Life*) states categorically that Chamberlain's distinction between Aryans and non-Aryans is groundless and is simply *etnografía para pasar el rato* ("ethnography to pass the time of day").[8] Larrañaga himself in another volume explains to his friend Stolz that differentiation between Aryans and Semites is a fantasy, then declaring roundly that there are no superior races. With the air of a true believer who has just lost his faith, Larrañaga adds that he and others like him had been taken in by false theories concerning Aryans, dolicho- and brachycephalics.[9] This seeming destruction of whatever faith Baroja once had in racial theories is part of the general disintegration of illusions which is the distinguishing mark of the *Agonías de nuestro tiempo* (*Agonies of Our Time*) trilogy, a series which might be read as Baroja's personal *Götterdämmerung*. Yet, if the old gods wane, they never quite die, and several years later Vacher de Lapouge, Chamberlain, and Gobineau rise, as it were, from their ashes in order to again provide Baroja with material for disquisitions on race.[10]

A note of hostility begins to be evident in the *Rapsodias* (*Rhapsodies*), published in 1936, when Baroja remarks that Chamberlain has an unsympathetic attitude toward the Basques. To the German essayist, St. Ignatius and St. Francis Xavier belong to the age of the cavedwellers and are natural enemies

of the "luminous European spirit of the Reformation."[11] In the
essay "Las desigualdades étnicas" ("Ethnic Inequalities"),
Baroja's resentment at Chamberlain's tendency to group Basques
along with Semites is exceeded only by his anger at the classification of the two Basque Saints as representatives of the evil
influence of Ahriman as against the beneficent influence of
Ormazd.[12] Equally critical is the essay "La raza y la cultura"
("Race and Culture"). Written in 1938, it contains the following
assertion: "These labels of Aryans, Semites, Latins, Germans
and Slavs . . . just produce confusion. Scientifically, they are
worthless."[13]

Baroja's oscillation between partial acceptance and rejection
of ethnic theories depended to a large extent on his preconceptions and existing opinions. If Chamberlain's or Gobineau's
theses often seemed to him to offend the scientific method, his
subjectivity tempted him to return for another view in the hope
of salvaging some valid observations. Baroja's obvious delight
in belonging to the superior family of long heads, his deep antipathy toward the Semitic type, and his instinctive desire to defend
the Basques against derogatory judgments combined to produce
a high degree of ambivalence and contradiction. It can be said
with some justice that racial theories provided the author with
a smorgasbord from which he selected only what he liked.

II Northerners and Southerners

Contrary to the distinction made by Menéndez y Pelayo
between *claridad latina* ("Latin clarity") and *nieblas germánicas*
("German mists," i.e., foggy Germanic thinking), both Baroja and
Ortega y Gasset maintained that Germanic culture is dedicated
to the discovery of deep realities, while Latin culture concerns
itself only with the surface. Baroja feels fully at ease only in the
grey, misty atmosphere of the North, in a landscape that mirrors
the interior landscape of the soul.[14] The South, with its clear
skies and vibrant light, is external brightness, hollow beauty.
To Baroja, Latin culture is dogmatic, while Germanic culture permits freedom of conscience and independence of thought;[15]
the beautiful aspects of old Paris, with its Sainte Chapelle and
Notre Dame de Paris is a reflection of "Saxon genius," but all
that is affected, graceless, and commonplace is the heritage of
the Romanized Franks.[16] The Romans, it goes without saying,
are a degenerate race.[17].

Baroja viewed Southerners and the inhabitants of the Mediterranean litoral as essentially vulgar, theatrical, resentful, dirty,
given to hyperbole, and prone to violence. The author's *bête*

noire, rhetoric, is the particular specialty of the Southerner. The
Mediterranean, he affirms, pays in words rather than in money,
thus uniting magniloquence and avarice.[18] The much-advertised
wit of Southerners is purely imaginary, for their talents are
oriented toward the stinging, wounding barb which, far from
constituting humor, is but one facet of the capital vice of envy;
Unamuno has captured the essence of this latent hostility in the
authentically witty question *¿contra quién va ese elogio?*
("against whom is that compliment directed?").[19] Dr. Aracil,
one of the major characters in *La dama errante* (*The Wandering Lady*) and *La ciudad de la niebla* (*The City of Fog*),
epitomizes the true Mediterranean: clever, insincere, his love
for words far outstrips his love for his fellow men. The ubiquitous
Dr. Iturrioz condemns him further by insisting that he is a victim
of "the aesthetic virus," adding: "It is not in vain that he comes
from the Mediterranean region."[20]

The novelist's puritanical tendencies rendered him far more
receptive to the severe geographical and moral climate of the
North than to the sensual, *dolce far niente* associations of the
South. As a Basque, he is a Northerner in a Southern country
and it is not unnatural that he arrogate to himself some of the
particular virtues that he discerns in the English, the Germans,
and the Scandinavians. Baroja notes in the *Memoirs* that he has
been best understood by Northerners[21] and his correspondingly
sympathetic attitude is reflected in the portrayals of Norwegians,
Russians, and Poles in the novels written both at the start as
well as toward the end of his literary career.[22]

III   *The English and the Germans*

England represented for Baroja freedom and order, practi-
cality and individualism, a sense of purpose and the will to
action.[23] It is the English heritage of Roberto Hasting of *The
Quest* and *Weeds* that gives him his single-mindedness and
strength of will and it was the English education of Quintín Roelas of *La feria de los discretos* (*The School for Rogues*) that
taught him to be strong and to win. The Englishman Hugo Riversdale, one of the principal characters in *Humano enigma* (*A Human Enigma*) is the embodiment of what the author considered
the best English qualities: he is calm, courageous, and optimistic,
endowed with a large measure of intelligent self-confidence. The
reasonable, ethical Jorge Stratford Grain of *El amor, el dandismo,
y la intriga* (*Love, Dandyism, and Intrigue*) is an elegant gentleman who detests all forms of exaggeration, all manifestations
of the mass mentality and who is repelled by the slightest hint

of vulgarity.[24] In Baroja's portrayals of Englishmen, the ethical and the rational are sometimes counterbalanced by the erratic and the comic: Mr. Bothwell of *El mayorazgo de Labraz* (*The Lord of Labraz*) is pleasantly eccentric, while the English dentist, Mr. Philf, has at his disposal a degree of comic resourcefulness bordering on genius.[25] Anglo-Saxon women are similarly given the benefit of either serious or comic treatment. In the former category are the sympathetically drawn young English girls who occasionally adorn the pages of the novels. Mary Sandow, Shanti Andía's wife, and Dolly Warden, the model mate of Captain Chimista, obviously belong to the select minority, at opposite poles from the Southern women who, Baroja maintains, promptly join the species designated as *ballenatus meridionalis* ("Southern whale") once they marry.[26] Victims of the author's tendency to caricature are the hapless English governesses with their bony frames and large feet, with the stereotype of the desiccated old maid reaching epic proportions in the portrayal of Miss Pich in *Paradox, Rey* (*Paradox, King*).[27]

Baroja's first trip to England in 1906, of which *The City of Fog* was the reflection, challenged some of his preconceptions and, inevitably, brought about some modification in his views. While expressing in his London novel great admiration for England's capacity to conquer the forces of nature and to breed men of action, he is adamant in his dislike of the hypocrisy and snobbery of the English, and uncompromisingly rejects their sense of hierarchy, their cold correctness, and the dullness of their lives.[28] In *The City of Fog* it is Dr. Aracil, himself the former butt of Baroja's anti-Mediterranean prejudices, who frequently expresses the author's biting comments on a society which had somehow failed to live up to his expectations. *Caesar or Nothing*, published in 1910, contains the observation that the English have everywhere imposed an atmosphere of coldness along with rare meat and bottled gravy. César Moncada, who is not in any event noticeably benevolent in his judgments, refers to the English as ridiculous sheep given over to worship of the monarchy and the aristocracy.[29] The adjectives "cruel," "dull," "hypocritical," "cold," "arrogant," begin to appear regularly in Baroja's disquisitions on the English. Although Hugo Riversdale does much to give England a good press in *A Human Enigma* (1928), in the same work Riversdale's friend Max Labarthe avows that it is very English to be unintelligent. Lord Clancarty, the English ambassador described in the Aviraneta series is arrogant and disdainful;[30] Mr. Piper, a minor figure in the same series,

is "a typical Englishman" with an ill-tempered manner and the
face of a bulldog.[31]

Both before and after the second trip to England in 1926 there
is an alternation of positive and negative views. *Sublimated
Sensuality,* published in 1920, contains an appreciation of the
English for their capacity to judge men according to individual
worth, and in an essay written seventeen years later Baroja
reaffirms his admiration of the English willingness to recognize
merit in all fields. In England, if not in Spain, scientists, writers,
dancers, are justly valued, because it is the individual and not
the mass that is esteemed.[32] The essay "Las ideas de ayer y de
hoy" ("Yesterday's and Today's Ideas") of 1933 sounds the
nostalgic note so frequent in the older Baroja: before the first
World War ". . . one could come and go, without any explana-
tions, without documents, without having to answer questions.
This did not prevent England from being great."[33]

It is in the essays written after the conclusion of the second
World War that Baroja expresses unmitigated disappointment
with England's failure to maintain her leadership in Europe. In
1947 and again in 1948, the author accuses England of sinking
back into a slow, routinized life, without interesting herself in
the fate of liberalism throughout the continent. Baroja insists
that England has lost her direction since the conclusion of the
War and is a nation fatally given over to the banalities of the
Laborites.[34]

If England at one time represented order, strength, and self-
confidence to Baroja, Germany won his admiration for her leader-
ship in science, industry, and organization.[35] Unlike Azorín and
Unamuno, Baroja did not support the cause of the Allies in World
War I, but declared himself on the side of Germany. In his
"Carta de un germanófilo a un suizo alemán,"[36] a letter written to
Paul Schmitz, Baroja goes to great pains to indicate that his
Germanophilia is in no way to be associated with that of some of
his ultraconservative countrymen whose love for Germany was
based not on admiration for its culture but on admiration for
its militarism and discipline. Baroja's reasons are entirely to the
contrary, for it is precisely the militarism that he detests and the
culture that he respects. The Spaniard considers the German
intellectuals far superior to those of any of the Latin countries,
and finds in German thought great precision, agility, and clarity.
While admitting to no particular competence in judging the
merits of either side in the first World War, Baroja hazards the
opinion that, from an ideological standpoint, neither side is
right. Without denying the aggressive nature of Germany's acts

in Belgium, for example, he mentions, by no means casually, that England and France had been equally violent in their past conquests, with England covering her aggressions in a cloak of hypocrisy while France ostentatiously inscribed on monuments the names of her victim countries.

As in the case of England, however, the abstract Germany was not matched by its concrete reality and when the author visited that country for the first time, less than a decade after the conclusion of the conflict, his commentaries were frequently less than favorable. Speaking via José Larrañaga, Baroja expresses his dismay at what he takes to be the true nature of Germany. Where before the War there was an air of nobility and evidence of a high degree of technical development, Larrañaga sees in the present and on the heels of defeat only the baser aspects of the German spirit. Saving, of course, Kant, Dürer, and Beethoven from the general condemnation, Larrañaga foresees no reason for a renaissance of Germanophilia.[37] A group of noisy Germans in a restaurant in Basle evokes from the author's spokesman the bitter comment: "so that's the sublime Aryan about whom Chamberlain has spoken . . ."[38] Larrañaga admits that he has lost his former enthusiasm for the Northern peoples and that it was an error to attribute to them the possession of the specific virtues that Southerners lacked.[39]

Scattered throughout Baroja's works are references to Germanic brutality, pedantry, and heavy-footedness, but he never failed to maintain in his later as well as in his earlier books and articles that Germany was unquestionably the first country in Europe in philosophy and music.[40] The author's insistence on the primacy of Germany in philosophy is wholly expected, given his own philosophical formation, but his apparent admiration for German music does not bear similar scrutiny. Although Baroja liked Beethoven and Mozart, the latter of whom he classifies vaguely as a German, his real enthusiasm was reserved for Italian opera and such Spanish composers of popular music as Chueca and Iradier. His fierce hatred of Wagner has already been noted.

In *Swan Hotel*, which is set in the period of World War II, one Gentil maintains that Germany could have become an important influence for good in Europe, had it not allowed itself to fall into the hands of "stupid and conceited musical-comedy adventurers . . ."[41] The characterization is scarcely adequate and suggests the same marginal understanding of political realities that made possible Baroja's too-rapid condemnation of England shortly after the second World War when that battered country could barely maintain itself, much less serve as an example of liberalism to Europe at large.

The Germans in the earlier Barojian novels are often unlikely pedants who discuss *das ding an sich* after listening raptly to a concert of music by Beethoven. In a novel of the Aviraneta series one Hermann Werner takes notes on everything he sees in Missolonghi; an exceedingly patriotic young professor in the same series holds forth on a variety of involuted aesthetic and philosophical problems; Hugo Werner in *El laberinto de las sirenas* (*The Labyrinth of the Sirens*), an astronomer with encyclopedic knowledge, had spent his life reading *lo legible y lo ilegible* ("the readable and the unreadable").[42] The novels in which the three characters appear all antedate the 1926 visit to Germany. Another variety of German in the novels is characterized by childlike ingenuousness and emotionalism. The baker Karl Schneider in *The Quest* has severe attacks of lachrymose sentimentality when under the influence of alcohol, and wanders through the streets reciting verses, weeping, and apologizing to passersby for imaginary affronts. Baroja's friend Paul Schmitz, undoubtedly his favorite Northerner, is transformed into the German Max Schultze in *The Way to Perfection*, resuming his Swiss nationality as Pablo Springer in *The School for Rogues* and as Paul Stolz in the *Agonies of Our Time* series. Springer is a romantic, fond of books and music; Stolz is an engineer who specializes in fantastic projects and unrealizable dreams. He is also a particularly robust physical type, strong, cheerful, and with a voracious appetite, undoubtedly Baroja's idea of the product of a healthy race in ascendancy.[43]

The Great Whirlwind of Life which, like the other two volumes of the *Agonies of Our Time* trilogy was written out of Baroja's first direct experience with Germany, presents concrete Germans with a degree of solid reality that must be distinguished from some of the stage Germans of the novels written before 1926. The Brinckmanns, a German family living in Denmark, are gloomy, strict, and prone to judge the worth of other nations according to whether or not they are in sympathy with Germany. Convinced as they are that the Germans are God's chosen people, all Southerners, particularly Catholics, are pagan idolators hopelessly enmeshed in the toils of wickedness and sin.[44] Stolz's circle of friends includes the chemist Lenz, a self-satisfied Communist, Dr. Haller, a specialist in nervous diseases who takes a dim view of psychoanalysis, and one Mr. Fisher who, having had no success as a violinist or as a reader of horoscopes, manages to make a fortune in California as a hotel-keeper.[45] Although in the trilogy Baroja's own opinions are often indistinguishable from those of his Germans and Swiss, it is highly probable that he drew more on his objective experiences than on a catalogue of well-worn clichés in presenting his figures in this series.

It is worth noting in passing that in *Los amores tardíos* (*Late Loves*), the last novel of the trilogy, Baroja's pride as a Spaniard comes unexpectedly to the forefront in response to the anti-Spanish atmosphere of Amsterdam, and Baroja-Larrañaga, without denying the acts of cruelty committed by the Spaniards in the Flemish wars of the sixteenth century, exalts their heroism and affirms his pride in claiming the Duke of Alva as his compatriot. Further, Larrañaga maintains that the myth of Spanish excesses as against Flemish moderation is the product of the bias of Protestant historians, who have deliberately set about blackening the reputation of a Catholic country.[46] This untoward defense of Catholic Spain, certainly not typical of Baroja, is clearly the expression of the wounded sensibility of a Spaniard traveling abroad as well as an implicit criticism of Protestant fanaticism. Apropos of the latter, as early as 1904 Baroja had defended Spain's manner of colonizing the New World, attacking at the same time the bias of the Protestant historians who had reported unfavorably on the role of the Spaniards.[47] While Baroja's patriotism took the form of a severely critical attitude within the confines of Spain, once outside, that same patriotism rendered him incapable of losing himself in immoderate worship of other cultures.

IV *The French*

France and the French preoccupied Baroja to an extraordinary degree, and throughout his writings there is evidence of an ambivalent attitude, a tension between admiration and resentment, a deeply-felt Gallophobia tempered by grudging respect. The geographical closeness which made invidious comparisons almost mandatory was one factor, to be sure, but of even greater importance was the influence of historical events. Since the author devoted several of the novels of the Aviraneta series to a recreation of the struggles of the War of Independence and to the ensuing period during which French intervention was instrumental in reimposing a regime of absolutism in Spain, it is not unnatural that this stirring up of old antagonisms should leave the sediment of hostility which lies below virtually all of his observations about the French, past and present. Further, Baroja's numerous trips to France between 1899 and 1936, as well as the years spent there during the Spanish Civil War, served to intensify his preoccupation, obliging him to sharpen and to clarify his point of view.[48]

The essay "Triste país" ("Melancholy Country") included in the *Tablado de Arlequín* (*Harlequinade*) of 1904 consists, in part, of a comparison between France and Spain in which the latter country is judged superior in terms of its great men, but lamentably inferior in terms of its daily life. France is an "amiable and smiling" country with a way of life that is as admirable as its inhabitants, but its cuisine and its wines are adjudged greater than its artists; Arcachon oysters are superior to the paintings of Delacroix, a bottle of Bordeaux is better than a play by Racine.[49]

Los últimos románticos (*The Last Romantics*) and *Las tragedias grotescas* (*Grotesque Tragedies*), both of which purport to depict French life in the closing years of the Second Empire, are accounts of the Parisian *haut monde* and the slow corruption of all those who live on its fringes. Baroja's love for the physical aspect of Paris is evident everywhere, but a stern moralizing finger is raised against the frivolous way of life then reigning. Carlos Yarza, an extraordinarily well-informed and courageous Basque living in France, provides a certain counterpoint to the protagonist Fausto Bengoa's effusions about Paris, and, as in the case of José Larrañaga in the *Agonies of Our Time* series, frequently expresses the author's point of view. Yarza loves the picturesque streets and blackened buildings of the old Paris, or, to use Baroja's distinction, Saxon Paris, but detests the inauthenticity and lack of moral fibre of the overcivilized French who surround him. Yarza admits that the general level of the Frenchman is far higher than that of the Spaniard, but then adds that Spain produces more astonishingly and deeply human individuals. He had already informed Fausto Bengoa, his usual interlocutor, that although France had brought forth over the centuries many men of great talent, it was too balanced a nation to create great geniuses.[50] The temptation to compare Spain with France, cancelling out the latter's overall superiority with the former's erratic eruptions of greatness is irresistible.[51]

In *Caesar or Nothing* and *The Restlessness of Shanti Andía* there are despective references to the French, criticisms which are repeated sporadically in many of the later works. César is scornful of the stupidity revealed by the French in all non-French matters; in another section of the novel he remarks on the sense of cruelty and vengeance displayed in French *graffiti*, in contrast to the clownishness manifested by the English in theirs.[52] The motif of cruelty is intensified as Baroja begins writing the Aviraneta chronicles, but already in *The Restlessness of Shanti Andía* there is the affirmation that the French were the cruelest among all the masters of the slave ships.[53] *El escuadrón del Brigante* (*The Brigand's Squadron*), the second novel in the *Memorias de un hombre de acción* (*Memoirs of a Man of Action*) series, is an account of the role played by Aviraneta in the War of Independence. The conceit, fatuity, and cruelty of the French officers are mentioned repeatedly, with Count Dorsenne given as an egregious example.[54] The narrator remarks resentfully on the indifference of the French to everything outside their borders, although he grants at the same time their talent for science and industry. Examples of adverse comments on the French abound in the later novels of the Aviraneta series. *Con la pluma y con el sable* (*With Pen and Sword*) and *Las furias* (*The Furies*) provide hair-raising examples of French cruelty; *La ruta del aventurero* (*The Route of the Adventurer*) characterizes the French Royalists in Pamplona as vain, stupid, fanatical, affected, and conceited;[55] in *Los caudillos de 1830* (*The Chieftains of 1830*) the French are accused of selfishness and stinginess vis-à-vis the Spanish liberals of 1830.

The essay "Alrededor de la guerra" ("Thoughts about the War") included in the *Nuevo tablado de Arlequín* (*New Harlequinade*) is an attempt on Baroja's part to present his views coherently.[56] The now-familiar note is sounded once again: France may be the first nation in the world, with a long and balanced tradition of outstanding men in all branches of endeavor, but it has been more of an enemy than a friend to Spain. French pornography, fashions, and wines are exported regularly, but doctors, engineers, and mechanics are carefully kept to the north of the Pyrenees; when political counsel is given, it leads to disaster.[57] A further defect of the French is their hostility to German culture, an attitude of animosity, Baroja believes, that prevented France from becoming the intellectual capital of Europe.

The following year there is a *ritornello,* a restating of the motif of the beauties and splendors of France unfortunately marred by the pride and vanity of the French; intelligence and bravery go hand in hand with a lack of empathy and warmth.[58] With an increasingly personal feeling of bruised national pride, Baroja inveighs against French writers who are full of antipathy and condescension and given to superficiality when writing on Spain; even the Hispanists among them are fundamentally ignorant of things Spanish.[59] In the *Agonies of Our Time* series France predictably fares worse than Germany: the French are too concerned with money and sex, they consider themselves the arbiters of taste, their language is the perfect vehicle for the utterance of commonplaces, etc.[60] There are continued signs of Gallophobia even in such an innocuous novel of adventure as *Los pilotos de altura* (*The Celestial Navigators*). Captain Verdillon hates impartially all Englishmen, Spaniards, Creoles, Cubans, Brazilians, and Argentines, while "The Viscount" is a conceited braggart who, unlike Captain Verdillon, has catholic tastes and all the vices; he not only loves women but loves men as well.[61]

It is in the *Memoirs* that Baroja makes a particular effort to deny the imputation of Gallophobia, an effort that is indeed curious. In *El escritor según él y según los críticos* (*The Writer as Seen by Himself and by the Critics*), no sooner does the author deny that he dislikes France than he demurely adds that it is merely certain French characteristics that he finds distasteful.[62] He protests again, in 1945, against the label that has been attached to him, declaring that he had always admired the French but that ". . . I have always suspected that the French do not really understand other peoples."[63] In a fascinating example of "Against whom is that compliment directed?" Baroja asserts without qualification that Paris is the best city in Europe. On closer examination, however, it becomes evident that the compliment is paid not so much to flatter France as to criticize Unamuno's stubborn refusal to accept as truly good anything that is not Spanish, Basque, and preferably from Bilbao.[64]

Dating from 1948 is an unexpectedly adulatory description of the French on the eve of World War II. Baroja expresses profound admiration for the dignified behavior of the Parisians, their lack of bravado, and absence of false confidence in a passage that inevitably invites comparison with the author's bitter remarks in *El árbol de la ciencia* (*The Tree of Knowledge*) concerning the absurd confidence of the inhabitants of Madrid on the eve of the Spanish-American War.[65] Characteristically, the favorable note is subsequently neutralized by its opposite. In "Nuevamente en París" ("In Paris Again"), a section of the *Memoirs* not included in the *Obras Completas* (*Collected Works*), and published in 1955, Baroja's deep hostility rises to the surface in a castigation of the French for their scornful treatment of the Spanish refugees who found themselves in Bayonne at the end of the Spanish Civil War.[66]

The opinions Baroja expressed about England, Germany, and other Northern countries were naturally influenced by his travels; his trips in 1906 and 1926 brought about some modification in his views but not to the point where the abstraction was totally supplanted by the reality. Over the years Baroja's feelings about the North were perhaps more bookish than visceral, more the result of the fusion of abstract thought with experience than of experience alone. The case of France was quite different. Aside from the greater frequency of trips to that country and the consequent contact with its inhabitants, France was an ultimately painful reality; it was not the idea of France so much as France itself that occupied the Spaniard's mind and emotions. Kant and Nietzsche often stood between Germany and Baroja, and he saw England transformed by Dickens, but he was left to face France alone, without the interposing shadow of a great figure. Even his idol Claude Bernard could not modify his view, for to Baroja he was first a scientist and only incidentally a Frenchman.

V The Basques

When Luis Murguía longs to share the religious beliefs of his fellow Basques, he does so not from any need for religion in this life so much as from the need to be able to look forward to reposing in the cemetery in Arnazábal . . . *al lado de los hombres de la misma raza, entre la ceniza de los antepasados* (". . . next to men of the same race, amidst the ashes of my ancestors").[67] To Baroja, being Basque was not merely an accident of birth; the sentiments expressed by his alter ego Murguía might have been his own as well. If Baroja first began to feel like a Basque only when he went to practice medicine in Cestona, the sentimental groundwork had already been laid. His mother spoke Basque and Don Serafín not only spoke it but wrote poetry in that language. Even the casual reader can not fail to notice the prodigal insertion of Basque songs in many of the novels, an abundance that suggests long and deep familiarity. Baroja was, however, quite distinctly not politically a separatist, nor could he share the views of the reactionary, ultramontane Basques. If he detested the religious fanaticism of the Basque region, he loved its damp, grey climate and its topography; if the ultratraditionalist Carlists repelled him, he was enormously attracted by the suggestion of magic and primitive rites in the misty hills and dark caves of the countryside. Even without a scapulary, as Baroja put it, he was none the less a Basque.

If a single thread emerges from Baroja's variations on the theme of the Basque country, it is the elegiac longing for the lost paradise. The naive sensuality and polytheism of the primitive Basques found expression in life-affirming rituals and magic; not Jaungoikoa, the Semitic Jehovah, but Urtzi (Thor),[68] not the law, but freedom and lawlessness. The Christianization of the

Basque country was, to Baroja, a fall, an expulsion from paradise.
The local gods were crushed under the weight of "Latinized
Semitic cults"[69] and, with the imposition of dogmatic unity,
Basque originality, goodness, freedom, and diversity were submerged. Nietzsche had said in the *Twilight of the Idols* that
"Christianity is a metaphysics of the hangman"[70] and it is precisely the role of the Church in restraining the vital impulses that
Baroja condemns. Sexual liberty was driven out and the idea
of sin made its entrance; sensuality and crime became synony-
mous. Whatever capacity the Basques might have had for
creativity and invention had been suffocated under the débris
of lifeless Latin formulae; the Catechism had become the sole
repository of all truth. Catholicism, in short, had deprived the
Basques of their fantasy.

The moralist in Baroja comes to the surface when he begins
to distinguish between the Basque of the city and the Basque
from the villages. The native of Bilbao, for example, is ignorant,
self-satisfied, limited in outlook; the men are conceited and noisy
and have execrable taste; there is no social life, no sense of
solidarity.[71] The city dwellers are the sons of Jaungoicoa and are
consequently bourgeois, religious, indifferent to their history, and
egotistically absorbed only in the present.[72] The countryside
is the realm of prehistory and it is there that pagan survivals
flourish; echoes of the Witches' Sabbath and the shadow of the
soothsayer still haunt the glens. The Basque village is the natural
habitat of the eccentric, the madman, and the individualist; the
fantastic "type" so dear to the heart of Baroja is an indigenous
product. The adventurer, the sailor, the guerrilla fighter are all
sons of Urtzi the Thunderbolt; primitive, barbaric, dionysian,
they embody the valiant spirit of the ancient Basques. The
author's mock-ideal state is the Republic of the Bidasoa "without flies, without priests, without guards."[73]

Baroja's love for the Basque countryside finds literary expression in *Vidas sombrías* (*Somber Lives*), a collection of short
pieces published in 1900. Among these lyrical, melancholy frag-
ments of imagination and experience is "La venta" ("The Inn"),
an ode to the joys of a countryside inn, remarkable for its celebration of physical satisfactions and comforts.[74] The tendency to
intellectualize, to speculate, to criticize is absent; the author is
at one with his surroundings, fusing with them rather than
standing outside. The sybaritic pleasure experienced in the
Basque inn was apparently never equalled by the amenities and
refinements available in the grander establishments in European

cities, for Baroja's rhapsodic tone was not to be duplicated in subsequent descriptions of lodgings.[75]

Joy, an uncommon thing in the works of Baroja, finds its most congenial home in the Basque region. "Elizabide el vagabundo" ("Elizabide the Vagabond") is a simple, romantic tale with a happy ending, reflecting the pleasure experienced by the young author at the festival in Aizarnazábal;[76] *La dama de Urtubi* (*The Lady of Urtubi*)[77] is essentially a vitalistic glorification of primitive pagan rites; *El caballero de Erlaiz* (*D. Adrián de Erlaiz*) contains an extensive interlude dedicated to the geography, superstitions, and songs of the Basque region. Basqueness plays a role in novels too numerous to mention, but perhaps the most explicitly Basque work is *La leyenda de Jaun de Alzate* (*The Legend of Jaun de Alzate*). Published in 1922, *The Legend . . .* is a novel in dialogue form and can be characterized to a limited degree as a Basque variation on the theme of Faust. Jaun de Alzate, who has always believed in the traditional Basque deities, suddenly finds himself surrounded by converts to Christianity. Passionately desirous of learning the ultimate truth, he gives himself over to reading and contemplation, only to become disillusioned with the limits of knowledge and to conclude: "Urtzi is as true as Jehovah or Christ."[78] The words "as true as" are to be interpreted as "no more true than," for Jaun dies a skeptic.

Jaun's study in many respects resembles Faust's and the scenes presenting a Witches' Sabbath, the magic mirrors, and a panorama of famous men are reminiscent of Goethe, as is the anti-Christian counterpoint supplied by Baroja-Mephisto. Jaun remarks that there can be no doubt that he is surrounded by Catholics: "I could tell because my books have been burned and my garden destroyed."[79] In the epilogue, Urtzi Thor bids good-bye for the last time to the ". . . haughty and jovial ancient Basques." What the work lacks in form it makes up for in imagination; with its poetic interludes it is Baroja's romantic recreation of the old, barbaric deities in whom, be it said in passing, he had as little faith as in their more modern replacements.[80]

The minor Basque characters in the novels range from the bold, energetic, and primitive Ollarra who, entirely uncorrupted by civilization, lives in close contact with nature, to the braggart Beluasteguigoitia, whose very name is the visible sign of his tendency to exaggerate.[81] Shagua, an illiterate old peasant, has such respect for all forms of life that the protagonist of *El cura de Monleón* (*The Curate of Monleón*) is naively amazed at this surprising manifestation of non-Christian Christianity; "El Arran-chale" of *Los recursos de la astucia* (*The Resources of Cunning*) speaks only Basque, knows nothing of the nature of the Carlist war raging about him, and feels a complete stranger when more than a few kilometers from his home. Baroja's noble savage is clearly Basque, but not all Basques are noble savages. Old Tellagorri of *Zalacaín el aventurero* (*Zalacaín the Adventurer*) is a completely free, independent spirit, individualistic to the point of mania, but not unaware of either Church or State, both of which he criticizes freely. A potential citizen of some impossibly antisocial community, Tellagorri makes his own clothes, cuts his own hair, even sews his sandals. His slogan, quite logically is: keep what you have and steal what you can.

If Baroja is attracted by the simplicity of the peasant and entertained by the fantasy of the eccentric, his pride in being a Basque flowers at the evocation of the warriors and adventurers produced by his region.[82] Generals Zumalacárregui, Eguía, and Espoz y Mina alternate in the pages of the Aviraneta series with the valiant hawk-like Basque foot soldiers; Basque seamen and adventurers crowd the pages of *The Restlessness of Shanti Andía* and *The Celestial Navigators*. To make a catalogue of the Basques appearing in all of Baroja's collected works would be almost an endless and probably futile task; their ubiquitousness is incontestable.

Toward the end of his life Baroja consented to dedicate a book to the Basque country, a book that was to be at once a geographical guide, a history, a poetic evocation. *El país vasco* (*The Basque Country*), published in 1953, was the result. In the prologue, the octogenarian author makes no attempt to hide the fact that the work is based on his former impressions of the Basque country; comparing himself to a weatherbeaten boat lying at anchor in port, stripped of sails and rudder, Baroja remarks: "I have to live and write according to my past impressions, copying myself."[83] The remembrance of the past brings to the fore the author's lyrical vein, and fills him with nostalgia for the charm and picturesqueness of the Basque country as he remembered it from his early years. The passage of time has not diminished his preference for the country over the commonplace vulgarity of the cities. "The authentic aspects of Basque life are to be found in the countryside."[84] The last section of the work is once more a paean of praise to Basque sailors, poets, musicians, artists, and scientists. There is an interesting section on Iradier, about whom Baroja had already written twice with some heat, since Bizet had "borrowed" the Basque composer's

Habanera for his *Carmen*.[85] *The Basque Country* concludes with the reproduction of some texts of old Basque songs—an appropriately sentimental return to the beginning.

VI *The Semites*

Baroja's idealized Basque is at home in the mountains or on the sea, living in close contact with nature and giving rein to his spontaneous impulses. The overcivilized, corrupted Basque lives in the city, his primitive past forgotten, his heroic impulse disintegrated; in his dogmatic observance of religious and political law, he reveals the influence of the Semite. Insofar as religion and politics reveal the malign influence of the Semite, Baroja finds them worthy of condemnation; neither his anti-Catholicism nor his anti-Socialism can be clearly understood in any other context.

The fanaticism and intransigence that Baroja sees as a characteristic of Spanish life in general he considers a direct reflection of Judaic dogmatism and authoritarianism. The solid construction of the monotheistic Jews, at opposite poles from relativistic Greek thought is too closed, too positive for the skeptical Baroja. Respect for the law, the insistence on unity as exemplified in the motto "Whoever is not with me is against me"—a motto Baroja considers quintessentially Judaic—were taken over by Christianity to the detriment of the individual; Nietzsche's affirmation in *Zarathustra* to the effect that Judeo-Christian morality is a manifestation of the herd instinct finds a fervent echo in Baroja. Extending the dogmatism of the Jews to the Arabs as well, the author insists that no pure Arab is ever a freethinker or a heretic. The flagrant example of Averroës is neatly sidestepped with the suggestion that some of the philosopher's ancestors may have been Visigoths or Iberians.[86] The desire to punish and to take revenge, the cult of language whose by-product is rhetoric, the tendency to equate misconduct with crime, are considered by Baroja to be Semitic characteristics.[87]

In the *New Harlequinade* Baroja maintains that the primacy of the state at the expense of the individual suggests Jahveh or Moloch; socialism has "a very Semitic air" and communism is "a plague of Judaic origin."[88] In a not wholly unexpected reversion to old and presumably rejected distinctions, the author states categorically in a work written in 1952 that liberty is to be associated with the Aryans, while despotism is to be associated with the Semites.[89]

If Marxism is a reflection of the doctrinaire Jewish spirit, the

same can be said of psychoanalysis. The latter, however, is held
in even lower esteem because of its utilization of erotic symbolism.
Freud, who is classified by Baroja along with Lombroso as the
opposite of the serious scientist such as Pasteur and Koch,
emerges as a cross between a theosophist and an avant-garde
opportunist who, by means of rhetoric and the clever exploitation
of neurasthenia, has managed to inherit the role of the Catholic
priest. Psychoanalysis is looked upon by the author with the
same suspicion as such other manifestations of "fakery" as
Cubism, Dada, and spiritualism.[90] In *The Curate of Monleón,*
Dr. Basterreche refers ironically to "Freud and company" and
their "discovery" of the libido; in a previous section he had
already impugned the originality of the contributions of psychoanalysis.[91]

Dr. Iturrioz, in *The Tree of Knowledge,* divides Spaniards into
two moral types: the warlike Iberian and the shrewd, rapacious
Semite. Although Baroja comments that this classification is
somewhat arbitrary, it seems to reflect his own view with a
fair degree of accuracy, particularly in light of the fact that
Arcelu makes an almost identical distinction in *The Way of the
World,* adding the detail that the Iberian lives in the country
while the Semite inhabits the city.[92]

The association of usury, banking, and commerce with Jews
is a commonplace in Baroja's novels and there is a veritable procession of materialistic and practical businessmen who are
involved in some way with finance. The figures in Baroja's
gallery of Jews are numerous but not distinguished for their
individuality. There is the materialistic, opportunistic Ernesto
Klein of *The Way of the World,* the oily, repulsive Santos
Toledano of *The City of Fog,* the bankers Benolié, Lione and
Silva in the Aviraneta series,[93] the usurer's son García Pérez
in *Los visionarios* (*The Visionaries*); Yaco, in *Weeds,* who though
kind is exceedingly stingy, Gómez Salcedo in *Love, Dandyism
and Intrigue* who is pleased to traffic in every available commodity, Manasés León, the small businessman in *The Wax Figures,* and a considerable number of others. Baroja's "instinctive
antipathy" to the dark, curly-haired type has been noted by Julio
Caro Baroja, but it is a superfluous commentary.[94] The novelist's
Jewish men are almost invariably described with an unmistakable
air of revulsion on Baroja's part, and often turn out to be physical
caricatures.[95]

The women fare quite differently, perhaps in part because the
hateful financial associations are lacking. The four daughters of
the widow Mesoda Ben Asayag in *Los contrastes de la vida* (*The*

Contrasts of Fortune) are all charming; *Juan Van Halen* contains
a rhapsodic description in almost Cervantine prose of two very
beautiful Jewish women.[96] Although Sara in *Love, Dandyism
and Intrigue* is a representative of the dark, curly-haired type so
unacceptable to Baroja, there is no evidence of antipathy in the
description, nor does the author take exception to a Rumanian
Jewess with an aquiline profile and "Semitic mouth."[97] Baroja's
bias in favor of the non-Catholic, preferably non-Spanish woman
undoubtedly saves the Jewesses in his novels; for the men there
is little hope.

Reference has been made in a previous chapter to the author's
association of the avant-garde in art with Jewish critics and merchants. The erotic symbolism of Freudianism, so distasteful to the
puritanical Baroja, is but one manifestation of the "vile mentality" of the Jews; the "Judaic sensuality" of *La Celestina* is another.[98] In the *Intermedios* (*Intermezzi*) of 1929, Baroja suggests
that the Jews will set the tone for the literature of the future. The
new literature will be unheroic, erotic, concerned with sexual
aberration; in short "plain filth."[99]

Baroja evidently believed that the Jews could distinguish
themselves in the sciences but not in the arts; for the arts he
considers them too strident. Kafka, aside from being a miniature
Dostoyevsky, is also an example of "Jewish hysteria," a judgment based on the author's vague indication that he had read
algo ("something") by the Jewish author, which he then
amplifies sufficiently to indicate that the one work in question is
obviously *The Metamorphosis*.[100] In a surprisingly ingenuous
series of conjectures, Baroja wonders if anyone could tell that
the theory of relativity was the product of a Jewish mind, if it
could be guessed that a symphony by Mendelssohn was written
by a non-Christian, if some of Heine's poems could not easily
be taken for those of a one hundred percent German.[101] To be
taken with a similar degree of good-humored skepticism are
the author's creation of honorary Semites. Julio Aracil, the practical and opportunistic friend of Hurtado in *The Tree of Knowledge* is a "Semitic type"; D'Annunzio is a "Judaic type"; Larrañaga wonders if perhaps Nietzsche is not "a Jew in disguise";
Stalin is apparently an Ashkenazi, and Baroja's contemporary
Valle-Inclán is under suspicion.[102] The reverse process is in operation when Baroja sees no point in attributing Montaigne's
philosophical orientation to his ethnic background; the author
doubts that the Frenchman's mother was Jewish in any case. He
then adds solemnly that it is not possible to associate any particular spiritual disposition to a particular race or group.[103]

Although he had said earlier that the Hapsburgs were correct in purifying Spain of its Semitic elements, in an essay written in 1938 there is the wistful statement: "If the Jews had not been expelled from Spain, Spinoza would have been a Spanish philosopher."[104]

Silvestre Paradox, Aviraneta, César Moncada, José Larrañaga, Jaun de Alzate, all make pejorative remarks about Jews with varying degrees of intensity. In the case of Larrañaga, the hostility is greatly mitigated for being shared; the critical Basque dislikes Catholics and Protestants as well. In a similar vein, César Moncada explains that his disapproval of Jews is based not on their anti-Christianity but on their super-Christianity.[105] That Baroja did not always devote himself to scurrilous remarks is evidenced by his admiration for Spinoza, Heine, Bergson, and Einstein. In the case of the scientist, however, there are reservations. In *The Caprices of Fortune* Dr. Haller sees "nothing new" in Einstein's theories, for Kant had already explained the philosophical aspects, and the mathematical concepts were not understandable anyway.[106]

In an evocation of memories of fin-de-siècle Paris in a portion of the *Memoirs* dating from 1945, Baroja devotes several paragraphs to the Dreyfus case, concluding that it was folly to resuscitate anti-Jewish phobias at a time when the Jews were becoming assimilated in France. Although, he adds, Jews and Moors ". . . seem like musical comedy actors to me,"[107] they should not be persecuted on that account. Such a return to the Dreyfus case in the wake of the mass slaughters of World War II might seem truly extraordinary if one were not already initiated into the Barojian method of seeking support in personal experience. Baroja had been in Paris at the time of the Dreyfus affair and witnessed the events he describes; World War II, only the beginnings of which he witnessed from his vantage point in Paris, was somehow remote and unreal. Like the souls in Dante's *Hell,* Baroja sees events that are distant far more clearly than the present, or in this particular case, the recent past.

El cantor vagabundo (*The Wandering Singer*), published in 1950, presents a series of Jews without tendentious commentary, and in the *Memoirs* it is evident that the author is truly aghast at accounts of Nazi brutality against the Jews.[108] In another section of the *Memoirs,* however, Baroja asserts that Jews form a powerful world-wide association by means of which "They control everything."[109] It does not seem to strike Baroja at any time that a particular mode of thinking may quite easily lead to a particular type of action, that there may very well be a link between theory and practice, that speculation is not always and everywhere idle. Baroja was greatly interested in racial theories and was obviously anti-semitic, but that such an attitude could lead as a consequence to concentration camps and crematoria simply never occurred to him. The loss of the link between thought and action as described by Azorín could scarcely be clearer.

VII *General Xenophobia*

If hostility towards foreign countries is indeed the negative side of patriotism, the more closely one examines Baroja's attitudes toward foreigners the more patriotic he appears. His South Americans, while not numerous, seem to have been created for the sole purpose of proving the rightness of the Monroe Doctrine. Such affirmations as "America has never given us anything" and "America is the stupid continent par excellence" give some indication of the tenor of the author's remarks.[110] Deceit, vengefulness, indolence, ostentation, vulgarity, servility, and near-illiteracy are qualities which Baroja bestows with largesse upon the luckless South Americans who occasionally make their appearance in his novels.[111] Pedro Leguía, the narrator of *Love, Dandyism, and Intrigue* obligingly explains that if South Americans are conceited and greedy, it is because of their drops of "Negro blood"; in St. Moritz, after commenting with horror on the number of members of the black and yellow races to be seen everywhere, Leguía predicts that there will be no real Europeans left after a few years because ". . . they will all be mixed breeds."[112]

Larrañaga also disapproves of mixed breeds, describing the modernist poet Rubén Darío as spiritually negroid, and adding in a later conversation that black societies seek only pleasure and the satisfaction of their vanity, with no thought for difficult accomplishment and self-improvement.[113] It is evident that Gobineau's *The Inequality of Human Races* often led Baroja down the perilous path of uncritical commentary and capricious judgment. Both *Paradox, King* and *The Celestial Navigators* display burlesque Negroes, bearing such names as Ugú, Funangué, and Bagú in the former work and Sambo, Kukula, and Nambulu-Bumu in the latter. While the comic intent is unmistakable, the underlying distrust and revulsion are equally so. Baroja's treatment of the Chinese Fang-Li in *La estrella del capitán Chimista* (*Captain Chimista's Star*) is similarly grotesque, with the author compounding the felony by observing on several occasions that the Chinese must always remain an enigma to the Europeans.[114]

North Americans do not play a prominent role in either the essays or the novels, but occasional comments indicate an uncritical propensity to surround commonplaces with an aura of authenticity. If American men are laconic and efficient, American women tend to lack character and decorum.[115] Perhaps the most noteworthy passage dedicated to the United States is the anti-Wilson diatribe written in November, 1918. Still a Germanophile, Baroja impugns the altruism of Woodrow Wilson, sardonically referring to him as "This Marcus Aurelius of the great Republic of trusts and sewing machines . . ."[116] The extermination of the American Indian, lynchings, American corruption and immorality, are all condemned in turn after which, surprisingly, Baroja refers to the United States as a country "that would conquer Puerto Rico or the Philippines when they belonged to a weak nation . . ." A rapid comparison with passages in *The Tree of Knowledge,* wherein Spain's inertness is held responsible for the loss of the colonies and wherein the author mentions the United States as the country of the sewing machine solely in order to mock the false optimism of his fellow Spaniards, casts an interesting light on the evolution of Baroja's sympathies.[117] The author's Germanophilia of that period clearly led him to adopt extreme positions against France and the United States, whether with or without justification. Before the outbreak of the first World War Baroja was accustomed to looking at the world primarily as a Spaniard, but with the taking of sides in 1914 and until the echoes of the war were heard but dimly, his phobias and "philias" reflected his sympathy for the German cause.

Wholehearted admiration for any one country, unmodified by adverse judgments on at least a few aspects of its national life, was not within Baroja's capacity; his critical sense usually rendered him incapable of viewing only one facet of, for example, French or English life, and he was not sufficiently naive to mistake a single part for the whole. But if neither France, England, nor Germany could fully satisfy him, Spain inspired a far more intense feeling of dissatisfaction, a discontent strongly mixed with rage.

CHAPTER 4

Church and State

I The Secular Image of Spain

THE critical spirit of the Generation of 1898 found its most virulent and insistent expression in the works of Baroja, who, undistracted by any concern for life in the next world, was free to concentrate the full force of his attention on this one. Few institutions and few social classes emerge unscathed after the Basque's scrutiny, for reality must fall short of the ideal. In the case of Spain, the merciless fustigation is more a consequence of familiarity and love than of cold hostility, since it is the true patriot who suffers most for the weaknesses of his country. In *Youth, Egolatry,* Baroja defines his position succinctly: he would like the Basque provinces to be the best region in Spain and Spain the best country in Europe, but he will not permit himself to falsify the truth.[1] This *amor amargo* (bitter love), to use Laín Entralgo's term, underlies the cries of anguish and shouts of protest with which Baroja and his cogenerationists reacted in the face of the Spanish reality, investing the sharp criticism with deep feeling and, at times, genuine poignancy. The image of Spain that emerges from the totality of Baroja's works is flavored with a consistent if not necessarily comforting amalgam of sarcasm and sympathy, impatience and understanding, anger and pain.

Harlequinade, which contains some of the novelist's most intemperate attacks on his native country, describes Spain devastatingly as the country of the minimum: minimum in brains, in vice, in passion, in food. Everything is so utterly insipid, in life as well as in art, that even adultery does not flourish. Spaniards are so enslaved to conformity that the novelist has to invent characters because there aren't any.[2] Ignorant, devoid of curiosity, with a passion only for the utterly useless, the Spaniard exists in a mummified state of monotonous lifelessness. Proud but not patriotic, dogmatic but not moral, he shows talent for neither science, order, nor civilization. Natural and intellectual resources are wasted, intelligence is not respected, change is anathema, and intolerance is rampant. Contrary to his romanticizing tendency to idealize the past, the author describes the Madrid of the eighteenth and early nineteenth century as backward, barbaric, dirty, its streets pullulating with the lame, the indigent, and the blind.[3] These Goyesque sketches in the Aviraneta novels indicate what there was in the capital at that time, but equally vivid are Baroja's descriptions of what there was not. In evoking the villages of Spain after the conclusion of the Carlist wars, the novelist writes, ". . . there is no society, there are no gardens, no books, no religion, no love affairs, no complications, neither good food nor good drink . . ."[4]

The Way to Perfection, as one of Baroja's earliest novels, contains some of his most strident passages. Both the aristocrats of the capital and the villagers of Yécora are weighed and found wanting in the most elementary human virtues. The high society of Madrid is a compendium of vice, and the life of the aristocracy is a series of variations on the theme of sexual immorality. Yécora, in contrast, provides the author with the ingredients for a chilling study of death in life. Baroja characterizes this pueblo terrible (dreadful village)[5] in terms of a series of negatives, supplying a catalogue of all the beautiful works of art and examples of traditional and noble architecture that are notable for their absence.[6] Present and strikingly evident, however, are the sun-baked rocks, the dusty roads and bare hills; with moneylenders, priests, corrupt political leaders, with sordid vices, hypocrisy, and gloom, Yécora is the realm from which all joy has fled.

The essay "Triste país" ("Melancholy Country") written two years later, contains a brief summation of all of Spain's Yécoras: "Our way of life is poor, dreadful."[7] Any sign of originality or of fantasy is crushed; effusiveness and sentiment are deemed shameful, and there is no élan, no joviality, no desire to please. The regenerationist tone is equally evident in many other essays in the Harlequinade, particularly in "Revisión necesaria" ("Essential Reforms").[8] The stress on appearance and outward show, combined with a refusal to face reality, point to the existence of a people whose sole interest is to seem rather than to be. The essay is a bitter protest against the cruelties and inequities of contemporary Spanish life and against the indifference of those who see no reason to change.

The Madrid of the Restoration painted in The Tree of Knowledge is a stagnant pool, immobile, unchanging, with only an occasional ripple on its surface. "Spain, and Madrid in particular, was living in an atmosphere of absurd optimism; Spain had the best of everything."[9] The press did all in its power to encourage this somnolent state, and with the outbreak of the Spanish-American war provided assurances that the United States was but ill equipped to conquer such a powerful nation. Alcolea del Campo, Baroja's rural counterpart of the capital, is another *pueblo terrible*, a village fallen into decay through indifference, through lack of interest and vitality. Each family lives exclusively for itself, guarding all possessions carefully, including wine, money, and women. Local political bosses rule Alcolea, with the conservatives and the liberals taking turns with results that presented no discernible differences in terms of dishonesty and corruption. Alcolea maintains its perfection—the perfection of a well-tended cemetery—by selecting for the most important positions only the most obviously unfit; to be qualified is to be unqualified and vice versa.[10] Envy, cruelty, and pride dominate every aspect of life in this bare, treeless village; egotism blooms, injustice flourishes, human warmth and cordiality are annihilated.

The Wandering Lady contains the following brief diagnosis of the defects of Spain, summarized by Dr. Iturrioz: false patriotism, vulgar regionalism,[11] and natural barbarism. In *The City of Fog* the same Iturrioz, perhaps in a fanciful mood, declares that Spanish irritability is the product of a dry climate; if Spain had England's dampness, hate would disappear.[12] Dr. Aracil, in the same novel, observes that if in England he is enraged only by the abstract, in Spain he is outraged only by the concrete—the Spaniards themselves.

In Spain there are no laboratories, no opportunities for experimentation; water is not used to generate electric power, rivers are not utilized for irrigation, natural resources are disregarded. The classical image of Spain is that of a country drunk with wine, sun, fanaticism, and violence, with poverty in the streets and pomp in the cathedral.[13] The relationship between the sexes is materialistic and profoundly antisocial, with the young men in the cities seeking mates with large dowries while the young ladies reciprocate in kind. Once married, the man lives in the streets while the woman remains at home.[14] In what appears to be a compliment, Baroja mentions that Spanish men, at least, are not hypocritical about their private immoralities, but then adds by way of explanation that the reason for this refreshing openness is that virtue is not a prized commodity in any case.

With its abundant and convenient sinecures, Spain is an ideal haven for the lazy. Luis Murguía has a position in the Ministry for which the only requirement is a monthly trip to collect his salary;[15] when he happens to appear, it is the occasion for a gathering of the bohemian clans. The *Memoirs* contains a similar description of free-for-all discussions in a Ministerial office, a phenomenon which surprised nobody but Paul Schmitz who was obviously accustomed to a different attitude toward governmental offices. Quintín, the protagonist of *The School for Rogues* is much admired because he does nothing, a state he has no wish to change for fear of offending the hordes of the indolent. Although in many cases Baroja contrasted the virtues of a former age with the vices of the present, the cultivation of idleness and the institution of the sinecure belong as much to the past as to the present. In *The Route of the Adventurer,* which is set in the early part of the nineteenth century, the English narrator J. H. Thompson secures a post at the Museum of Natural History in Madrid and is astonished to discover that of all the employees, only he possesses the naiveté to come to work. Not entirely disassociated from the sinecure is the custom of securing positions, passing courses, or obtaining a favorable judicial decision by the use of *recomendaciones* (personal influence). References to this procedure are far too abundant to enumerate, but it is noteworthy that Baroja himself had no qualms about taking advantage of the corrupt practice of *recomendaciones* in order to pass a course in Chemistry and in order to avoid military service.[16]

The Spaniard's lack of social sense and of solidarity, his unconcern for others, and his profound indifference constitute another target for the author's arrows; the essay entitled "Indiferencia" ("Indifference") included in *Harlequinade* is a synthesis of the antisocial attitudes illustrated in such novels as *The Way to Perfection, The Tree of Knowledge,* and *The Way of the World.* The theme of hatred and envy, elaborated by both Unamuno and Antonio Machado,[17] figures prominently in the novels and essays of Baroja. In *The School for Rogues* envy is labeled the national vice and in *The Last Romantics* scorn and envy are characterized as the only truly strong passions in Spain.[18] The author writes in the essay "De Madrid a Tánger" ("From Madrid to Tangier"): "We look at each other with the hatred typical of Spaniards when they are looking at each other,"[19] an observation that suggests that there are more Hispanophobes in Spain than outside its borders.

Against this black view of Spain's spiritual and economic ailments there is a countervailing tendency to acknowledge at least a few national traits worthy of praise. Among these virtues are compassion, the sympathy that a Spaniard feels for the poor, and the manner in which the poor treat their own children. In one of his xenophobic comparisons, Baroja notes that in England the offspring of the impoverished are sad, dirty, and unsociable, while their Spanish counterparts are lighthearted and happy. It must be pointed out, however, that this observation appears in *The City of Fog* and is at variance with the author's opinions when he is comfortably within his own borders; in the essay "Nietzsche y la filosofía" ("Nietzsche and Philosophy"), Baroja remarks that while he is writing the essay the prospect from his window reveals a group of shabby, squalid children, for whom life is only pain and misery.[20] If Baroja's viewpoint in this question was subject to variation, his pride in Spain's distinguished past and the greatness of her men was not. The novelist points with awe and admiration to the brio and bravery of the conquistadors, to the valor of Spain's great guerrilla fighters in the Carlist wars, and to the heroism of his people in defending their land against the French in the War of Independence. Of equal importance are his country's great figures: Cervantes, Velázquez, El Greco, Goya, Loyola, St. Theresa, Miguel de Molinos, and her universal types—El Cid, Don Juan, and Don Quixote.[21] It is the Spanish way of life that is to be condemned, not the individuals who somehow came forth and distinguished themselves. The select man, the person capable of surpassing himself, is always saved from the general shipwreck. Miguel de Lara, a fellow guerrilla fighter of Aviraneta in *The Brigand's Squadron,* is the embodiment of the qualities the novelist prizes most. He is generous, disinterested, brave, possessed of a firm sense of justice. With the pride that belies all charges of hatred for his country, Baroja declares that only Spain produces this type of man, albeit in insufficient quantities.

As is natural in a true patriot, Baroja felt himself at liberty to say whatever he wished about his country, but took a dim view of non-Spaniards who attempted to exercise the same freedom. A South American who presumes to characterize Spain as a backward, dreadful country is informed with some asperity that ". . . when you travel with Spaniards, you don't vilify Spain."[22] Further, in *The Caprices of Fortune,* the author portrays as a complete fool an expatriate Spanish professor who equates anything foreign with excellence and who considers himself far too good to live in his homeland.[23] If bitterness is the dominant tone of Baroja's commentaries, love is a necessary complement.

II *Politics*

Baroja's conception of the state is essentially Augustinian; no matter the form of government, the result is the secular equiv-

alent of organized sin. This image of the state is matched by
the author's vision of man as a creature of evil—cruel, perfidious,
and egotistic. Enrique Olaiz in *La Voluntad* paints the *animal
humano* ("human animal") as a ferocious beast, more fit for
the jungle than for Arcadia.[24] Baroja-Olaiz is fully aware that
Utopian dreams based on the assumption of man's innate goodness are foredoomed to failure; evil must first be destroyed
before progress can become a reality. Baroja was convinced
that the only form of progress so far achieved was in the realm
of science, for in all other respects man was no more civilized
than a troglodyte.

Naturally skeptical, Baroja had little faith in the efficacy of
any form of political organization, since the very concept of
organization was inimical to his belief in the sacrosanct nature
of the individual. The writer aligned himself with no political
cause, supported no political party, applauded no leader. In a
parody of Kierkegaard's *Either/Or*, Baroja summarized his political slogan as Neither/Nor.[25] The novelist was prodigal, not to
say indiscriminate, in his censure of all "isms," but was particularly hostile to socialism, which he attacked repeatedly and
repetitiously.

A. *Socialism and Democracy*

In an article which appeared in the *Homenaje a Pío Baroja*
(*Homage to Pío Baroja*), Antonio Elorza suggests that one of
causes for Baroja's lifelong hostility to the Socialist movement
might be traced to the difficulties caused by his employees'
organizations when he was running the bakery.[26] In the same
collection Martínez Laínez makes a similar although less specific
conjecture.[27] The influence of personal rancor on Baroja's ideology
is not to be underestimated, but in this case there are enough
external reasons to account for his animus toward socialism
without necessarily invoking old resentments.

Starting with *Aurora roja* (*Red Dawn*) in 1904 and continuing
through the *Memoirs,* Socialists are characterized as despotic,
opportunistic, pedantic, hypocritical, and inquisitorial. The
pseudo-scientific and messianic air that Baroja attributes to
socialism derives from the financial talent and theocratic spirit
of the Jews in general and from the *mesianismo semítico* (Semitic
messianism) of Karl Marx in particular.[28] To Baroja, socialism
is yet another version of Semitic monotheism, with requirements
of discipline, order, and faith. It is enlightening to observe the
frequency with which the author attributes to political organization the same defects he finds in religious organization: intoler-

ance, arbitrariness, the need to unify and to codify. Enrique Olaiz describes socialism as a variety of Catholic dogma for all of humanity, while in *The Visionaries* Communists are the ". . . priests from the other side of the street."[29]

An interesting explanation by the author of his anti-socialism appears in *Harlequinade* in the essay "Burguesía socialista" ("Socialist Bourgeoisie"). With the Socialists forming the new bourgeoisie, numbers, the mass, will inevitably triumph and the individual will be engulfed. Nietzsche's aristocratism and the prophetic vision of the anthill in Dostoyevsky's *Legend of the Grand Inquisitor* are echoed by Baroja, who witnessed with repugnance the mounting influence of the Socialists both in and out of Spain.[30] To Baroja and his cogenerationists, to be bourgeois was to be unimaginative, mediocre, enslaved to the security of a routine life.[31] Once Socialists are identified with the philistinism of the middle class, they necessarily become an object of opprobrium. Baroja, certainly, shared Flaubert's belief that hatred of the bourgeoisie was the beginning of virtue.

Related to Baroja's hostility to socialism is his distrust of democracy which manifested itself, in Spain at least, as ". . . the most sterile, superficial, and stupid institution."[32] Although the author does not use the particular word, he implies that democracy is mediocracy, where every sign of superiority and distinction is an offense and where the majority, no matter how ignorant, is alway right;[33] as Kierkegaard had stated sardonically: "Where the mass is, there untruth is." The democratic rule is the rule of the masses, and the masses are vile, cowardly, uninformed, and pedantic. Heraclitus, one of the novelist's most-admired philosophers, had said that one good man was worth ten thousand,[34] and Gracián, Schopenhauer, and Nietzsche utilized only the most pejorative adjectives in their comments on the herd. Baroja might have said, again with Flaubert, that the dream of democracy was to elevate the proletariat to the level of stupidity of the bourgeoisie.[35]

B. *Anarchism*

Philosophical anarchism exercised a certain attraction for Baroja since it accorded well with his own rebellious individualism, but practical, militant anarchism was almost as distasteful to him as socialism, and for similar reasons. With the transformation of an abstract idea into a concrete organization, dogmatism makes its appearance as an inevitable adjunct, and the beauty of the theory is irrevocably destroyed by the harshness of its practice. The idealism and utopianism of theoretical anarchism cannot fail to have an appeal, but according to Dr. Iturrioz in *The Wandering Lady,* anarchism is ". . . a ridiculous and humanitarian utopianism . . ."[36] Olaiz had called dogmatic anarchism a form of atheistic mysticism, based on the false premise of the innate goodness of mankind.

Baroja devoted *Red Dawn,* the last novel of the *Lucha por la vida (Struggle for Life)* trilogy, to a study of Anarchists and anarchism.[37] There are, in accordance with the author's literary theories, many figures and many episodes, but the purported central character is Juan Alcázar, an ex-seminarian whose anarchism is artistic-humanitarian rather than doctrinal. His favorite authors are Tolstoy and Ibsen; he rarely reads political tracts. With Juan are the philosophical Anarchists Prats and El Libertario, both of whom proclaim as their program the destruction of the State, the Church, and the Army. The discussions and arguments that form the substance of the novel make clear the author's critical attitude. If Anarchists are admirable in their idealism and in their zeal for change, they are fatally flawed by their vanity and narrow-mindedness. The faces at an Anarchist meeting are described as neither intelligent nor benevolent, and El Libertario concludes: "The truth of the matter is that with people like that we cannot get anywhere."[38] In the lecture entitled "Divagaciones acerca de Barcelona" ("Thoughts on Barcelona"), delivered on March 25, 1910, Baroja indicates that the only revolutionary philosophy among the masses is the Anarchist philosophy, but unfortunately it is not only sentimental, absurd, and childish, but also bears an uncomfortable resemblance to religious dogma.[39]

The Wandering Lady, which followed *Red Dawn* by four years, was inspired by the attempted assassination of the King and Queen of Spain on May 31, 1906, the day of their marriage. According to the author's words in the prologue, the Anarchist Nilo Brull who throws the bomb in the path of the royal couple is not intended to represent his historical counterpart Mateo Morral, but is rather a synthesis of the Anarchists who came from Barcelona to Madrid after the Montjuich trials. In the *Memoirs*[40] the author recalls having met the journalist Francisco Iribarne who had spoken to him at length about his friend Mateo Morral some time after the novelist's return from London in 1906; if, at the time of writing *The Wandering Lady,* Morral's person was unknown to Baroja, evidently his deeds were not. In the same section of the *Memoirs* Baroja remembers having become acquainted in London with the Italian Anarchist Malatesta, and having been most favorably impressed by his simplicity and humility.[41]

Nilo Brull, who looks upon himself as another Raskolnikov, a lion in a hencoop, is a vain, theatrical, and thoroughly disagreeable megalomaniac who thinks only in capital letters. Dr. Aracil, his mentor and temporary benefactor, is an Anarchist in words only, for he prefers the resounding phrase to the heroic deed. The vitalist Iturrioz proclaims that it is the duty of the individual to cast aside the old morality and worn-out institutions and to destroy the mummified society of the present, but cautions that these aims must be accomplished only by means of the strength and vigor of ideas. Anarchist terrorism brings death in the midst of life and is therefore inadmissable. Iturrioz speaks in Nietzschean terms of vitality and natural barbarism, but his conclusions are scarcely less humanitarian than the idealistic dreams of Juan Alcázar.[42]

C. *The Second Republic*

The Spanish Republic which came into being in 1931 was the disappointment to Baroja that it was foreordained to be.[43] Fermín Acha, the author's spokesman in *The Visionaries*, calls it the bourgeois republic, and "bourgeois" is a scurrilous epithet in the vocabulary of the period. Baroja sees neither outstanding men, nor vital ideas, nor a genuine renewal of values; vulgarity, bureaucracy, and the repetition of worn commonplaces will be the distinguishing mark of this unimaginative Government.

In the *Rapsodias* (*Rhapsodies*), published in 1932, Baroja accuses the Republic of violence and repression and of having occasioned more deaths in the streets in one year than the monarchy had caused in forty.[44] From the somewhat greater distance of *Ayer y hoy* (*Yesterday and Today*) and the *Memoirs*, there is no softening in attitude: the author's verdict is that the Spanish republicans were devoid of political talent and that the Republic was despotic and arbitrary.[45] Baroja's animosity toward the Republic is particularly consistent with his romantic view of history. In an essay entitled "Riego y su himno" ("Riego and his Hymn"), the writer draws a series of invidious comparisons between the pedestrian republicans of 1931 and the heroic republicans of 1820; to the worshipper of individual effort and private distinction, the practical politician is but a dim figure alongside the charismatic revolutionary chieftain.

The Visionaries, the last novel of *La selva oscura* (*The Dark Wood*) trilogy, is a disquisition on the Syndicalists and Communists—the *visionarios* of the Second Republic. The garrulous and restless Fermín Acha drives about ceaselessly, meets various Communists and Syndicalists, and there follows a series of exchanges of opinions and information. Acha's point of view is familiar: negative and pessimistic, he has no faith in political panaceas. *La familia de Errotacho* (*The Family of Errotacho*) and *El cabo de las tormentas* (*The Cape of Storms*) deal with the Anarcho-Syndicalist coup in Vera and the republican uprising in Jaca, respectively. *The Family of Errotacho* resembles a chronicle far more than a novel, and whatever interest it may have is journalistic rather than aesthetic. The preparation, the uprising, the killing of the Civil Guards, the subsequent imprisonment of the leaders, and the execution of Enrique Gil Galar and Julián Santillán Rodríguez make up the bulk of the novel. *The Cape of Storms* treats in a similar fashion the premature attempt to establish the republic in Jaca by Captains Fermín Galán and Angel García Hernández and their execution in December of 1930. Fermín Acha once again provides the lessons in history as well as the commentary. The Republicans of Jaca are compared unfavorably with the Vera Anarchists, for anarchism, although "absurd and pathological,"[46] is at least somehow literary and picturesque; republicanism, especially military republicanism, is dull and "very bourgeois." The nostalgia for the old warriors is very strong, and Acha is quick to point out the difference between General Mina in 1830 and Captain Galán in 1930.

The Anarchists and Republicans who appear in the trilogy are not calculated to inspire faith in either movement; Gil Galar, particularly, is described as a degenerate afflicted with acute paranoia; the terrorists el Mecánico and el Negre have the mentality of sentimental pirates, and one either very clever or completely insane Robinsón is a vegetarian who believes in metempsychosis.[47] It may be mentioned in passing that if neither Anarchists nor Republicans are looked upon with favor, neither is the Royal Family. The Bourbons occupy the author's attention for three chapters in *The Visionaries,* supplying material for historical background tinged with backstairs gossip. The role of Alfonso XIII, the "mummified Bourbon," in forcing the execution of Galán and García Hernández is sharply censured by Acha not only as a tactical blunder but as an act of barbarism. Legal killing, as opposed to killing on the field of battle, is a revolting act worthy only of the Jews in the Bible, lawyers, judges, and other vile people who are governed by a superstitious reverence for the law.[48]

There can be little doubt that Acha speaks for Baroja throughout the trilogy. Acha is a Basque, a bachelor, a rationalist, a reader of Dostoyevsky, Nietzsche, Ibsen, and Schopenhauer; his ideals are analysis and criticism, and his loves are liberty and culture.[49] *The Dark Wood* testifies to Baroja's chronic dissatisfaction with the present and the real; he is suspicious and ill at ease at the prospect of involvement in events which he wished only to report as a disinterested observer. The past alone grants immunity.

D. *The Civil War and Dictatorship*

Baroja's allegiance in the Civil War was vouchsafed to neither side. In *Yesterday and Today* he describes both sides as equally "poor and miserable" and accuses both the Nationalists and the Republicans of hostility to Spanish writers; the *blancos* ("Whites") attack those writers who, in their opinion, discredit religion and order, while the *rojos* ("Reds") object to the writers who give their readers a sense of disobedience and skepticism. Both sides are cruel, but Baroja distinguished between the desire of the Republicans to conquer and punish, and the purely militaristic wish of the Nationalists to conquer only. While technically speaking the author's decision is still Neither/ Nor, there is a decided inclination to view the Republicans (to whom he always refers as "Reds") as under the domination of Bolshevik Jews from Russia, international apaches, and criminals from all over.[50]

Over a long period of years Baroja had many observations to make about the feasibility of a dictatorship, but his particular requirements were usually so Platonic that it is obvious that he was merely spinning theories. Roberto Hasting recommends an enlightened despotism and in *Harlequinade* the author advocates rule by the intelligent, a suggestion that is repeated decades later by Fermín Acha in *The Cape of Storms*.[51] César Moncada in *Caesar or Nothing* proposes that Spain should attempt to organize "extrareligious individualism." What Spain needs, he continues, is a military discipline of iron: ". . . men like us, each isolated from the other, join together only through discipline."[52] Moncada then adds with true Barojian irony that Spaniards require a leader for the sole purpose of subsequently destroying him. Aviraneta propounds a dictatorship of justice, intelligence, and liberty in *El aprendiz de conspirador* (*The Apprentice Conspirator*), and in *Vitrina pintoresca* (*Picturesque Showcase*) Baroja remarks that he would welcome a "good tyrant" provided that he were just, intelligent, and well-intentioned.

The Utopian nature of these requirements did not, of course, escape the author's notice, but the deep gulf between theory and practice, between thought and deed favored the cultivation of pure speculation. The difficulty of maintaining the distance between public theorizing and private opinion occasionally placed Baroja in an awkward position from which he found it necessary to extricate himself by means of denials and refutations. In *Yesterday and Today,* published during the Spanish Civil War, Baroja declares that authoritarianism is preferable to the bestial caprice of the masses,[53] but while advocating a military dictatorship to control the vengefulness of both sides in the conflict, is careful to qualify his suggestion by utilizing the phrase *en estos momentos* ("at this time").[54] That his apparent support of a dictatorship evoked unfavorable response is abundantly clear from his insistence in the *Memoirs* that his recommendation was intended as a temporary measure, that a dictatorship might be feasible in critical moments, but "only as a stopgap."[55] After stating in *Yesterday and Today* that if it is a choice between a Fascist or a Communist dictatorship he would favor the former, if only because a military dictatorship is predictable, Baroja asserts in the *Memoirs* that both forms of control are alike in their means and in their results: both communism and fascism end as a banquet for barbarians in which each guest seizes whatever he can.[56]

In an article written in 1940, Baroja takes an unequivocal stand against totalitarianism, defining it as a dangerous monster of treachery which will ultimately devour liberty and honor. While the country to which Baroja makes indirect reference is scarcely in doubt, the author makes a desperate attempt to save the shreds of his faith in Germanic culture by maintaining that traditional German thought cannot be held responsible for the aggressiveness displayed by the Third Reich.[57]

Although Baroja maintained throughout his long life that he was a liberal, he adds in the *Memoirs* that he is not intransigent: an enlightened despotism would do as well as any other form of government provided that it did not interfere with the freedom of the mind.[58] Baroja's ideal society, aside from the fly-free, religion-free and guard-free Republic of the Bidasoa is a society based on individualism and liberty, freedom of conscience and tolerance. The customary association of anarchism with Baroja's name can be understood only in this light: free thought, freedom from dogma, freedom from repression, the right of the select individual to be different. *Être comme un autre* ("To be like everybody else") was no more the Spaniard's ideal than Stendhal's, and Ortega's alarm at the revolt of the masses was matched if not exceeded by Baroja's. Gonzalo Sobejano has referred to the members of the Generation of 1898 as *anarcoaristócratas* ("anarchoaristocrats");[59] it would be difficult to describe the novelist in more accurate terms. Like Ibsen's Stockmann, Baroja believed that the strongest man is indeed he who stands most alone.

If the author's refusal to take sides in the Civil War was not particularly admirable, it was at any rate consonant with his genuine hatred for politics; he had maintained that he is not a citizen of the *polis* but a rustic, a country-dweller, and hence reserves the right to be antipolitical.[60] To the disabused candidate for political office, all politicians are swindlers, actors, and rhetoricians. Incapable of sustaining a dialogue since they are incapable of listening to each other, all political "discussions" are an aggregate of monologues. Baroja does not deny the good intentions of liberalism, but insists that it has failed in practice.[61] *Youth, Egolatry* summarizes with complete accuracy the novelist's attitude: first an enemy of the Church and second an enemy of the State. In a struggle between the two, he will support the latter, but once the State gains control he will be at odds with the State.[62] It is evident that Baroja's self-proclaimed liberalism was genuine but so profoundly anti-establishment and so completely impractical as to ultimately negate itself.

III   *The Church*

Baroja traces the beginning of his anti-Catholicism and anti-clericalism to a terrifying childhood experience which he recounts in *Youth, Egolatry*, thirty-six years after the event. After watching a funeral procession, Ricardo and Pío Baroja, accompanied by several friends, entered the Cathedral of Pamplona whereupon a canon, hearing the younger Baroja humming part of the religious service he had just witnessed, jumped out from behind a confessional and throttled him violently. The Canon, whom Baroja identified as Don Tirso Larequi, announced that he was going to see his victim's father, and rushed out of the cathedral "like a bull."[63] Baroja affirms, with perhaps more than a trace of fancy, that the ferocious Don Tirso became for him a symbol of the Catholic religion. An earlier and more tranquil memory is associated with his childhood in San Sebastián. The young Baroja used to watch a certain Don Fernando, who was reputed to be a Protestant, reading a book and feeding the swallows whose nests were near his balcony. Once Don Fernando moved away, the owner of the house destroyed all the nests. In the dictionary of Baroja's childhood the following distinctions were henceforth made: "A Protestant: a man who reads and

who likes swallows' nests. A Catholic: a man who does not
read anything and who destroys swallows' nests."[64] It may be
noted that the sardonic definition of a Catholic is not too far
removed from Jaun de Alzate's previously quoted statement
apropos of the burning of his books and the destruction of his
garden.[65]

Baroja's anti-Catholicism is militantly aggressive as is his
anticlericalism. The Spanish tradition of anticlericalism is long
and, so to speak, respectable, but Baroja's vehement anti-
Catholicism is by no means traditional and the degree to which
it is not respectable will presently be illustrated. Chapter XXXVII
of *The Way to Perfection* contains one of the author's most
intemperate attacks on the religious education of the day—so
much so that the last four paragraphs were expurgated from
the *Complete Works*.[66] The Piarist school in Yécora, which Baroja
designates contemptuously as a barracks, is the chief cause of
Yécora's moral anemia and the chief producer of the village's
political bosses, immoral priests, usurers, and ne'er-do-wells who
pass their time in idleness in the local casino. A child condemned
to that torture chamber soon suffers the loss of his intelligence,
the atrophy of his memory, the perversion of his good instincts.
Before leaving the school, the education to which the hapless
youth has been subjected has already transformed him into an
idiot, a fanatic, a coward, and a hypocrite. And above his head
there hangs the overwhelming concept of sin. Baroja's indictment
is reminiscent of Schopenhauer's essay on religion, in which
the German philosopher maintains that the education given the
young by the clergy results "in a kind of partial paralysis of
the brain."[67]

The destruction of individuality by means of the demand for
obedience *perinde ac cadaver* (like a corpse) makes of Catholicism a school of humiliation; Catholicism brings in its wake
ruin, misery, decay, superstition, and resignation. If Spain is
poor and fanatical, it is because of the pernicious influence of
religion; if women are scorned and treated without consideration,
it is a manifestation of the effect of Semitic ideas on Catholicism.[68] Dogmatism and intolerance take the place of true
religious feeling, and there is no connection whatever between
the practice of the cult and morality. The Spanish Renaissance
philosopher Luis Vives had said that Christianity continues
but fails to turn people into Christians, and it is evident that
Baroja has the same objection. Religion has engendered wars
and hatred, but it has not made people more virtuous; rather

than an opiate, it has served as a stimulant, driving men to fury and to violence.[69]

The Route of the Adventurer contains the illuminating idea that Christianity grows in inverse proportion to cleanliness, running water, and rationality, and also suggests that the most accurate indication of the cultural level of a country can be procured by adding the amount of wine consumed to the total number of flies and priests, and then dividing by the number of trees.[70] A similar association of religion with backwardness and a lack of sanitation is made in a letter signed by "P.B." which reads in part, "When I think of Christianity, I immediately imagine ghettos, scrofula, scabies, and friars." In *The Antichrist* Nietzsche declares with reference to the attitude of Christianity toward hygiene that "The body is despised, hygiene repudiated as sensuality; the church even opposes cleanliness . . ."[71]

César Moncada, in Rome, denominates Catholicism "Jewish meat, Roman style" and in *Picturesque Showcase* Baroja remarks that both Catholicism and Protestantism are "Jewish meat," each served with a different gravy.[72] José Larrañaga, predictably, is anti-Catholic and anti-Protestant; Catholicism is too Latin, Protestantism is too Judaic. The difficult Christianity of Kierkegaard, however, receives an unaccustomed nod of approbation. As the religion of the solitary individual, it is exempt from the anathema placed by Baroja on all collective and uniform creeds. At the same time that Larrañaga admits to a certain admiration for the Danish philosopher, his interlocutor Olsen raises objections to the "religious masochism" of the followers of such a demanding theology. The terror of condemnation and an obsession with the eternal life, both of which are illusory, are rooted in the brooding sense of sin awakened by the imperatives of either/or. To Baroja, Kierkegaard is a latter-day St. Ignatius, who in turn is a Don Quixote in clerical garb; if Quixotism is social mysticism, Kierkegaardism is religious mysticism.[73]

The idolatry which Baroja finds in Catholicism is in no way to be distinguished from the magic arts of the African tribes, and most Catholics are *hotentotes honorarios* ("honorary Hottentots").[74] In the African kingdom of Bu-Tata, Silvestre Paradox sighs nostalgically and with heavy irony for the beauties of Spain, not the least of which are its numerous monasteries, charming friars, and clean and intelligent priests. In the account of Paradox' youth it is noted that the charlatan Macbeth's shadow play includes "dogs, cats, rabbits, Spanish priests, friars, and donkeys."[75] There are statistical surveys of Coria, Jaca, and Cuenca, for the sole purpose of indicating the extent to which the clerical overshadows the secular,[76] and a trip to San Sebastián in 1918 reveals to the disappointed Baroja that there is a scarcity of everything but nuns and priests.[77]

Priests in general are characterized as fanatical despots who dominate the towns and cities of Spain, conspiring with the military to poison the sources of life. The clerical influence extends into the home via the women, whom priests dominate with their masculinity; if the men are not persuaded by this show of strength and brusqueness, the Jesuits are there to capture them by other means.[78] The pejorative references to Jesuits that appear here and there in the author's works apply only to the modern age, for Baroja held St. Ignatius and St. Francis Xavier, the Basque founders of the Order, in very high esteem. In an essay entitled "Los jesuitas" ("The Jesuits"), the novelist extols the military and heroic spirit of the Order, a spirit that presently changed and produced a great blossoming of theologians and moralists—Escobar, Soto, Mariana, Suárez, Molina. The casuistry and subtlety that became the mark of the Jesuits, however, found no favor with the uncompromising Basque.[79] The question and ensuing answer, "What connection is there between the Basques and that clever Jesuit spirit full of subtleties? None," make plain what was in any case a growing suspicion; it is the Basque origin of the Order with its warlike spirit that is acceptable to the anti-Latin.

In *Caesar or Nothing* the obscurantism of the church is exemplified in the behavior of the priests in Castro Duro. Profoundly suspicious of the printed word, they demand the right to examine all books before they are made available to the parishioners. In *The Restlessness of Shanti Andía*, the vicar Don Benigno decides to burn books written in French and in English, neither of which language he reads, because they must of necessity convey dangerous, subversive doctrines.

The customary scabrous note is not neglected, nor could it be, given the author's literary heritage. According to a popular ballad, all the inhabitants of Sigüenza are the children of priests and friars;[80] in *The Tree of Knowledge*, a priest is reputed to be the proprietor of two brothels; Don Sebastián Miñano, of *With Pen and Sword*, is *todo un clérigo* ("every inch a priest") for he had fathered children, had been both a Mason and an extreme reactionary, and finally died a Protestant; in the same work the Trappist Antonio Marañón is a thief and potential rapist. *The Curate of Monleón* includes an episode involving a homosexual priest, an account of an affair between a young girl and the curate Don Clemente, the arrest of a priest on charges of corruption of a minor. Don Jacinto in *The Quest* tells obscene stories, the seminarian Tiburcio Lesmes in *The Ship of Fools* gambles with marked cards, the priest Macorra in *Las mascaradas sangrientas* (*Blood-Stained Masquerades*) is a drinker and a womanizer.

The "Judaic cruelty" of the priest is illustrated in the example of the Penitentiary Sansirgue of *The Resources of Cunning;* like his counterpart in Galdós' *Doña Perfecta,* he is hypocritical and vengeful, completely unscrupulous in the choice of means to secure his ends. The clerics José de Calasanz, Vicente de Valencia, and Martín Lafuerza in *Caesar or Nothing* are all fanatical, despotic, and reactionary, while the Bishop of Pamplona in *The Family of Errotacho* is authoritarian and choleric, without compassion for the anarchists of Vera on the eve of their execution.[81]

The humorous aspect of anticlericalism is not entirely absent from Baroja's writings, although it must be admitted that it does not occupy a prominent place. The abbot in *The Lord of Labraz* is the author's prime zoological specimen—*clericus catolicus hispanicus.*[82] The abbot's cassock is an ocean dotted with islands of grease, his hat is encrusted with grime, his well-fed appearance suggests that he is a "Napoleon of the digestive tract."[83] His mental equipment parallels his physical aspect: his sermons consist of three or four hours of howls of imprecation directed against liberals and Freemasons.

Animosity toward clerics is not limited to the Catholic clergy, to judge from an episode recounted in *Ciudades de Italia* (*Cities of Italy*). Baroja describes his instantaneous antipathy toward a Protestant pastor who shared his train compartment; in every gesture, in every act, Baroja sees only hypocrisy. To further fortify his dislike, the pastor appears in Bologna when the author is happily admiring a park, and it immediately begins to rain: ". . . it could not have been otherwise."[84]

In mitigation of his prevalently truculent tone, Baroja portrays a small number of priests in a sympathetic light. The curate Don Ramón in *Caesar or Nothing* is humble, gentle, generous; the village priest Father Anselmo in *El sabor de la venganza* (*The Taste of Vengeance*) is an angelic spirit, without malice; in *Captain Chimista's Star* Father Martín is chaste and neither fanatical nor despotic. A different type of priest is Don Fermín Esteban de Uranga of *D. Adrián de Erlaiz.* Don Fermín is a dedicated botanist, with a growing interest in astronomy, music, and meteorology. Don Luis Arvizu, in the same novel, is cultivated, amusing, given to discussing Horace, Virgil, and Ovid. Both Don Fermín and Don Luis are, of course, Basques. Don Francisco Chirino, who preceded the implacable Sansirgue in Cuenca, has the reputation for great virtue and learning, and died in the odor of sanctity; a perusal of his annotated books revealed him to be a Voltairian and a secret enemy of the Church.[85]

Characteristically, Baroja undertakes to defend himself against the charge of anticlericalism, insisting that he does not believe that priests lead irregular lives and denying that he had ever made such an accusation. He then adds virtuously that the priests in the Basque country, at least, are not given over to vice.[86] If priests in general are hypocritical and despotic, it is the fault of the country in which they live. Larrañaga maintains similarly that if the Spanish priest is fanatical it is because he is a Spaniard, further echoing his creator in insisting that he has never hated the clergy.[87] It must be noted, however, that in another essay of the *Solitary Hours* Baroja remarks that behind the Spaniard there always lurks the priest, thus closing the circle.[88] In the case of a nation where state and religion are one, such distinctions have little meaning. The evidence in support of the accusation of Baroja's anticlericalism is even stronger than the proofs of Gallophobia, and denials are to no avail.

Dr. Basterreche who, as a Basque and as a physician sometimes speaks for Baroja in *The Curate of Monleón*, expresses admiration for the lower clergy but has only disdain for the bishops and cardinals.[89] Later, in *Yesterday and Today*, Baroja objects to the persecution of the lower clergy by the Second Republic and, in what appears to be a curious reversal of opinion, takes the republicans to task for interfering with the customs of the country by prohibiting the religious feasts and processions which harm nobody.[90] This unexpected defense of the Church can be explained in part by Baroja's fierce hostility toward the Republic; it is a question of priorities, and in virtually any comparison, the Republic is the loser. There is also the paradoxical possibility that the anti-traditionalist was unwilling to part with the old traditions.

If Baroja excoriated Christianity for its failure to foster brotherhood and to establish peace, he did not include the figure of Jesus Christ in his condemnation. *The Curate of Monleón* contains the statement that "Christ is the most human part of Judaism,"[91] and Aviraneta explains with great deliberation that animosity toward the clergy does not necessarily imply hostility toward Jesus Christ. Addressing Father Chamizo, Aviraneta exclaims, "You [priests] have nothing to do with Jesus Christ. How could you possibly have!"[92] Once again the outstanding figure is saved; it is only the dogmatic crystallization of a religion about the individual, whether human or divine, that is execrated.

CHAPTER 5

Diversity: 1900-1911

O N the occasion of his reception into the Royal Spanish Academy in 1960, Juan Antonio de Zunzunegui dedicated his acceptance address to Pío Baroja, a dedication made particularly appropriate since the chair he was to occupy had belonged to his countryman and mentor. Zunzunegui's "En torno a D. Pío Baroja y su obra" ("Considerations on Pío Baroja and his works") is the more or less conventional tribute required by the nature of the occasion and is, therefore, predictably adulatory. Speaking about the novelist's art in general, Zunzunegui insists that the distinction between the author and his characters must be kept, that the more intense the life of a novelistic character, the less he is subject to the will of his creator, that, in short, an authentic novelist must be able to jump over his own shadow.[1] Zunzunegui admits that Baroja is incapable of this self-transcendence, but considers this inability to jump over his own shadow a source of strength and originality rather than a weakness.[2]

The question of self-transcendence is crucial. The frontiers of reality and invention, experience and fantasy, are peculiarly blurred in Baroja's novelistic world, and hints and clues must be sought in the essays and in the *Memoirs*. The definition of these boundaries is essential to a coherent presentation of the author's works, for it is true that Baroja's originality does not consist in the degree to which he resembles nobody else, but in the degree to which he resembles himself. The egolatry of Baroja is the continuous thread, the essence; all else are accidents. It may be noted in passing that while Zunzunegui spoke about Baroja in his acceptance speech, when the latter was similarly inducted he spoke only about himself.

I The Beginnings: Short Tales and Two Basque Novels

Baroja's first collection of short stories was published in 1900 under the general title of *Vidas sombrías* (*Somber Lives*). Before that date the author's literary efforts had been confined to articles and brief, fictional pieces for such publications as *La Justicia*,

78

El País, and *Revista Nueva.*[3] Some of the titles in *Somber Lives,*
"El vago" ("The Vagabond") and "Errantes" ("Wanderers"),
for example, had already been published in *El País* in the course
of the previous year.[4]

The stories in the 1900 collection strike many notes, ranging
from the sentimental and lyrical effusions of "Mari Belcha" and
"Playa de otoño" ("The Beach in Autumn") to the compassionate realism of "Hogar triste" ("A Sad Home") and "La trapera"
("The Ragpicker"). The Basque country and its ancient superstitions which were later to receive such detailed attention in
The Legend of Jaun de Alzate and *The Basque Country* are
evoked with the simplicity of the folk tale in "El trasgo" ("The
Goblin") and "La sima" ("The Pit").[5] "Marichu," with its pessimistic lament for all mankind, announces in a significant way one
of the author's most persistent themes. The description of every
town as ". . . a huge hospital filled with ailing flesh,'"[6] so similar
to T. S. Eliot's "The whole earth is our hospital/Endowed by
the ruined millionaire" or Heine's Krankenhaus, indicates the
deep preoccupation with pain and suffering that was to constitute
a motif in so many of Baroja's novels. The symbolic tales "Pará-
bola" ("Parable"), "La sombra" ("The Apparition"), and "Nihil,"
particularly, are fresh with impressions from other writers. The
figure of Schopenhauer looms behind the scenes in "Parable,"
and the shadow of Dostoyevsky hangs over "The Apparition"
and "Nihil." In "Parable" the author states for the first time a
theme from Ecclesiastes, a theme inherent in the later, philosophical works: *En la mucha sabiduría hay mucha molestia
y quien añade ciencia añade dolor* ("For in much wisdom is
much grief; and he that increaseth knowledge increaseth sorrow").[7]

In the prologue to *Somber Lives* Baroja mentions the influence
of Dostoyevsky on some of his stories, and freely confesses to
certain literary similarities to Poe and Dickens, but at the same
time points with pride to the originality of such tales as "Mari
Belcha" and "Angelus."[8] In an article on *Somber Lives* Unamuno
remarks that "Bondad oculta" ("Hidden Goodness") reminds him
of Dostoyevsky, while "Médium" suggests Poe.[9] It is precisely
these two stories that Baroja recalls many years later in his
Memoirs in order to give a brief indication of their genesis.
"Médium" was based on a story he had heard when his family
was living in Valencia. The author remarks that, although he
did not believe the supernatural aspects of the story, he nonetheless chose to retain them in his own version.[10] The inspiration for
"Hidden Goodness" came several years later when Baroja, al-

ready a physician in Cestona, accompanied his father on a trip
to inspect some mines in Alava. In the mining village of Barambio
the young Baroja met a rather mature woman, "a rose among
thorns," to whom he was immediately attracted. His first plan
was to ask her to abandon the man with whom she was living
and to come with him, but practical considerations promptly
supplanted the romantic impulse, and all that was left was to
write about her later.[11] Art as a substitute for life could scarcely
find a more apt illustration.

"Noche de médico" ("Doctor's Night"), which, like "La venta"
("The Inn"), had appeared the previous year in El País, clearly
marks the path that Baroja was to follow faithfully until the
end of his literary life. It is a return to experience, a literary
version of a portion of his life; in The Basque Country, published
when the author was eighty-one years old, Baroja writes that
he still remembers his "nights as a village doctor."[12] A different
aspect of the author's temperament is revealed in the antic
humor of "La vida de los átomos" ("The Life of the Atoms"),
wherein a silvery laugh is rendered as "Ag . . ., ag . . . ag . . .!"
The revolt of the atoms is transformed many years later in
Swan Hotel into the rebellion of objects: elevators that elude
would-be passengers, phonographs that refuse to change records,
sirens that wail as the fancy strikes them.[13] "Un justo" ("A Just
Man"), the story of the village priest Javier, anticipates The
Curate of Monleón but also looks back to the author's days in
Cestona. While practicing as the village doctor, Baroja had lived
in the house of Dolores, the sacristan's wife; Javier lives in the
house of the sacristan's daughter, and both women are depicted
as rabid traditionalists.[14] Javier is an unpretentious, disinterested
cleric who is on the side of morality and ethics; his transfer to
an isolated parish as punishment for his virtue is an expression
of Baroja's critical attitude toward conventional society—an
attitude that is evident from his literary beginnings.

As the title suggests, Somber Lives is a melancholy book, full
of delicate feeling poetically expressed. The concerns of the
Generation of 1898 for everyday life, for the enduring traditions of the humble people, in short, for "infrahistory,"[15] is
particularly apparent in this collection. The vein of tenderness
in Baroja, which diminished with the passage of time and with
the concomitant acquisition of many opinions, is at its freshest
and most poignant in this youthful work.

La casa de Aizgorri (The House of Aizgorri), published in
the same year as Somber Lives, stands somewhat apart from
the mainstream of the author's production in both form and

content. At first conceived as a play, it is in effect a novel in dialogue form. Baroja had stated in his *Memoirs* that he was often moved to write after contemplating a particular place or meeting a specific person;[16] a distillery in Pasajes, near San Sebastián, provided him with the inspiration for *The House of Aizgorri*. Baroja's distillery is transformed into a symbol of decadence, of the ruin and degradation of the inhabitants of Arbea. Don Lucio and his son Luis, two of the remaining members of the once illustrious Aizgorri family, are corrupt and degenerate; the others, according to Don Lucio himself, are madmen and idiots. Agueda, the daughter of the family, is almost driven to madness by her bizarre visions, but, in keeping with the youthful tone of the work, succeeds in overcoming her weakness by an act of will. The distillery with its poisonous fumes is counterbalanced by the foundry with its clean iron: iron roars, alcohol hisses. The destruction of the distillery in the midst of a workers' strike closes the era of decadence in Arbea, and the dawn of the new day glimpsed by Agueda and her fiancé Mariano announces a future full of optimism and hope.

It is the derivative nature of the work that both sets it apart from the bulk of Baroja's production and links it with some of the pieces in *Somber Lives*. The idea of the hereditary taint owes much to Ibsen and Nordau[17] and the sharp line of demarcation between the symbols of good and evil recall the stylized, rhetorical dramas of the nineteenth century. Everything is clear in *The House of Aizgorri*, there are no ambiguities, there is no greyness.

The Basque background plays a minimal role and is largely confined to the superstitious recitals of the servant Melchora. Arbea has its mandatory village idiot and its resident madwoman, but Baroja dwells on neither; there are few side-excursions into the picturesque. It is worthy of note that Don Julián Aróstegui, the village physician, is the first of a series of portrayals of the author's scientific side. Don Julián is eminently reasonable and entirely ethical, and his intervention in the action is unequivocally on the side of right and justice.

Similar in ethical intent is *El mayorazgo de Labraz* (*The Lord of Labraz*), published three years later. *The Lord of Labraz* is a somber novel, medieval in atmosphere, and romantic in spirit. Baroja had gone to Labraz, a decrepit and moribund *pueblo terrible* because its lugubrious atmosphere was in keeping with his anguished spirit, deeply saddened by "the destruction of [my] romantic illusions."[18] Availing himself of an old and respectable fictional device, Baroja states that his novel is merely a transcription of a fantasy imagined by the Englishman Mister Samuel Bothwell Crawford. Mister Bothwell, as he is usually designated in the novel, therefore plays the dual role of playwright and actor, mirroring the double role often played by Baroja. When Bothwell begins to express the author's opinions, the reader is introduced into a hall of mirrors.

The central figure of the novel is Juan, the blind Lord of Labraz. Stoical, ascetic, long-suffering, his atony makes him a suitable victim for the outrages committed by his persecutor Don Ramiro. The plot of the novel is purely operatic, and includes near-murder, seduction, robbery, escape, economic ruin. As in *The House of Aizgorri*, the lines are cleanly drawn: Ramiro is Evil, Juan is Good. A medieval morality play could not have made a more obvious distinction. Don Ramiro is intended to be a satanic figure, but he lacks the necessary grandeur and magnificence; he is merely a commonplace seducer and unimaginative thief. The Lord of Labraz is more complex; at first resigned and apathetic, he suddenly turns on his tormentors with the righteous wrath of Christ driving the money changers from the temple, and setting fire to his fields, abandons Labraz to become a wanderer. This withdrawal from life is plainly Schopenhauerian, but months after his disappearance, Don Juan reappears in Labraz and asks Marina, the innkeeper's daughter, to accompany him on his wanderings. The travels, however, will not be aimless; both he and Marina will go to live in a house belonging to his family on the shores of the Mediterranean. Like Agueda and Mariano in *The House of Aizgorri*, Juan and Marina go toward light and hope.

The creaky melodrama of the plot recalls the worst moments of nineteenth-century fiction, but the atmosphere and landscapes are undeniably authentic. On the same mine inspection trip that brought Baroja to Barambio where he met the future protagonist of "Hidden Goodness," both he and his father continued on to the village of Abornícano. In the village inn the young Baroja met and was enormously attracted by the innkeeper's daughters Blanca and Marina; both are recreated in *The Lord of Labraz*, with Marina singled out for special attention. The geographical details of the wintry crossing of Navarre in the snow are recollections of a trip to Viana with Ramiro de Maeztu,[19] combined with memories of the ascent of the Urbión with Paul Schmitz in 1901.

The secondary characters are not numerous, and there are few extraneous episodes. Mister Bothwell, the Englishman who hates England,[20] and Blanca's fiancé Antonio Bengoa, the scion of a noble family whose only ambition is to be a pharmacist, express Baroja's point of view between them. Bothwell, who likes to *épater*, dresses in checked or striped suits and sometimes wears a top hat to go fishing; his mind is teeming with extravagant projects, none of which he plans to realize. Bothwell gives voice to the author's skepticism, his lack of faith in progress, his dislike for any form of political organization. Justice, he maintains, is not of this world, for nature herself is unjust.[21] Bengoa, less disabused, believes in the regeneration of Spain through the love of justice and liberty, a statement that draws an indignant reaction from the Carlists who are compelled to listen to his heresies and a long speech from the canon to the effect that liberals like Bengoa are destroying society and threatening the Church.[22] If the form and plot of *The Lord of Labraz* are traditional, the voice of the outraged regenerationist makes itself heard at every turn. Labraz is another Yécora, ruled by selfishness and hypocrisy, inhabited by indolent so-called Christians who neither think nor read. Everything is accomplished by influence, usurers flourish, two *Celestinas* (intermediaries) arrange for the surreptitious amatory escapades of the male inhabitants, and whatever marriages are celebrated are marriages of convenience. The violence of the author's criticism may be somewhat diluted by the plot, but the sting is unmistakably there.

It is evident that Baroja's view of mankind made it relatively easy for him to depict collective evil and vice, but what he fails to do in this novel is to portray evil successfully in an individualized fashion. Don Ramiro is an unrealized idea, a hollow receptacle, a Don Luis Mejía without a wager. The evil that the author sees is a characteristic of the generic *homo sapiens*, for nowhere are there concrete, full-scale villains, capable of overflowing a page and filling a book.

Three secondary characters are worthy of note, for all embody ideas that were to be repeated in later novels in various guises. The first is the indispensable doctor, in this case Don Martín Echenique, who diagnoses Juan's passivity as a weakness of the instincts and a death of the will. His prescription is the collective recommendation of the Generation of 1898: be free, be strong, be armed for struggle. The second character is the beggar who has shaken off the chains of society in order to wander through the countryside. He has no name and lives nowhere, but his indication that he comes from a region where Castilian is not spoken despite which fact he thinks he is Spanish, suggests that he is one of Baroja's free-spirited Basques. His preference for the country over the city reinforces the probability. The third character is the fierce bandit Melitón, whose views on life can best be summarized in the Plautine axiom, *homo homini lupus* (man is a wolf unto man). The law of destruction, the survival of the fittest, the struggle for life are synthesized in one paragraph by this Darwinian.[23] In *The Tree of Knowledge,* is is Dr. Iturrioz who takes up the subject and elaborates on it with all the accumulated knowledge of his long scientific career; Melitón states the theme in 1903 and eight years later Iturrioz supplies the variations.

The romantic nature of *The Lord of Labraz* places the work at the head of a long line of rather melodramatic novels of fantasy produced by Baroja over his long life-span. In works of this type the critical note becomes attenuated over the years while the melodrama is noticeably accentuated.

II *Silvestre Paradox: The First Portraits*

Between *The House of Aizgorri* and *The Lord of Labraz,* neither of which is distinguished for its originality, Baroja wrote *Aventuras, inventos y mixtificaciones de Silvestre Paradox* (*Adventures, Inventions and Hoaxes of Silvestre Paradox*), the first novel that can be labelled, *a posteriori,* genuinely Barojian.[24] In the *Adventures* . . . , published in 1901, Baroja finds his authentic style, and the texture and tone are as unmistakably his in this early work as they are in *The Tree of Knowledge* or *Sublimated Sensuality.*

According to the author's testimony, parts of the novel were written in the bakery, between the settling of bills and arguments with deliverymen, while parts were composed amidst the tumult of a café. Written in accordance with Baroja's belief that a novel should be porous and invertebrate, it is a series of episodes held together by the presence of the principal speaker. Silvestre Paradox is inventive, impractical, and slightly mad by conventional standards. His first appearance in the novel sets the tone: when he comes to Madrid he moves into an attic accompanied by a dog, a snake, and a stuffed bustard. He seems to own nothing useful. A portrait of Silvestre provides the information that he has reddish hair (balding) and a beard of the same color, is of indeterminate age, and is an obvious brachycephalic; this last detail is supplied, no doubt, to account for his turbulence and restlessness. The memories of his unruly childhood and rebellious youth in Madrid and Pamplona, which also include such details as the funeral processions along the Calle Real, his indifferent success as a student, his early introduction to *Robinson Crusoe,* Jules Verne, and Mayne Reid, his later study of

Kant and Schopenhauer, his recollections of Paris, all recreate the author's personal experience.

The inventions undertaken by Silvestre Paradox with the aid of his friend Don Avelino Diz de la Iglesia have antecedents in the author's past, as he clearly specifies in the *Memoirs*.[25] Baroja relates that he and his brother Ricardo, along with their friend Riudavets, used to make strange artifacts in the attic of their home; Julio Caro Baroja mentions Ricardo's sketches for submarines and flying machines, and his plans for fantastic voyages.[26] That Baroja met many inventors while he was in charge of the bakery is clear from his acceptance address before the Royal Spanish Academy as well as from the aforementioned *Memoirs;* one Lamotte in particular was the inspiration for most of the inventions attributed by Baroja to Paradox' overheated imagination.[27]

Avelino Diz de la Iglesia is a reformed philatelist, numismatist, and collector of prehistoric archaeological remains. A former victim of acute bibliomania, he was in the habit of presenting fresh contributions daily to his disastrously disorganized library until, having finally managed to lose the key, he was forced to resort to the expedient of firing the recent acquisitions in through the transom.[28] An *auto-da-fé* is subsequently held to weed out such undesirable items as works on literature, philosophy, and history, and Don Avelino is free to dedicate himself to Paradox' schemes.

Before his Madrid period and partnership with Don Avelino, Paradox had had a series of picaresque adventures with the charlatan Macbeth, serving as unpaid straight man for his protector's tricks of sleight of hand and hypnotism. When the Englishman is arrested, Paradox has to shift for himself, which he does by working on his inventions, writing murder stories for a serial called "Los crímenes modernos" ("Modern Crimes"), hiring himself out as a tutor to the two children of the Ossorio family, and then finally devoting his talents to the marketing of some extremely original ideas. The most noteworthy of the projects invented by the partners is the establishment of the Eternal Life Insurance Company, the purpose of which is to send, in exchange for a small sum, a sufficient number of prayers up to Heaven to insure life after death. Other projects include an elaborate Christmas panorama and crèche, the artistic aspect of which was to be the responsibility of Fernando Ossorio. With the proceeds of these activities the partners are solvent, a happy and short-lived state of affairs which is abruptly ended when Silvestre's secretary-servant Pelayo makes off with every-

thing but the stuffed bustard. Forced to escape from the attic
to avoid their creditors, Don Avelino pawns his watch and with
the proceeds Paradox and his friend, still confident that success
lies ahead, leave for Valencia.

Geographical displacement as a remedy for spiritual displacement, suggested at the end of the *Adventures* . . . becomes
a motif in many of Baroja's novels, early and late. Unamuno
remarked that the reason for travel is often not love for where
one is going but hatred for where one has been. When Paradox
complains that he feels poisoned by Madrid, he immediately
adds, "I have to leave, I have to go away."[29] Paradox seems to
be a fey eccentric, an innocent, one of society's natural victims.
Like Baroja, he was born on December 28. He moves untouched
among the bohemians of his acquaintance, leading a life of
unexceptionable moral probity and chastity. He is repelled
by the examples of criminality and perversity that surround
him in Madrid, and desperately oppressed by the uselessness of
life; his desire for purity and tranquillity, his Baudelairian longing
to go "anywhere out of the world" is constantly present and constantly frustrated. He feels lonely, old, and sad, condemned to
witness the eternal repetition of the same things again and again,
a galley slave rowing endlessly with no lighthouse in sight.
Paradox describes, decades before Sartre, his "nausea at living,
nausea at the sight of people and things."[30] This *taedium vitae*,
this melancholy realization of the futility of life, suggests to Paradox the need for an abattoir for all of society's rejects, a
slaughterhouse that would provide one hour of paradise before
death.[31]

Silvestre Paradox' opinions—he dislikes socialism, democracy,
and the rule of the masses—are consistent with his aristocratic
outlook, but his experience of futility and nothingness and the
anguish and melancholy that periodically beset him seem to
belong more properly to his creator. Further, Paradox describes
himself as lacking in will and incapable of perseverance, although
there is little concrete evidence of either weakness in the course of
the novel. At the end of the *Adventures* . . . Silvestre Paradox is
full of plans for the future, defiantly proclaiming the indestructi-
bility of his spirit in the face of a cold and indifferent universe—a
universe symbolized by the frigid temperatures of a snowy
December night. To be capable of such metaphysical defiance,
the *soi-disant* weak-willed pessimist would require the sort of
revelation experienced by Meursault at the conclusion of Camus'
The Stranger, but there is no revelation. There is only flight, and
Silvestre's final "Hurrah! Hurrah!" has a hollow ring.

Paradox' internal reality exists almost independently of external reality and scarcely responds to it. His *Weltanschauung* seems predetermined, and his melancholy appears to spring less from the depths of his being than from the author's. In the *Adventures . . .* Baroja's tendency to set a static preformed personality against a changing background is already evident. The scenery changes, unrolling as in a film, but the character remains the same. The dynamics of the Barojian novel, for the most part, are external, moving the reader from place to place and from episode to episode; the inner change that usually arises from collision with external realities is neither implicit nor explicit. The spiritual disposition of the protagonist is as predetermined as the moral disposition of a Christian in the Augustinian schema, with the difference that in Baroja's world there is free will only by exception.

Not content with grafting some of his own preoccupations on to the person of Silvestre Paradox, Baroja also presents himself in this novel as Dr. Labarta. The doctor and his brother, who is a painter, own a bakery which they run quite disastrously since the doctor has attacks of misanthropy and the painter, who does not paint, spends his time on his inventions. Dr. Labarta is partially bald, seems to be of no particular age, and appears melancholy and unsociable. He is badly dressed and, of course, writes.[32] A slightly different description follows in a later chapter: Labarta's beard is yellowish, his eyes are amiable and smiling: ". . . he looked like a spiritual but gluttonous friar, like a pessimist and an Epicurean, both waggish and romantic."[33] Baroja gives to Dr. Labarta his complete physical identity and his varying moods insofar as they are reflected in his appearance; Silvestre Paradox receives from the author his spiritual anguish and his imaginative fancies.

Among the secondary characters in the novel are Pérez del Corral, who is Baroja's satirical version of Valle-Inclán, Lamela, a medical student who later reappears in *The Tree of Knowledge*, and Fernando Ossorio, the future protagonist of *The Way to Perfection*. With the Labartas is a nameless German watchmaker who knows something of Nietzsche; Baroja had become friendly with Paul Schmitz the year before and this shadowy German is Schmitz's first literary incarnation.[34] Baroja indulges his interest in evoking the atmosphere of turn-of-century Madrid in the scenes involving Pérez del Corral and other bohemians,[35] and the brief hospital sequences, for which the dying Pérez del Corral provides the excuse, recall the author's medical school period. *Adventures . . .* anticipates the later novels in which the author projects his personality through one central character and suggests the large canvas and the multiplicity of figures and episodes that were later to become the hallmark of a Barojian novel.

III *The Confluence of Nietzsche and Nordau:* Camino de perfección (The Way to Perfection)

With the publication of *The Way to Perfection* in 1902, Baroja emerges as a serious novelist-critic, joining Azorín as spokesman for the Generation of 1898. The vitriolic tone is an augury of the sharply critical novels and essays yet to come, and the central themes reflect the readings and synthesize the preoccupations of his cogenerationists. Baroja describes this work as consisting almost exclusively of travels, and adds, "to get to the end, one has to put up with many descriptions, a lot of sun and dust, many roads in Castile . . ."[36] The author admits at the same time that the work is not just a travel book but has a psychological aspect as well which, to his mind, is "not at all bad."

Fernando Ossorio, the protagonist of the novel, had already made his appearance in the *Adventures* . . . as an artist who signed his drawings "Mephisto."[37] Ossorio is described by his Aunt Laura as a rake and ne'er-do-well who leads an irregular life with a mistress who had once been a prostitute; Ossorio points to himself as an example of the excessive eroticism that is characteristic of his entire family, men and women alike, from generation to generation. The Ossorios are aristocratic, but their vices and perversions leave Zola's most flamboyant inventions in the shade; Fernando's Aunt Laura is a lesbian and a sadist, her nephew Octavio is a homosexual, other so-far unspecified members of the family are either imbeciles or degenerates. Ossorio confesses to Paradox that he is ashamed of himself, his family, of all the infamy he has had to witness.[38] His spirit is bruised, his will broken.

In *The Way to Perfection* Ossorio makes his appearance as a medical student who collects scapularies, amulets, and religious medals from the corpses in the dissection room. He is also an artist who alternately seems to his fellow students a man of great talent or a complete fool. It is customarily assumed, no doubt on the basis of some of the later novels wherein Baroja paints himself in the guise of the central character, that Ossorio reflects the author to a greater or lesser degree,[39] but since Baroja was not noticeably reticent in revealing the inspiration for his plots and characters, it seems indeed unwise to disregard his own version of the genesis of Fernando Ossorio. In the *Memoirs* the author clearly states that the figure of Ossorio is based in the main on a medical student who had been an acquaintance of his while he too was studying medicine. This acquaintance, whose name Baroja can no longer recollect, is described as young, elegant, and ". . . an avid reader of Baudelaire and somewhat decadent and satanic."[40] The same passage of the *Memoirs* contains the information that the author fused the figure of this acquaintance with that of *el pesimista* ("the pessimist"), about whom he had written in his student days. This vague reference is somewhat clarified in a preceding section where Baroja mentions having started a novel which he called either *El pesimista* or *Los pesimistas*;[41] like *Las buhardillas de Madrid* (*The Attics of Madrid*),[42] it was abandoned.

The transformation from medical student to artist—for the medical school is soon forgotten in *The Way to Perfection*—can best be understood by reference to the relevance of Max Nordau's *Entartung* (*Degeneration*) to the fleshing-out of Ossorio's portrait. *Degeneration* was translated into Spanish in 1902 but was already known in Spain via the 1894 French version.[43] In his essay "Nietzsche y la filosofía" ("Nietzsche and Philosophy"), written in 1899, Baroja describes his reaction to Nordau's work in the following fashion: "When I finished reading it, I felt as if I had just escaped from a madhouse, from a madhouse in which, as in a tale by Poe, the supervisor was mad as well."[44] Nordau classified as degenerate the works of Wagner, Ibsen, Wilde, Manet, Swinburne, Rossetti, Baudelaire, Verlaine, Nietzsche—the list is interminable. George Bernard Shaw had said of Nordau's work that it created a European scandal ". . . by declaring that the greatest creative artists of the century are barren and hysterical madmen."[45]

Ossorio's decadence, already suggested by the figure on whom he is modelled, is amplified by the association of degeneracy with art as outlined in *Degeneration*; if artists are degenerates, then degenerates may be artists. Ossorio's personality is poorly integrated, and it is his opinion that his particular weaknesses are a manifestation of hysteria and degeneracy, taints which he attributes to his heredity—a mad aunt, a cousin who had committed suicide, an alcoholic uncle—and to the corrupting influence of his three years in the Piarist school in Yécora.[46] Ossorio mentions the disappearance of his brilliance in the course of his education, a loss Baroja evidently attributed to the nature of the education itself, but it is not without interest that Nordau gives as one of the effects of hereditary degeneration the following: ". . . the boy who, only yesterday, was a model scholar, be-

comes an obtuse, clumsy dunce . . ."[47] Nordau further describes the
typical degenerate as follows: he is egoistic and impulsive, emotional and easily moved by music; he is pessimistic and suffers
from *aboulia*; he is tormented by doubts and susceptible to
"mystical delirium."[48]

There is evidence throughout the first section of the novel
of the degree to which Ossorio qualifies for inclusion in Nordau's
catalogue of degenerate artists. Ossorio is without will, inert,
fatigued, oppressed by a sense of nothingness;[49] the degenerate,
Nordau declares, despairs of himself and the world; he is fatigued
and his fatigue produces hysteria.[50] Despite the possession of
sufficient funds for an independent life, Ossorio prefers to drift,
and in order to postpone a decision, moves in with his aunts.
With his tendency to hysteria accentuated by his sexual excesses,
Ossorio begins to have strange, quasi-religious hallucinations
which leave him weak with terror and more and more convinced that he is on the verge of insanity. Ossorio's eroticism
and frightening visions seem like a page from Nordau's case-
book. Religious fervor, Nordau affirms, usually accompanies
"morbidly intensified eroticism,"[51] and the mystical degenerate
"in extreme cases" suffers from hallucinations.[52]

To escape from himself and from his obsessions, Ossorio takes
to the road. Baudelaire had said that life is a hospital where
each patient is filled with the desire to change beds; like his
predecessor Paradox, Ossorio suffers more from topophobia than
from philotopia. In the course of his wanderings through Castile,
the protagonist repeatedly seeks to recover some lost religious
emotion by immersing himself in the atmosphere of old churches.
As if in obedience to Pascal's exhortation, Ossorio takes holy
water, but he does not for all his efforts succeed in believing.
It is as an artist that he reacts to the incense, the candles, the
somber colors in the Cathedral of Toledo; the censing of the
altar reminds him of the old Byzantine paintings. He loves the
music, the solitude, the poetry of religion, but dislikes the
dogma and the words used to convey it. His emotional and
aesthetic response reveals to the modern reader a romantic
sensibility that refuses to recognize itself; for Nordau it is the
mark of the degenerate.

Ossorio's previous religious history, a product of the double
influence of his Voltairian grandfather and a fanatically religious
nurse, was marked by contradiction and ambiguity; a brief
period of religious exaltation, following upon the agreeable
effect of his first confession, was soon to subside under the influence of his grandfather's rationalism.[53] On the basis of this

and later passages, Laín Entralgo suggests that perhaps Baroja too had suffered a similar religious conflict and that behind his anticlericalism there may be . . . *cierta religiosidad vaga, un deísmo de tinte unamuniano* ("a vague religious feeling, a deism of the Unamunesque type").[54] The conjecture seems little justified in light of the similarity between the details of Ossorio's pseudo-mysticism and Nordau's prototype of the fin-de-siècle degenerate.

Since *aboulia,* pessimism, or what Baroja himself called "hamletism" is often implicit in the spirit and work of the Generation of 1898 and is a general characteristic of European fin-de-siècle decadence, it is not necessarily in obedience to Nordau that Baroja ascribes these characteristics to a fictional protagonist, but the addition of exacerbated eroticism, pseudo-mysticism, an over-emotional response to music, hallucinations, and general hysteria suggest that in Ossorio's case the author was indeed following Nordau, and rather closely at that.

The Castilian landscape serves as backdrop for Ossorio's peripatetic existence, and Baroja evokes its colors and textures with the eye of an artist. Throughout the novel there are recollections of the author's visits to Illescas and Toledo, vivid reminders that it was not only in theory that Baroja believed that the interest of a work lay in the details.[55] The stoical Polentinos, whom the author designates as a King Lear of La Mancha, is one of the many minor figures to weave in and out of the novel, providing a glimpse into Spain's "infrahistory." Ossorio's apparently aimless wanderings lead him to the cemetery of the abandoned monastery of El Paular, and it is here that there is a shift in the center of gravity of the novel, a shift that becomes apparent only much later.

In El Paular, Ossorio makes the acquaintance of one Max Schultze, a German who is greatly interested in Spain. When Ossorio confesses to him his neurasthenia, Schultze recommends exercise and the reading of Nietzsche's works as an efficacious cure. Ossorio imagines the German philosopher's doctrine to consist only of the glorification of the ego, but Schultze insists that Nietzsche is eminently ethical, sensitive, and pure. Together, the new acquaintances climb the Urbión, descend, and separate, Schultze to return to the monastery, Ossorio to continue to Segovia. The three chapters that comprise this section[56] consist in the main of poetic landscapes and little dialogue, but the ultimate consequences for the protagonist are far-reaching.

Baroja had visited the monastery of El Paular in 1900 and had climbed to the top of the Urbión in the company of Paul Schmitz in the period previous to the publication of *The Way to*

Perfection.[57] It was in the cemetery of the monastery that Schmitz translated for Baroja some of Nietzsche's letters,[58] converting him from his former negative view to one of understanding and admiration. Baroja wrote in "Nietzsche and Philosophy" that the German philosopher's name first became known to him and to many others of his generation by means of Nordau's *Degeneration.* In Nordau's work Nietzsche is painted as a super-decadent, combining the dandyism of Barbey d'Aurevilly with the satanism of Baudelaire; the characterization of the model for Fernando Ossorio as a reader of Baudelaire and as "somewhat satanic" resembles Nordau's description of Nietzsche and may very well have suggested to Baroja the triangular association of Ossorio-Nordau-Nietzsche. In his first essay Baroja considers Nietzsche as an implacable egotist, full of violence and sadism, but after his indoctrination in El Paular, he wrote in 1901 two articles favorable to the German philosopher in *El Imparcial*;[59] the following year Baroja wrote an essay entitled "El éxito de Nietzsche" ("Nietzsche's Success"), a compendium of opinions on the philosopher collected by the novelist.[60] The intervention of Paul Schmitz in Baroja's philosophical orientation at this period in his life is obviously of great importance, and it may not be idle to speculate about the name Max Schultze which Baroja assigns to him. It was partly through the influence of Ernst Schulze, a professor at the University of Göttingen, that Schopenhauer became interested in philosophy. In the same way, Baroja became interested in Nietzsche partly under the influence of this new "Schulze."

The brief exchange of remarks between Ossorio and Schultze could not logically be expected to have significant consequences, but such is not the case, for by Chapter XLVI Ossorio's tone is rapturous and lyrical as he sings a paean of praise to the beauties and vitality of springtime. The vigor of nature awakens a corresponding vitality in the observer, and at last, free of his melancholy and atony, Ossorio feels at one with his surroundings and, for the first time, affirms the positive value of life. "To live and to keep on living . . . that is the question" is his anti-Hamletian conclusion.[61] One may well wonder what has brought about this transformation. Between the scene with Schultze and the apparent disappearance of his neurasthenia, Ossorio visited Toledo, where, among other things, he attempted an unsuccessful courtship of a nun, resisted the temptation to seduce Adela, his landlady's daughter, and then went to Yécora to look for a girl he had deceived many years before. From the point of view of logic, the external events so far summarized should not have had sufficient bearing on Ossorio's spirit to effect a change from apathy to vigor, from anguish to self-affirmation. The *deus ex machina* is Nietzsche, not the fragmentary, shadowy Nietzsche of the dialogue between Schultze and Ossorio, but the living and vivid Nietzsche of the letters read to Baroja by Paul Schmitz.

On the same ascending note Ossorio goes to Castellón to visit his uncle and there falls in love with and marries his cousin Dolores. The death of their first child, born prematurely, casts a shadow on their happiness, but presently a robust son is born to them and it is to this second child that Ossorio dedicates the coda of the novel. His son will be free to follow his instincts, he will know nothing of art and religion, for art and mystical longings had marked the father as a weakling and a decadent; the child will be uncorrupted by pedantic teachings and will live close to nature, deriving ever-renewed strength and vitality from the contact: ". . . should he be a lion, he would not remove his claws; should he be an eagle, he would not clip his wings."[62] Even if he should be a monster, ready to violate law and morality, he would be free to follow his impulses.

This Nietzschean hymn is not without its counterpoint. When Dolores had informed her husband of her pregnancy, it was to the accompaniment of liturgical music floating out into the cloister of the Cathedral of Tarragona to drown the songs of the birds and the sounds of nature. The conflict between the denial and the affirmation of life, between repression and freedom, is carried to the last line of the novel, for as Ossorio plans for his son the complete liberation he himself had not heretofore experienced because of his sinister education and life-negating preoccupations, his mother-in-law prepares the child for a future ruled by superstition and conventional religion.[63]

Ossorio's first child, the symbol of his previous existence, is doomed, an unripe fruit from a diseased tree. The second child, born when the father had come into full possession of his natural instincts, is sturdy and vigorous; if the first child was Nordau's, the second is Nietzsche's. The simultaneously affirmative and negative tone of the ending of *The Way to Perfection* indicates that the conquest of nihilism as recommended by Nietzsche and effectuated by Ossorio found only a faint echo in Baroja, whose enthusiastic acclaim of vitalism was inevitably tempered by pessimism and skepticism; the painful reality of Spain had still to be taken into account.

The style of the novel is alternately lyrical and strident; while the landscapes of Spain, sometimes radiant, sometimes grim, are painted with the delicate brush of the impressionist, the institutions of Spain are probed with a merciless scalpel. With its harsh social criticism and its portrayal of a fundamentally flawed protagonist, *The Way to Perfection* takes its place next to Azorín's *La Voluntad* as one of the earliest authentic literary manifestations of the temper of the Generation of 1898, but does not fully indicate the path that Baroja was later to follow with such consistency in his major works. The progression from the representation of a partial alter ego, as exemplified by Silvestre Paradox and Dr. Labarta in 1901, is irregular and full of gaps; the free utilization by the author of Nordau and Nietzsche in the delineation of Ossorio's personality indicates strongly that the latter is not a link in the progression.

IV *The Madrid Trilogy*

La lucha por la vida (*The Struggle for Life*) is the trilogy published in 1904 which earned for its author the Orteguian designation *el Homero de la canalla* ("the Homer of the rabble").[64] In *The Quest*[65] and *Weeds*, the first two novels of the series, the writer becomes the photographer and poet of the slums of Madrid; thieves and prostitutes, murderers and Don Juans, confidence men and degenerates, the hungry and the needy, crowd the pages of a work dedicated to the exploration of all the manifestations of abject misery that an urban center can produce. The wind and the cold, the rain and the snow are chronicled with the precision of a meteorological report, and the teeming sublife of Madrid at night and by day is observed and catalogued with the zeal of a scientist. Baroja has called both novels a copy from nature, with antecedents in the Spanish picaresque novel, in Dickens, the Russians, and in French serial literature of the *bas fonds* (lower depths).[66]

The Darwinian title of the trilogy announces the dominant theme: *homo homini lupus*. The unifying thread of the novels is the figure of Manuel Alcázar, who comes to Madrid at the age of fifteen to serve in Doña Casiana's boarding house, and who, after a series of many different occupations and adventures, is finally integrated into the bourgeois society of his time to marry and to become an upstanding and respectable citizen. Given Baroja's view of the bourgeoisie, Manual's progress does not necessarily constitute a success story but reflects the trajectory of the prototype of the picaresque novel *Lazarillo de Tormes*. Martínez Laínez, however, suggests that this is indeed a happy ending, and shrewdly concludes that Baroja's ideal is obviously conformity rather than change.[67]

In keeping with the picaresque tradition, Manuel moves from

one employment to another; after leaving the boarding house he works successively in the shoe repair shop of Ignacio, in the grocery store of tío Patas, in a bakery, and in other less edifying occupations too numerous to mention. At one time he momentarily joins the night people of the city in their marauding, but comes to the conclusion at the end of *The Quest* that he is destined to join the day people: "For some, pleasure, vice, and the night hours; for others, work, fatigue, and daylight. And he thought too that he had to belong to the latter group. . . ."[68] Manuel is a spectator both in the world of gamblers and thieves, of writers, artists, and anarchists, reacting, like Paradox, with horror and compassion at the sight of malevolence and suffering. Pessimistic and hopeless, Manuel sees life as sad and incomprehensible and is convinced that human motives are invariably vile and egotistical. Manuel Alcázar is generally passive but, in common with Juan de Labraz, can be driven to rage and violence in extreme situations. Unlike the Lord of Labraz, however, who stands out in relief against the anodyne background of Labraz, Manuel is often a vague and shadowy figure, barely visible in a crowded canvas pulsating with activity and movement.

Baroja's predilection for stamps of a defective issue, to use Torrente Ballester's phrase, is fully in evidence for the first time in this trilogy. *El Bizco*, "a sort of chimpanzee," *el Besuguito*, "the little porgy," with his fish face, *el Conejo* (the rabbit), with his quivering nose, Don Alonso, *el Hombre Boa* (the human boa) pass in review along with all the other rare specimens in Baroja's zoological park. The language of the untutored alternates with the argot of the underworld to produce a dense texture of reality, harsh and cruel.

Roberto Hasting y Núñez de Letona is a brisk wind blowing across this generally fetid atmosphere, and it is he who unequivocally exemplifies the influence of Nietzsche on Baroja's thinking at the time. Hasting, who is partly English, is determined to prove that he is the legitimate heir to a large fortune left by Don Fermín Núñez de Letona, curate of Labraz. A man of iron will, energy, and self-discipline, Hasting dedicates himself singlemindedly to his task; kindness and compassion play no role in his life-plan. "To know how to want something passionately is the first thing one has to learn."[69] His slogan is all or nothing, and it is in accordance with his character and behavior that he ultimately achieves all. In his dynamism and strength of character Hasting symbolizes the Northerner as imagined by Baroja before his first trip to England, serving as contrast to the supine

Spaniard Manuel Alcázar, whom he periodically attempts to spur to action.

Hasting, an individualist and "anarchoaristocrat," is scornful of the masses and fearful of their tyranny: "I would rather obey a tyrant than obey the crowd . . ."[70] Enlightened despotism is preferable to democracy, and a society in which the select man can rise above the general level of mediocrity is preferable to the society which aspires to an unjust equality. If the author's voice is clearly audible in the preceding pronouncements, in the following Hasting speaks only with the voice of Nietzsche: since action and struggle are the essence of life, each individual must bring into play his strong will and warlike instincts if he is to survive and conquer.[71] Hasting's ringing call to action would be more persuasive were his own energies employed in a better cause; the conquest of a fortune is not, after all, equal to the rhetoric with which he surrounds it.

Hasting roams through the pages of the trilogy, but whatever color and interest these novels possess depends less on him than on the cumulative effect of the multiple episodes and characters. A hideous beggar nicknamed "La Muerte" ("Death"), and described both in *The Quest* and the *Memoirs* is infinitely more vivid than the robot-like Hasting or the curiously blurred Manuel Alcázar.[72] Some of the places and persons observed by the author in the slums of Madrid are incorporated into the novels with but few transformations and constitute their most appealing aspect; the shop which competed with Ignacio's "shoe regeneration" establishment is but one example.[73] In *Picturesque Showcase* and in the *Memoirs* Baroja provides the source for a few of the episodes in *Red Dawn*, observing that such characters as Don José the housebreaker and Monzón the sculptor are copies rather than inventions.[74] The whole of *The Struggle for Life* is in fact an illustration of Goethe's statement that reality has more genius than invention. Baroja paints observed details and creates multitudes of rapid vignettes; the total number of figures in the three novels is enormous and the variety of episodes and subplots makes a detailed summary extremely lengthy.[75] If the vision of *The Struggle for Life* is Goyesque, the execution is by Breughel. When Don Alonso, "the human boa," states sadly, "My life is a continual Waterloo," he is speaking for all the disinherited; Gorki and Baroja meet across a wide geographical expanse but over a chronological distance of only two years.[76]

Baroja's view throughout the work is compassionate and humane, yet at the same time puritanical in its insistence on morality, work, and steadfastness. For all its crude realism, the note of sentimentality is not absent, for the death of Manuel's idealistic brother Juan at the end of *Red Dawn* seems inspired more by Dickens and nineteenth-century Italian opera than, for example, by Zola. The last paragraphs of *Weeds* are equally attenuated; Manuel's friend Jesús dreamily describes a Golden Age, an idyll of love and freedom in a world free of hate and constraint. Although the total effect is dreary and pessimistic, each of the three novels ends on a note of hope similar to that of *The House of Aizgorri, Adventures . . .,* and *The Lord of Labraz.* Baroja is not yet ready to follow his own thinking to its logical conclusion but seeks, however artificially, to mitigate the consequences of his apparent nihilism.

V   A *Morality Tale*: La feria de los discretos (The School for Rogues)

One year after the publication of *The Struggle for Life,* the puritanical collector of specimens from the lower depths again takes up the cudgels in defense of morality and decency. In *The School for Rogues* what has been implicit all along is now explicit: paradise is reserved for the pure in heart. The ex-Etonian Quintín García Roelas, protagonist of the novel, is neither a gentleman nor a scholar despite his proper education. He is ambitious but lazy, clever and unscrupulous, hypocritical and calculating; if he is brave he is also frequently cold and indifferent. A Julien Sorel *manqué*, Quintín laments the fact that he was born too late to serve under Napoleon.[77] The author's preoccupation with Nietzsche, evident in Hasting's pronouncements on action and in Ossorio's later rhetorical flights, is carried over to Quintín with ambiguous results. When he decides on the heels of a disappointed love affair to become a man of action—as if such things can be decided—his first act is to become inebriated and to behave aggressively.

The novel is set in Córdoba before the Revolution of 1868 and Quintín's numerous undertakings include an alliance with the Freemasons for the purpose of fomenting a revolutionary plot, a connection with a libelously satirical newspaper called *La Víbora (The Serpent)*, a series of cloak-and-dagger adventures, escape from Córdoba, and finally a triumphal return six years later. The six years are accounted for with the vague indication that Quintín "Went from one success to another."[78] Now a wealthy member of Congress, the former opportunist and arch-egoist unexpectedly feels unworthy of the girl he loves and resorts to the usual remedy: flight. Filled with self-pity, Quintín weeps over his moral defeat at the hands of the trusting

Remedios. Baroja's point of view is eminently clear: such moral exemplars as Juan de Labraz, Marina, Agueda, and Mariano go toward the sun, but Quintín is forever condemned to inhabit the region of shadows. The author's distinction between success and failure is evident in this early work; sentimental success is a necessary adjunct to public success, for without it the latter is transformed into its contrary.

The mystery surrounding the hero's origin as well as the proliferation of subplots and episodes involving gambling, kidnapping, and robbery, *inter alia,* make the association with serialized novels inevitable and give the reader the uneasy feeling that he has inadvertently stumbled into a theatre specializing in plays of the Romantic era. Baroja had been in Córdoba in 1904 with the painter Regoyos, and it was this visit that inspired the setting for the novel. Quintín, however, was invented, and it does not seem unfair to say that it is for this reason that he lacks substance and interest; he is all surface, all gesture, a figure in a museum in which the exhibits already include Don Ramiro of *The Lord of Labraz.* The voice of the author is heard intermittently, particularly when invidious comparisons are drawn between Andalusians and the English, but it is through Escobedo, one of Quintín's acquaintances, that Baroja speaks most directly. Escobedo is a Pangloss in reverse, convinced that he is living the worst possible life in the worst of all possible worlds. Knowledge, he affirms, is the enemy of happiness and a state of beatitude or *ataraxia* can be achieved only by not knowing, for "he that increaseth knowledge increaseth sorrow." Happiness, sincerity, and friendship are an illusion and every man who looks in the mirror sees only a *poseur.* Yet, continues Escobedo, the black view is but one side of the coin, for the other is comic and grotesque: "I am changing from a tearful, gloomy man into a jovial misanthrope."[79] If Escobedo's Schopenhauerian pessimism reflects Baroja's vision of mankind and the world, the figure of the jovial misanthrope had already been suggested in the description of Dr. Labarta in the *Adventures* . . . and was later to be amplified in *La caverna del humorismo* (*The Grotto of Humor*).[80] Heraclitus, the weeping philosopher, and Democritus, the laughing philosopher, are sometimes inseparable.

VI *Silvestre Paradox Revisited*

Paradox Rey, (*Paradox, King*), which followed the *Adventures* . . . after a period of five years, is a sequel only in the sense that Silvestre Paradox and Don Avelino again figure prominently in the plot. *Paradox, King,* like *The House of Aizgorri,* is a dialogued novel, a form Baroja used infrequently but with considerable skill. When the work opens, Paradox and Don Avelino are in a town near Valencia and the restless Paradox is once again beset by his mania for movement and change: "I'm a born vagabond," he affirms.[81] His plan is to join an expedition to the Republic of Cananí, presumably organized for the purpose of establishing a Jewish colony in Africa. The two friends go to Tangier to meet the organizer of the expedition and his company of naturalists, explorers, soldiers, and assorted adventurers. Their ship founders on the way to their destination and crew and passengers are taken captive in Bu-Tata, capital of Uganga. They presently escape to the Fortunate Isles where, by a common effort, they build "Fortunate House" and even put out an issue of the *Fortunate House Herald*. After aiding their former enemies, the inhabitants of Bu-Tata, in repelling their attackers by the device of diverting a river and thereby converting a valley into a lake, the foreigners are requested to supply a replacement for the tyrannical King Kiri the Bu-Tatians had just assassinated. Paradox is proclaimed ruler and with his reign there is established a model community. The new king's slogans are: down with art, down with science, down with universities and conservatories, down with deans and professors. "Let us live the free life, without restraints, without schools, without laws, without teachers. . . ."[82] If schools must be established, Latin, history, rhetoric, psychology, logic, and ethics will not be taught. Paradox' plan for a positive contribution to the social life of Bu-Tata is the construction of a carousel in the public square. The earthly paradise, unfortunately, is doomed. The French invade Bu-Tata and raise it to the level of European culture by introducing tuberculosis, alcoholism, and prostitution; in short, their civilization is "syphilization."

The motley nature of the adventurers who share Paradox' life in Bu-Tata gives the author the opportunity to display his preferences and dislikes. The Frenchman Ganereau believes in liberty, equality, and fraternity in theory, but in practice is keenly aware of social distinctions; the Englishman Sipsom is practical and hardheaded and, unlike Paradox, advocates war as a tonic for weakened nerves; the alarming Miss Pich, an immoderate feminist, asserts that Socrates, Shakespeare, and King David were all women; the geologist Thonelgeben is scientific and knowledgeable; Kiri, King of Uganga, is a sensitive soul whose idea of amusement is a beheading, etc. Through the rulers of Bu-Tata Baroja satirizes Spanish society: the aristocracy, the clergy, and the military all receive their share of blows.

Despite the novelty of Africa, Paradox is soon restless and eager to return to his attic in Madrid: ". . . I am a man of ideas, with plans, fond of struggle. . . ."[83] There is virtually no sign of the melancholy and apathy that beset him sporadically in Madrid. In *Paradox, King* he displays his ingenuity, a deeply aristocratic contempt for the masses, and the indomitable optimism that he expressed so belatedly and unconvincingly at the end of *Adventures*. . . . *Paradox, King* is a regenerationist work in many respects, but there is little of the bitterness and violence of, for example, *The Way to Perfection*. The positive aspects of Baroja's philosophy are clearly discernible in the "Elogio metafísico de la destrucción" ("Metaphysical Ode to Destruction"), one of three prose poems included in the work.[84] The refrain of the poem is *Destruir es crear* ("To destroy is to create"), for to destroy is to change and to transform. In the essay "La labor común" ("The Common Task"), included in the *New Harlequinade* (1917), the author reaffirms the positive value of destruction, insisting that the sole mission of the intellectual is to destroy "tenaciously, implacably."[85] The parable which constitutes Chapter XIV of *Paradox, King* presents an image of *las dos Españas* ("the two Spains"): the petrified Spain that neither knows nor wants to know anything finds its authentic voice in the frog, while the new Spain, the country that welcomes knowledge and with it progress and change, is appropriately symbolized by the moon and the creatures of light and movement.

The inspiration for the expedition to Cananí came to Baroja partly from his trip to Tangier in 1903 and partly from discussions held by some of his contemporaries, most notably Manuel Sawa, on the feasibility of emigrating to Cunani, a territory between Brazil and French Guiana. This story is related by Baroja both in the essay "La república de Cunani y sus hombres" ("The Republic of Cunani and its Men") and in the *Memoirs*.[86] In the same section of the latter work, written in 1947, the author recalls having heard about fifty years before some very exotic stories of black countries from an individual whose name he vaguely remembers as Orejón. A particular friend of this Orejón was an African king named Cataclysm who was in the habit of reading the Bible in English and retreating periodically to his domain in order to consume a succulent child which he ate, apparently, accompanied by fruits in season.[87] He also entertained himself by poisoning his courtiers and guests when they began to bore him. King Kiri is plainly a descendant of King Cataclysm.

Baroja classifies *Paradox, King* as half-fantasy, half-satirical poem[88] and it is in this work, particularly, that his formidable comic talents are most apparent. The arthritic, the author informs his readers, is timid and melancholy, ill-tempered and hypo-chrondriacal, but ". . . comedy often emerges in the midst of ill temper."[89] The misanthropy in *Paradox, King* is obviously of the jovial type described by Escobedo in *The School for Rogues*. The opportunity to feel *robinsoniano* (like Robinson Crusoe) fills Baroja with youthful cheer and vitality, and it is this vigor that gives to the work its bright ebullience.

VII *Paris and London*

Los últimos románticos (*The Last Romantics*) and *Las trage-dias grotescas* (*Grotesque Tragedies*), published in 1906 and 1907 respectively, reveal in a more convincing manner than *The School for Rogues* the author's consuming interest in nineteenth-century history, an interest that he presently cultivated extensively in the twenty-two volumes of *Las memorias de un hombre de acción* (*Memoirs of a Man of Action*). In accordance with his belief that only relatively recent history can be recreated with any sense of reality and vividness, Baroja sets both novels in Paris in the last years of the Second Empire. The materialism, vanity, and corruption as well as the revolutionary fervor of the era are conveyed through the descriptions of the amatory escapades and the political involvements of a group of French aristocrats, Spanish émigrés, and miscellaneous adventurers and idealists. The Franco-Prussian War, the struggles of the Com-mune, and the establishment of the Republic as well as the Revolution of 1868 and the dethronement of Isabel II in Spain serve as the background against which the amorphous pro-tagonist Fausto Bengoa lives out his inauthentic life. Romantic, timid, and lacking in character, Bengoa floats over the surface of the dynamic historical events which are unfolding all about him, wandering endlessly through the streets of Paris while sustaining himself with the illusion that he is a writer of some consequence. The fact that his articles are written by Carlos Yarza, whom he pays for his services, in no way interferes with his self-satisfaction. He has no personal life, properly speaking, since he is neglected by his ambitious and unscrupulous wife to the point where his room is sometimes used as a storage place for furniture; like Gregor Samsa, he is regarded as a non-person, an encumbrance.

Some of the non-historical aspects of the two novels again reveal Baroja's love for romantic fiction: a letter, a picture, black-mail, discoveries of hidden identities, the claiming of a fortune, still mar the author's plots. The valuable aspects of the work

lie in the sensitive descriptions of the old and picturesque Paris
and in the evocations of the Spanish émigrés living in that city in
the 1860's. Data on the lives of the latter were supplied by an
ex-minister of the First Spanish Republic, Don Nicolás Estévanez,
whom Baroja used to meet in the Café Flore in 1906.[90] It is only
Don Fausto's ghost-writer Carlos Yarza who stands out sharply
against the procession of *arrivistes,* revolutionaries, and reaction-
aries who appear in *Grotesque Tragedies.* A strong-willed and
outspoken Basque, Yarza lives according to his principles, dis-
daining the morally decadent Parisian society which surrounds
him. In some respects he is a mirror of Baroja: he is antireligious,
he considers himself a solitary and a stoic, he scorns social
climbers and the peaceful bourgeois life to which so many
"bovine" men and women aspire. In other respects he is a successful reworking of Quintín Roelas, the misguided man of action.
"One must be a wolf," is his motto, and he is faithful to it. Yarza
admires only the strong man who breaks in upon life with the
fury of a bull, sweeping all obstacles from his path.[91] Following
his convictions to their logical conclusion, Yarza joins the ranks
of the Commune and disappears in the subsequent melee. Baroja
creates the impression that Yarza was shot along with his friend
Pipot and the others, but in *Caesar or Nothing* Yarza reappears
in Paris, surprisingly enough, as a banker and broker.[92] The
French Stock Exchange becomes the stalking ground for this
wolf, now grown old and conventional. Within the limits of
Grotesque Tragedies, however, Yarza is another of the author's
Nietzscheans, modified by sentiment if not by sentimentality.

The cosmopolitan air of the work seems to be fortified by the
introduction of Germans, Italians, and South Americans, but is in
reality diminished by the author's provincial attitudes; South
Americans are presented as but one step removed from the
jungle,[93] while the German engraver Stahl, to give but one
example, falls into the same conventional category as the baker
Karl Schneider of *The Quest.*[94] Whatever qualities these foreigners possess have been bestowed by Baroja *a priori,* in accordance
with his own rigid scheme. The author was in Paris at the time
he began to write *Grotesque Tragedies,* and he attributed the
melancholy air of the work to his autumnal strolls in the Luxem-
bourg Gardens,[95] but a geographical shift does not necessarily
bring with it an intellectual and spiritual shift, and the author
is always himself no matter where he goes.

With Yarza no longer on the scene, the ending of *Grotesque
Tragedies* belongs to Fausto Bengoa, and, as in the case of most
of the early novels, it is vaguely optimistic. Paris in flames is not

so much a tragedy as an augury of the Golden Age still to come, and Don Fausto himself, old and abandoned, is nonetheless full of hope. Almost as an afterthought, Bengoa adds that life never ends: "We are always at the beginning . . . and at the end."[96] The cyclical view of history suggested here, natural in a disciple of Heraclitus, has interesting artistic consequences. As Baroja proceeds further into his novelistic world, it becomes increasingly evident that there is progress only in a restricted sense, for as soon as the author reaches a certain point he feels the inexorable need to slip back to the beginning. Ossorio, Hasting, Quintín, and Yarza are all returns at close intervals to his sympathetic interest in one aspect of Nietzsche, and the recollection of his own childhood in the early adventures of Silvestre Paradox is but the first of several such returns. Baroja is sustained as much by memory of the past as by observation of the present, and it is the ultimately stronger, more emotional, pull of the former that distinguishes the works of maturity.

The recent past rather than the nineteenth century supplies the material for *The Wandering Lady* and *The City of Fog*, published in 1908 and 1909 subsequent to a visit to London and a walking trip along the Tiétar River to Yuste undertaken by the author in the company of Ricardo Baroja and the writer Ciro Bayo.[97] The inspiration for the plot of *The Wandering Lady,* as already noted, was the attempt on the life of King Alfonso and his bride by the anarchist Mateo Morral, but the novel is in many respects a travel book of the variety cultivated first by Azorín and Unamuno and later by Ortega and Cela, the plot merely serving as a pretext for the evocation of landscape and incident. Dr. Enrique Aracil, Baroja's archetypal Mediterranean,[98] befriends the anarchist Nilo Brull until the latter, in obedience to Aracil's principles as outlined in his *El anarquismo como sistema de crítica social* (*Anarchism as a System of Social Criticism*), throws a bomb in the path of the royal couple. Horrified at the application of what was, for him at least, only vague theorizing, and fearful of possible arrest for complicity in the plot, Aracil and his daughter María make for the safety of Portugal. With the help of Dr. Iturrioz, an English journalist, and María's uncle Venancio Arce, they reach their destination and then embark for England. As the Aracils proceed across Spain, Baroja indulges his penchant for description and disquisition; unfavorable opinions on Spanish women, on Spain, on Latin wit and superficiality are set forth in a series of discourses suggesting the still-aggressive critic of contemporary society. The introduction of one Don Alvaro Bustamante serves the

double purpose of voicing the author's negative views and
exemplifying the national malady of *aboulia*. Don Alvaro's assertion, "I have no will . . . my will is dead," is an echo of similar
asseverations by Paradox, Ossorio, and Juan de Labraz.[99]

The City of Fog is the London novel for which *The Wandering
Lady* was the preparation. Baroja had gone to London in 1906
partly out of curiosity to see how he would react to the alien
atmosphere, partly out of an avid desire to visit the scene of
some of Dickens' novels. Ortega, with whom Baroja traveled as
far as Paris, apparently considered the trip an incomprehensible
caprice since, insofar as he knew, nothing in particular was
happening in London at that time.[100] What the novelist was
seeking in London, from the artistic point of view, was its grimy
buildings and rank corners, the shadow of Jack the Ripper rather
than Westminster Abbey. Just as the Paris of Hugo and Sue
stimulated Fausto Bengoa's imagination, the London of the
disinherited and the dispossessed attracted Baroja. The anarchist
Arapahú, the Indian with a celluloid eye, and his companion
Maldonado, an impoverished adventurer and wanderer, are more
pleasing to the novelist than the more representative and
respectable office workers who become María Aracil's daily companions. The countryside and the slums, Covent Garden and
Whitechapel are made the object of detailed examination as
shopkeepers, anarchists. police spies, and a variety of Russians,
Norwegians, Scots, and Poles cross María Aracil's path.

María Aracil is at first independent, critical, courageous, but
ultimately proves unable to sustain the weight of her freedom.
The emancipated woman finally capitulates, returning to Spain
to marry Venancio Arce and to become a calm, sedentary
bourgeoise. The courage and decisiveness which marked all her
actions in *The Wandering Lady* give way to passivity and
inaction. ". . . María is a case of unsuccessful emancipation" are
the words of Iturrioz.[101] It appears that marriage, in Baroja's
view, often undermines character.

The discursive tone that is usually associated with the Barojian
novel is more in evidence in these two novels than in the previous
works. The set pieces are assigned to Don Alvaro Bustamante,
to Aracil, and to Iturrioz. The latter makes his debut in *The
Wandering Lady* and is described as looking older than his
years; he is bald, unsociable, and taciturn.[102] His words have the
familiar Nietzschean ring: since life is based on violence and
injustice, man's brutal instincts should be given free rein. An
oligarchy, a strong and violent individual aristocracy, must rise
up to destroy society and then itself be destroyed in turn at the

first sign of decadence. Every intelligent man, the doctor continues, must say no to the stupidity of prevailing laws and customs until such time as he is too worn out to rebel any further; if anarchism is a dream, the individual, at any rate, is real. "Whatever favors life is good, whatever interferes with it is bad," is the conclusion of this vitalistic pragmatist.[103]

The Paris novels and *The City of Fog*, in particular, are of greater interest for their atmosphere than for their ideological content, and the poet is far more persuasive than the social critic. The Madrid, Paris, and London novels are antivalentines, loving evocations of the abject and dismal as well as of the romantic and the picturesque; the authentic valentine can be addressed only to the Basque countryside and to its heroes.

VIII   *A Basque Romance*: Zalacaín el aventurero
(Zalacaín The Adventurer)

As a man of his era, Baroja looked both out and in, both beyond Spain and within its borders for his literary inspiration. There is also the polarization between past and present, country and city, the idealized, romantic painting versus the brutal sketch. If the great cosmopolitan centers yield up sharp photographs, the countryside provides innumerable portraits; if deeds of courage, loyalty, and devotion are to be sung, the bard is most at home in the green Basque countryside. The idea for *Zalacaín the Adventurer*[104] first came to Baroja in 1907 when he was in Saint Jean Pied-de-Port. Darío de Regoyos had suggested that the novelist go there not only because he would find it agreeable, but because he might find a suitable landscape to serve as background for a novel. Regoyos apparently understood his friend's methods, for Saint Jean was presently transformed into Urbía, one of the settings for *Zalacaín*. A visit to San Sebastián placed the author in contact with some of his father's friends who obligingly supplied him with details of the second Carlist War; one Fuentes, a former *jai-alai* player who had at one time belonged to the Carlist faction of the curate Santa Cruz, also furnished first-hand information on his fellow warriors. With the locale and the historical facts in hand, Baroja wrote *Zalacaín*, which appeared in 1909, the same year as *The City of Fog*.

Zalacaín found great favor both in Spain and abroad, and was considered by Baroja to be one of his best novels. The popularity of *Zalacaín* may have done much to bring the name of the author to the public, but its merit lies less in its intrinsic excellence than in its interest as a rehearsal for the Aviraneta series. Zalacaín is a vigorous young Basque, confident, ambitious, with a love for danger and action. With the Carlist wars as a background, Zalacaín moves from place to place as an agent for the Carlists. Smuggling, imprisonment, escape, adventures involving Rosita, Linda, and Catalina, the three women who love him, his marriage to Catalina, his death at the hands of "el Cacho," friend of Catalina's envious brother Carlos Ohando, contribute to a novel of almost constant movement.

Mi país es el monte ("My home is in the mountains"), declares Zalacaín, and the sedentary life of others inspires him to violence: ". . . cities are made to be sacked by strong men."[105] Zalacaín is yet another Nietzschean, but instinctive rather than intellectual. His faith in his good fortune is limitless if unjustified, for he is killed in 1876, having reached the age of twenty-four. To conclude that Baroja's men of action invariably fail, however, as has been done by several critics,[106] is to equate failure with death. If that were the case, history would record no successes. Zalacaín's fate is sealed from the beginning, with the recital of the details of the death of one Martín López de Zalacaín, in 1412, at the hands of a relative of Mosen de Sant Pedro d'Ohando, Zalacaín's enemy.[107] The violent death is in keeping with the romantic conception of *Zalacaín*, and the three roses deposited on his grave by Linda, Rosita, and Catalina, suggest the hero of the tragic folktale or ballad. Zalacaín is Baroja's entertainment and distraction, expressing in his constant activity the author's need to create life.

Zalacaín is the most objective of Baroja's early novels and it is his only extended work that is truly redolent of youth. Basque songs are interpolated into the text, and Baroja's almost Cervantine custom of including independent narratives sometimes yields surprisingly happy results. Chapter IV, "Historia casi inverosímil de José Cracasch" ("The Almost Unbelievable History of José Cracasch"), is a masterpiece of absurdity. The more or less obligatory criticisms of Spain and the Church are expressed by a variety of foreigners,[108] and Baroja himself intervenes directly with an extensive catalogue of the Basque supporters of the Carlist cause, but Zalacaín, with his dynamic self-affirmation, rises above all political considerations, a jeweled link in a strong chain of Basque warriors.[109]

IX *A Regenerationist Work*: César o nada (Caesar or Nothing)

In 1908 Baroja conceived the idea of visiting Rome to gather material for a novel on Cesare Borgia, a figure that had attracted him from the time he went to Viana de Navarra with Maeztu to contemplate the burial place of that eminent son of Pope

Alexander VI. Once in Rome, however, the novelist almost immediately abandoned the project because it would have involved too much meticulous research and a too-protracted stay in Italy. He also feared that the work would turn out to be boring, a prospect that invariably filled him with horror. As a substitute for the Renaissance novel, Baroja decided to compose a work with a modern setting, but with reminiscences of the Borgia type; *Caesar or Nothing,* which was published in 1910 after having appeared serially in *El Radical,* was the result.[110] Aside from its function as a surrogate historical novel, *Caesar or Nothing* is also the reflection of the author's first serious brush with politics, for it was in 1909 that Baroja ran unsuccessfully for municipal councilman on the side of the Republican leader Alejandro Lerroux.

The novel unfolds in three countries, combining portraits of the clergy, the idle rich, and the social climbers in the inevitable hotels of Italy and Switzerland with sketches of politicians and opportunists in the town of Castro Duro in Spain. In Rome, César Moncada hopes to profit from his relationship to the influential Cardinal Fort, but it is his acquaintanceship with a fellow Spaniard Don Calixto García Guerrero that finally launches his career. Don Calixto promises to have César named Congressman for Castro Duro, and it is only in the second part of the novel, when César takes an active part in Spanish politics, that the putative man of action begins to act. In the course of innumerable conversations in the first part of the work, Moncada reveals his conviction that only the useful is good; art, architecture, and music are not worth knowing, and the formulation of aesthetic doctrines is the occupation of fools. His ambition, which he takes few steps to fulfill be it said in passing, is to be a Philistine "of the active life," to be a financial wizard, a man of decision and consequence. He freely dispenses unfavorable opinions on Christianity, the Church, the aristocracy, on the Germans, the English, and the French, while taking no pains to conceal his own astonishing lack of culture, a lack that seems deliberately imposed by the author to distinguish between the intellectual and the man of action.[111]

Moncada makes his first appearance in the prologue to the novel, wherein Baroja describes an interview in Cestona with his future protagonist. César announces that morality consists of strength and tenacity, the willingness of the individual to bend his efforts toward a single goal. His ambition is to be a success, an instrument of progress; action is the only solution to life's confusions, and struggle alone can sustain man in his high purpose. In this life, he declares later on, ". . . one must not defend oneself, but attack, always attack."[112] If César seems to join the ranks of Baroja's Nietzscheans, there is no concrete evidence of his dynamic self-assertiveness until he is elected Congressman in Castro Duro. At first he distinguishes himself more for his successful speculations on the Stock Market than for his role in Congress, but presently the new Congressman begins to carry out much-needed reforms in his constituency, attempting to solve the problems of irrigation and transportation, and planning to build a library and schools despite opposition from the conservative Catholic parties. The program of this Darwinian pragmatist is to break the power of political bosses, restrain the bourgeoisie, distribute land to the farmers, destroy theocratic rule: in short, the regenerationist program.

In a lecture delivered in Barcelona in 1910, Baroja declared " . . . I call transformation revolution. And to accomplish this, war must be declared against everything that is established."[113] The simultaneous process of destruction and creation, already elaborated in *Paradox, King,* will constitute Moncada's chief preoccupation.

With his reelection, Moncada becomes the *cacique* (political boss) of Castro Duro, *un cacique bueno* ("a good political boss"); the determination to do away with bossism apparently has a limited application. While affirming the necessity for hardness as a requisite for success, however, Moncada suspects that he himself is lacking in this essential quality.[114] He is often invaded by depression and more frequently manifests the restlessness and nervousness of a neurasthenic than the sangfroid of a purposeful man of action. His brief love affair with the Countess Brenda virtually shatters his already weak nerves, and his courtship of the American Susana Marchmont reveals a similar lack of elasticity and vigor; indifference and inertia take the place of enthusiasm and passion. Even the experience of love via-à-vis Amparito, his future wife, is bound up with pain and anguish, and if their marriage assuages the suffering it also dissolves his energies. "I am a sickly man, with a wounded, ulcerated spirit," are the words of the same person who was lost in admiration for Cesare Borgia's slogan *Aut Caesar, aut nihil* ("Caesar or Nothing") and who had declared, "One must live and struggle out in the open."

Moncada's at best uncertain aggressiveness is further threatened by compassion: the intercession of a mother in behalf of her murderer-son breaks Moncada's resolve to punish objectively and he laments that he is no longer hard.[115] His solution to the problem of this lack of strength is escape; he and his wife go to Italy and shortly thereafter César announces his intention of withdrawing from politics. Shamed into returning to Castro Duro, Moncada again becomes involved in the elections, which soon take on monstrously corrupt proportions. The Conservative faction, led by the priest Martín Lafuerza, among others, is determined to maintain the status quo and to eliminate subversive influences. Moncada is ambushed and shot at while his followers are betrayed to the police; the Conservatives are predictably victorious, and Castro Duro returns to its former state of paralysis, sunk in apathy and "enveloped in dust, filth and grime, asleep in the sun in the midst of its unwatered fields."[116]

The condemnation of the twin forces of theocracy and political corruption is openly violent and bitterly felt; the regenerationist sentiments are expressed with the same fervor that found its way into the essays of the *Harlequinade* of 1904. The strength of the novel lies in the tension between the patriotic Spaniard's overriding zeal for reform and the opposition to all change on the part of the equally zealous upholders of Spain's dearest and most destructive traditions; in short, the two Spains as symbolized in the parable in *Paradox, King.*

The problematical aspect of *Caesar or Nothing* is César Moncada. While on the one hand making pronouncements about strife, action, and a morality of convenience, on the other he is full of doubts,[117] subject to melancholia, and periodically all but inert. One of his first statements is that he sees life in general as a dark and mysterious web, devoid of attraction, a vision that should more properly lead to a Schopenhauerian withdrawal than to a Nietzschean affirmation and celebration. The grandiose declaration of strength and invincibility, "Caesar! I will be Caesar," is less of a battle cry than a prelude to defeat.[118]

The brilliant outer apparel of a latter-day Renaissance prince conceals a deeply tormented, indecisive spirit, for César's proclamations of aggressiveness and power leave a string of hesitations and suggestions of weakness in their wake. While Fernando Ossorio is a decadent who becomes a Nietzschean, Moncada partakes simultaneously of two opposing personalities which exist one beneath the other, as in a palimpsest. Moncada is one of Baroja's hybrids, in whom the imaginative recreation of a man of action reminiscent of Cesare Borgia is diluted by the infusion of the author's characteristically antivitalistic outlook. Moncada shares with Ossorio some of the characteristics of fin-de-siècle degeneracy, but his literary configuration resembles more closely that of Silvestre Paradox. Moncada is, after all, neither an artist, nor a pseudo-mystic, nor is he noticeably consumed with eroticism. His pessimism, self-doubts, and *Angst* bring him close to the author and mirror as well the nihilistic tendencies of the generation of which Baroja was so intimate a part.

Baroja's ambiguous portrayal of Moncada has given rise to contradictory interpretations. Gonzalo Sobejano considers Moncada *el hombre de acción que más cerca está de la Voluntad nietzscheana* . . . ("the man of action who comes closest to the Nietzschean Will . . .")[119] while Sherman Eoff considers *Caesar or Nothing* to go counter to Nietzsche's aggressive egoism, for César ". . . attempts self-glorification in a Machiavellian way and is made to know . . . the futility of his ego."[120] Moncada's dual nature, which Granjel has so accurately described, accommodates either interpretation.[121]

The *Adventures, The Way to Perfection,* and *Caesar or Nothing* can be regarded as Baroja's modern reworking of the medieval debate between water and wine, between carnality and self-denial. The elements of the modern debate have been transformed and the new struggle is acted out between affirmation and negation, between vitality and passivity, between life-giving and life-destroying tendencies. To the so-far uncommitted author, neither side appears to win and the contest ends in a draw.

X *Action and Contemplation*: Las inquietudes de Shanti Andía (The Restlessness of Shanti Andía)

The Restlessness of Shanti Andía made its appearance one year after the publication of *Caesar or Nothing,* and on the surface at least, it is difficult to conceive of two more widely differing novels. The complex clerical and secular society of Rome and the equally complicated structure of liberal and conservative politics in a representative town in Spain are abandoned for an idyllic evocation of the Basque fishing village of Lúzaro and its seafarers. The plot of this intricate tale of maritime adventure, some aspects of which were inspired by Mayne Reid and R. L. Stevenson, has been summarized by Nallim, and the fourteen pages of text devoted to the details reveal *peripeteiae* worthy of a Byzantine novel.[122] A considerable portion of the narrative is taken up with the life story of Shanti's Uncle Juan de Aguirre, and tales of mysterious identities, piracy, mutiny, buried treasure, and slave ships accumulate with cinematic rapidity and gusto.

These memoirs of the now old Shanti Andía contain authentic details on the slave trade provided the author by two old seamen in San Sebastián, while the prototypical Basque village of

Lúzaro is an amalgam of the author's childhood memories of San Sebastián modified by a later visit to other coastal Basque towns.[123] Shanti's Aunt Ursula is a lightly fictionalized version of Baroja's Aunt Cesárea, and many of the objects described in the novel were recognized by the author's sister Carmen as belonging to the Baroja household.[124] A painting of the frigate "Bella vascongada," which sailed under the command of Captain Don Justo Goñi in 1849, may have had some part in inspiring this novel; Captain Goñi was an ancestor of Baroja, and the original painting of his ship is in the author's home in Vera.[125]

The Restlessness of Shanti Andía begins with a rhapsodic description of the old days of the sailing vessel, and the nostalgia is both strong and delicate. The association of past time with heroic adventure is everpresent in this twentieth-century Romantic, and the conviction that the Basque ports and countryside produced the finest exemplars of bravery and virility is once again plainly evident. Martín Zalacaín and Juan de Aguirre differ in their modes of transportation and in the details of their adventures, but there is a marked family resemblance between them. Juan de Aguirre is strong and self-possessed, with a stubborn and tenacious will; even life on a prison ship cannot break his iron resolve to emerge unconquered.

It is the "rough sailor" Shanti Andía who is of real interest in this novel, despite his subordinate position as mere narrator. In the early pages of his memoirs, he reveals that in his youth he was reputed to be apathetic, indifferent, and sentimental; this "rough sailor" also refers to his innate Epicureanism. Life has no purpose, no end, Andía affirms, for "The end is a point in space and time, of no greater importance than either the point that precedes or the point that follows it."[126] Because of the purposelessness of life, this sailor would have liked to live more, every hour, every minute. *Vivre le plus possible* (to live as much as possible) could well be the motto of this Basque existentialist. Shanti Andía considers himself a patriot in his fashion and an antitraditionalist; at age twenty-eight he characterizes himself as old, disillusioned, and melancholy. In his early years it had been said of him, "This boy is worthless," and later on there are various references to arthritis or rheumatism; the identification with Baroja can scarcely be in doubt. Shanti Andía's opinions and his pessimistic world view bring him close to Silvestre Paradox, to the Paradox who feels nausea at the emptiness of life. Perhaps the sailor expresses his experience of hollowness in different terms, but the substance is the same: "The senselessness of objects troubles me; I have no hope."[127] Both Silvestre Paradox

and Shanti Andía reflect Baroja's anguished view of the futility
of life, a view shared periodically by César Moncada as well.
Juan de Aguirre asserts his will and affirms the positive value of
action as Shanti Andía functions as a languid observer; Hasting
and Alcázar at first display a similar relationship in *The Struggle
for Life* trilogy.

Baroja could have said with Faust *zwei Seelen wohnen, ach!
in meiner Brust* ("two souls are housed, alas, in my breast"). One
of Baroja's tendencies is dynamic and restless, craving constant
movement; the innumerable adventures in *Zalacaín* and *The
Restlessness of Shanti Andía* and the veritable shower of episodes
in *The Struggle for Life* fulfill this need. The other tendency,
contemplative and philosophical, lies just below the surface, a
variety of figured bass. All is vanity, the author whispers, all
effort and life itself are futile. In *The Restlessness of Shanti Andía*
the novelist seeks once again to mitigate the consequences of
his lucid pessimism. Although Shanti Andía does not shout
"Hurrah, hurrah" like his predecessor Silvestre Paradox, neither
does he succumb to the languor that his vision of life might
dictate. The author's compromise is to convert him into a good
bourgeois not too unlike Manuel Alcázar, a solid citizen ready at
all times to bore his friends with tales of the sea. If in the first
edition of *Caesar or Nothing* Moncada spent his postpolitical days
as a collector of objets d'art, Shanti Andía becomes a collector of
adventures lived by others. The conflict between affirmation and
negation remains unresolved.

XI   *Towards a Philosophy*: El árbol de la ciencia
(The Tree of Knowledge)

Baroja maintained in his *Memoirs* that *The Tree of Knowledge*
was his best philosophical novel and his most complete. Written
in 1911 when he was at the height of his intellectual powers, it
contains ". . . a vision of life in the past, a recapitulation."[128] It
was towards this recapitulation that the author was moving from
the beginning of his literary career, and it is in *The Tree of
Knowledge* that the tentative gropings in the direction of autobiography are fulfilled. The composite portraits of Silvestre
Paradox and Shanti Andía, the partial self-portrayals in Dr.
Labarta and César Moncada are abandoned in favor of an unequivocal alter ego who duplicates Baroja's spiritual disposition
as well as his intellectual identity. The protagonist of the novel
is Andrés Hurtado, and his friends, his experiences as a medical
student and as a doctor, the particular time and place allotted
to him all correspond to details of the author's biography.

Andrés Hurtado comes to Madrid as a medical student and is immediately struck by the incompetence of his professors and the indifference of his fellow students; as he progresses in his medical training, he finds more and more reasons for pessimism and discouragement. The doctor who should serve as a model for his internes treats his patients with cruelty and rancor, the professor who should inspire his students with respect for knowledge is an egotistical showman interested only in self-advertisement. Madrid reveals the worst aspects of Spanish society, and examples of ignorance, corruption, hypocrisy, and apathy multiply before Hurtado's outraged eyes. Nor does his home life provide him with motives for celebration. His father is arbitrary and despotic, his brothers are egregious examples of indolence and frivolity; although he esteems his sister, the two quarrel constantly. It is only the small brother Luisito who engages his warmest affections, and it is this child who dies of tuberculosis while Hurtado is still a student.

Once Hurtado earns his degree, he is appointed to serve as physician in Alcolea del Campo, a position he fulfills with more good faith than skill. Alcolea, like Yécora and Castro Duro, is a narrow-minded, provincial backwater, and Andrés is finally compelled to abandon his post and return to Madrid. After a brief but devastating period as a doctor in Public Health, Hurtado removes himself from the active practice of medicine and earns a living by translating scientific articles. Lulú, the young girl he had met in his student days, now becomes his wife and the two enter into a time of tranquillity and happiness, a period that is terminated by Lulú's insistence on her biological rights. With the eruption of the unpredictable forces of nature into the rationally ordered framework of their lives, Hurtado, Lulú, and the ill-fated child are destroyed.

The assertion that Baroja drew many of his characters from life and that he was given to revealing aspects of his own thought and personality in his works is hardly a novelty; what is striking in *The Tree of Knowledge* is the fidelity with which the author has been impelled to paint his intellectual history and to trace his true philosophical orientation. Baroja's readings are Hurtado's: first Dumas, Sue, Montepin, the whole repertory of serialized novels of crime, mystery, and adventure; then philosophy, history, astronomy. His youthful diversions—the discussions in the café, the evenings in the gardens of the Buen Retiro are also his protagonist's.[129] Hurtado mirrors the novelist's preoccupation with sincerity, his deep puritanism, his interest in and sympathy for the downtrodden.

Andrés Hurtado is a Schopenhauerian, a pessimist with leanings toward spiritual anarchism, an anarchism based on kindness
and compassion. His violent indignation in the face of cruelty
and injustice, his intense hatred for hypocrisy and bad faith
indicate his incapacity and unwillingness to accommodate himself to the prevailing morality of society. Unlike his classmate
Julio Aracil, whose only concern is for convenience and material
gain, Hurtado is a delicate, sensitive spirit, easily bruised by
contact with a competitive and hostile world. The true nature
of the competition is defined by his uncle Dr. Iturrioz in a
Darwinian disquisition on the survival of the fittest in the animal
world, followed by a summation of strife in the human race with
the familiar Plautine sentence, *homo homini lupus,* a sentence
quoted by Schopenhauer in *The World as Will and Idea.*[130] Since
justice is relative and more a matter of utilitarianism than abstract
right, the only solution for a man of integrity is either to with-
draw from the turbulence of life or to restrict his field of action
to a narrow sphere.[131]

As Andrés sees before him more and more examples of egotism,
stupidity, and malice both in Madrid and in Alcolea del Campo,
he begins to long for a state of complete indifference; it is his
desire to turn away from the conflicts of life, to achieve a state of
ataraxia. This Epicurean paradise is of course denied him as the
world insists on impinging itself upon his consciousness, and so,
obviously unsuccessful in carrying out the first suggestion made
by Iturrioz, Hurtado, perhaps not consciously, begins to carry out
the second. From a village doctor he becomes a Public Health
physician, restricting the nature and range of his medical
practice. Repelled by the human misery and degradation that it
is his lot to contemplate in the course of his treatment of prostitutes, Hurtado gives up his already limited practice of medicine
and confines himself to translating medical treatises. There will
be no more patients, and the limitation imposed upon himself
is now almost complete. He occupies with his wife an apartment
which he has made over into one large room, and as the novel
nears its finish, Hurtado's life consists only of this: one companion, one room, one occupation. Baroja's path is the same
in essence: after looking outside of himself and dealing with
the world as a doctor and as a man of business, Baroja abandons
both pursuits for the inwardness and privacy of the writer.

The relationship between Lulú and Andrés, perhaps best
described as love in a minor key, is given the benefit of a
humorous introduction based closely on Schopenhauer's *Metaphysics of Love.*[132] The sexual instinct at the root of the romantic

mirage, the theory of neutralization according to which each individual seeks his opposite, the vision of love as service to the species, are themes elaborated by Hurtado in close obedience to his master's precepts. Wherein Baroja differs from Schopenhauer is in his ability to envision a menage in which disinterested love, for a time at least, can create an island, a refuge from the anxieties of living with and in society.

The withdrawal from the external world into the realm of the self is not, however, without danger. Once outside distractions are eliminated and Andrés is left to contemplate his apparent tranquillity, his deeply-rooted pessimism suggests that the state of equilibrium attained after so much effort will not last. Existence begins to become a burden, and the image of a window opening onto an abyss becomes the symbol of his fragile human happiness. Akin to the "nausea" experienced by Paradox and Shanti Andía's perception of the "senselessness of objects" is Hurtado's realization that life is lived on the edge of the abyss; the thinking reed is constantly threatened with dissolution. Hurtado's anguish is heightened when Lulú reveals her longing for a child. What Schopenhauer termed "the genius of the species" must be served, even though Hurtado considers himself a tainted product, unfit for fatherhood.[133] As Lulú, once pregnant, becomes possessive and jealous, Hurtado's apprehension mounts to the point where he must have recourse to morphine injections in order to sleep.[134]

In an earlier chapter Hurtado had consulted Iturrioz on the feasibility of marriage between a nervous arthritic and a young girl who is weak and somewhat hysterical, and the doctor had responded with a warning that such a pair runs the risk of producing sickly children, and that only a robust couple has the right to procreate. *El delito mayor del hombre es hacer nacer* ("Man's greatest sin is procreation") and absolution can be granted only if the product of the union is a successful creation in every respect.[135] The subsequent death of Lulú's child serves to verify the accuracy of the doctor's remarks, echoing Book V of Plato's *Republic* as well as the law of the survival of the fittest.[136] Lulú's death, a product of her general debilitation, is a further example of unfitness for survival in the biological sense; it is more a question of incapacity than of will.

The cause of Hurtado's death is quite otherwise, for its origins are essentially philosophical and, of necessity, more complex: he is the chooser, not the chosen. With Hurtado's suicide, Baroja carries out in spirit if not in detail the cure for the intolerable miseries of life as prescribed by the model for Fernando Ossorio:

". . . if [life] became too burdensome all that was necessary was
to eliminate it by taking an injection of morphine."[137] Upon contemplating Hurtado's corpse, Iturrioz remarks that his young
nephew was an Epicurean, an aristocrat, lacking in the strength
necessary for life. Unable to summon the inner resources to
withstand the arbitrary and adverse decisions of nature, Hurtado
succumbs, paradoxically, with a final assertion of his will.[138] His
experience of the contingent nature of human existence and his
inability to accept the chance workings of an unintelligible universe lead him to total rejection and flight; with his own destruction he annihilates the world as well: "When our mind dies,
the world dies."[139]

Hurtado did not aspire to certainty, but only to peace. Such
nineteenth-century deities as positivism, liberalism, and meliorism
left him skeptical, but he shared his contemporaries' belief in
science. This sole article of faith is shattered with the death of
Lulú when one of the doctors attending her suggests that perhaps the birth would have gone otherwise had there been no
medical intervention. Hurtado's life plan had constituted a shift
from the human to the non-human, from the natural to the
artificial. Nature, which had been left out of account, avenged
herself fully. To live in the shadow of the Tree of Life is to live
on life-sustaining fictions and illusions, but to cling to the Tree of
Knowledge is to run the risk of destruction. "Beginning to think
is beginning to be undermined," are the words of Camus in
An Absurd Reasoning[140] or, in biblical terms, "He that increaseth
knowledge, increaseth sorrow."

The closing lines of the novel, "But there was something of
the precursor in him." although far from explicit, have the effect
of mitigating the tragedy of Hurtado's death. The latter can be
considered a precursor to the extent that he prefigures the new
man who will be capable of both contemplation and action, who
will be able to sustain his vitality and exercise his will despite his
knowledge, despite his awareness of the precarious nature of
existence. In a reminiscence of Zarathustra, Baroja implies that
what is not fulfilled in the present will be fulfilled in the future:
the new man will affirm life in the face of death. He will be, in
short, the existentialist hero.

Baroja's readings of both Schopenhauer and Nietzsche come
together in The Tree of Knowledge, with Hurtado reflecting the
former while Iturrioz reflects the latter philosopher. As in The
Wandering Lady, Iturrioz speaks for strength and struggle,
utilitarianism, the support of any myth or illusion that serves to
sustain life. The author's preoccupation with Kant led him to

assign to Hurtado the task of explicating some aspects of Kantian philosophy to a dubious Iturrioz, a questionable procedure from the standpoint of the novel's organization, but a natural one to a writer engaged in revealing the genesis of his philosophical orientation. If Baroja can be classified at all, he is a Kantian in so far as he conceived of the world as a representation, a creation of the subject, the Transcendental Ego.

Many of the secondary characters in *The Tree of Knowledge* support the theme of *homo homini lupus*: Antoñito Casares, the Andalusian journalist who preys on women, Manolo, "el Chafandín," who lives on the work of his mother-in-law Venancia, the implacable moneylender Don Martín, "el tío Miserias," his nephew Victorio who exploits gamblers, women, and Don Martín himself. Society's executioners are balanced by society's victims: the laundress Venancia,[141] the impecunious bohemian Rafael Villasús, the stoical Don Cleto Meana. Baroja's love for the purely picturesques type is not entirely absent, and such characters as Don Blas Carreño, who speaks in the florid style of the novels of chivalry, and "el Chuleta," a funereal type who has found suitable employment in a mortician's establishment, are reminders of the humor that Baroja liked to consider a by-product of his arthritism.

The Tree of Knowledge is Baroja's most authentic novel because it is his least contrived; invention is subordinated to reality with respect to atmosphere, incident, and character. Nothing was ever to be more vivid to the author than the years of his youth, and the inclusion in the novel of many real characters recollected from his student days is indicative of Baroja's reluctance, not to say refusal, to sever the link with his earlier self. The recapture of the past begins on the first page of the work when the young student attends his first class. The chemistry professor whose every experiment is a performance and whose entrances and exits are accompanied by loud and ironical applause is identified elsewhere by the author as Don Ramón Torres Muñoz de Luna. Don Ramón is again recreated in the *Intermezzi*, the Acceptance Address before the Royal Spanish Academy, and in the *Memoirs*.[142] Don José de Letamendi, Baroja's *bête noire*, is presented in *The Tree of Knowledge* as the type of universal man common in the Spain of his day: nobody outside of the country had ever heard of him. Letamendi is another of Baroja's Mediterraneans, all pompous rhetoric and verbal brilliance, a purveyor of fraudulent intellectual commodities. Like Don Ramón, he appears periodically in his ex-student's works, always in an unfavorable light;[143] Dr. Cerezo, the model

for the sadistic physician in charge of the ward for venereal
diseases in San Juan de Dios, fares similarly.[144]

Hurtado's two friends, Julio Aracil (the cousin of Dr. Enrique
Aracil) and Montaner, are a reflection of Baroja's classmates
Venero and Riudavets. Although the novelist found himself
constantly in the company of the two young men, he was not
fond of either; Hurtado is equally critical of Aracil and Montaner.[145] Antonio Lamela, the Galician medical student mentioned
in the *Adventures* . . . appears in *The Tree of Knowledge* as one
of Hurtado's older classmates. The model for Lamela was
Maximiano Limeses, a student of architecture and a man entirely
dedicated to his love for an actress who appears to have impressed no one else with her supposed perfections.[146] Limeses
intrigued the author because he was an anomaly; had he been
a character in a novel, his exaggerated love would have seemed
normal, but in real life, affirms the sometimes cynical novelist,
such a case verges on the miraculous.

Perhaps the most haunting figure in Baroja's student years was
el hermano Juan, a male nurse who was in his element only
when surrounded by pain, squalor, and misery. There are descriptions of this ambiguous type in at least five separate passages,
vying for a place in the author's morbid memory with the repeated recollections of executions and executioners.[147] With a
combination of pride in his ability to recreate a monster of
perversity, and scorn for the official purveyors of decadence—
Wilde, D'Annunzio, Huysmans—Baroja claims for *el hermano
Juan* the one quality that can make such a repellent figure
attractive: authenticity.[148]

Hurtado's uncle Iturrioz was apparently modelled on a real
person, but Baroja does not provide a clue to his identity other
than the indication in the prologue to *The Wandering Lady*
that "he must have died some time ago." It is possible that the
personality of the Barojas' Uncle Justo may have supplied some
of the ingredients for the fictional character's total identity.[149]
In any event, Dr. Iturrioz appears to be a composite portrait,
uniting many of Baroja's then-current ideas with observations
culled from others. One of the philosophical doctor's many dicta—
what is natural is bad and only what is artificial is good—is a
clear echo of an idea expressed many years before by one Don
Paco Lecea, an acquaintance of the author who was to appear,
briefly, in *Las noches del Buen Retiro* (*Nights in the Gardens
of the Retiro*).[150]

The principal female character in *The Tree of Knowledge* was
modelled on a young girl, also named Lulú, whom Baroja knew

during his student days. He used to converse with her and her mother in the Café de Zaragoza, and they were sometimes joined by a pharmacist who obviously held Lulú in high esteem. According to the pharmacist, Lulú's air of ill health was traceable to tuberculosis, a disease her mother refused to recognize since such an acknowledgment would put an end to her daughter's working days, a prospect she was unwilling to entertain. Further, one of Baroja's fellow students was courting her as a pastime, preferring the role of Don Juan to that of serious suitor. Distressed by what was evidently a gloomy outlook for Lulú, Baroja ceased going to the café. Some time later when he met the pharmacist, he was informed that Lulú had died.

The descriptions of the flesh-and-blood and the fictional Lulú are essentially the same, with emphasis placed on their air of fatigue and ill health as well as on their premature cynicism.[151] The classmate whom Baroja characterizes as both a friend and an enemy at the same time becomes Julio Aracil in *The Tree of Knowledge*, but the object of his callous attentions is transferred to Niní, the sister of the fictional Lulú. When Hurtado first comes to visit the sisters, it is their mother's hope that he will establish a similar connection with Lulú, a hope that is doomed to disappointment from the start, given Hurtado's puritanical nature and ethical standards. The pharmacist, at first seemingly forgotten in the novel, makes a delayed appearance as a frustrated candidate for Lulú's hand.

It is around the brief but poignant story of Lulú that Baroja weaves his themes of biological decadence and unfitness for survival in *The Tree of Knowledge*. Worthy of note, however, is the accompanying motif of a turning away or withdrawal in the face of misery, a theme that is stated casually, almost unconsciously, in the course of the narrative in the *Memoirs*. When Baroja realizes that Lulú's future looks grim, he states: "Since the situation seemed bad, I stopped going to the café. . . ."[152] Possible action is rejected in favor of inaction, with physical removal or, quite simply, flight, adopted as a method of abolishing reality; it was not in vain that Baroja was a Kantian.

If many of the characters in the novel are reworkings of Baroja's professors, classmates, and acquaintances, some of the episodes are equally reminiscent of events in the author's life. The illness and subsequent death of Luisito, Hurtado's small brother, mirrors the tragedy of the death of Darío Baroja in 1894, at the age of twenty-three, and the removal of the Baroja family to Burjasot is recounted both in the novel and in the *Memoirs*.[153] The period spent in Cestona and the competition between Baroja and Dr. Pedro Díaz is transformed in *The Tree of Knowledge*, with Don Juan Sánchez serving as Hurtado's professional rival in Alcolea del Campo.[154]

The purely autobiographical character of many aspects of the novel accounts for its dense atmosphere of emotion recollected and incident relived, but it is the principal character who gives *The Tree of Knowledge* its never-to-be-repeated vitality. Andrés Hurtado is perhaps Baroja's only fully realized fictional protagonist; he lives, he suffers, and he changes, responding to his environment with the sensitivity of a finely-tuned instrument. Paradoxically, it is his role as Baroja's mirror that gives him his authenticity and freedom. As the author unwinds the film of his earlier life, Andrés is on each successive frame, appearing to have no prior identity, but observed in the process of becoming. It is this becoming that gives to Hurtado his particular flesh-and-blood quality, a quality noticeably absent from most of the novelist's main characters. Hurtado has what Ortega called a *quehacer vital* (a vital task), and the content of his life is the attempted fulfillment of this *quehacer*. The fact that the task itself is more of a beginning than an end does not diminish its value; the search for an acceptable method of confronting the world is the proper occupation of the philosopher. Where Hurtado failed, others would succeed.

Baroja's anguished vision of the contradiction between the irrationality of nature and the rational constructs of man hovers over the novel, tingeing it with a quiet despair. Yet, the tendency to mitigate the consequences of his own thinking—a process not sufficiently noticed by critics of Baroja's work—is still in evidence. Hurtado dies in the physical sense, but he is theoretically the first in a series of philosophical conquerors. That Hurtado was himself incapable of transcending his *Angst* is a measure of Baroja's rejection of radically affirmative resolutions; what Heidegger has called "freedom-toward death" brings no transformation into authenticity in the existential sense, but escape instead.

The anxiety-ridden Barojian hero is fully awake and aware of the absurdity of the human condition, but, except in the case of Andrés Hurtado, the question of the risks involved in such awareness is side-stepped. The experience of nothingness is but one sensation more, and fails to produce dramatic spiritual transformations. Silvestre Paradox disappears from view, for he is finally forgotten by the author towards the end of *Paradox, King;* the tormented César Moncada, having failed in his endeavors, becomes an art collector; Shanti Andía, for all his despair at the hollowness of existence, is difficult to distinguish ultimately, from the other sea dogs of Lúzaro. What Heidegger has termed "resoluteness" in the face of the ineluctable fact of death is nowhere evident. Among the partial self-portraits, only Carlos Yarza lives dangerously, and this purely in obedience to his theories on action and violence, for he is not concerned with the abyss. He is authentically himself, but not because he has become so; the author presents him already fully created. Yet, even Yarza is spared the penalty of his courageous commitment for the author refuses to kill him, saving him instead for a stolid and comfortable middle age. Only in Hurtado's suicide is there manifested a clear cause and effect relationship, and the decision to be conquered by death rather than to be the conqueror is indicative of Baroja's virtually obsessive need to flee rather than to confront, to terminate an unbearable reality by ultimately refusing to deal with it in positive terms.

CHAPTER 6

Uniformity: 1912-1953

CAMILO José Cela once remarked that he wrote many different types of novels just to show that he knew how, and until the autobiographical mold became solidified the same could have been said of Baroja. With the completion of *The Tree of Knowledge* the novelist had already cultivated the short story, the dialogued novel, the tale of adventure, philosophical and political novels, fictionalized records of travels, the evocative Basque novel. After *The Tree of Knowledge* the autobiographical note becomes increasingly insistent while there is a corresponding tendency to look backward rather than forward. The world of fantasy, subservient to the world of reality in almost all of the early novels, begins to offer competition to its former master and at times succeeds in gaining a place of pre-eminence, pushing into the background momentous political problems and offering as a substitute agreeable if unlikely diversions.

I   *A Double Image*: El mundo es ansí (The Way of the World)

After the "recapitulation" of *The Tree of Knowledge,* Baroja was prepared to retreat into a somewhat more recent period in his past, and *The Way of the World,* published in 1912, was the product. Recollections of the author's travels in Switzerland and Italy supply part of the background for this novel, with yet another projection of the novelist's personality in the foreground. Properly speaking, there are two characters who share the burden of conveying Baroja's point of view. Through José Ignacio Arcelu the author transmits his philosophical ideas, and through Sacha Savarof, a Russian medical student, his despair at the callousness and indifference that lie at the root of human relationships.

If Sacha's geographical displacements are many—she is seen in Biarritz, Geneva, Florence, in Russia and in Spain—her mood is constant. Passive, capable of powerful indignation but not of strong love, cultivated, analytical, and of a melancholy disposition, Sacha is the first feminine member of Baroja's family of aboulic pessimists. Sacha drifts into two relatively short-lived marriages, one to Ernesto Klein, a Swiss Jew, and one to the Spaniard Juan Velasco, but these experiments in internationalism have catastrophic results, for she is wounded first by Klein's opportunism and materialism, then by Velasco's brutal indifference and egotism. Ultimately left to contemplate the shards of her shattered existence, her black conclusion is that life consists of a mutual lack of consideration, scorn for the weak by the strong, violence, cruelty, ingratitude. The realization that she had caused José Arcelu intense unhappiness out of her own egotism and insensitivity is the final confirmation of the accuracy of her definition of life.

Arcelu, whose Basque name permits of no misunderstanding, is bald, about forty, and is always badly dressed. An individualist and essentially a solitary, his principal defect is a weakness of will; every decision requires cautious reasoning at every step. Arcelu is fond of discoursing on the author's familiar topics— Spain's incapacity for social life and order, the irresponsible aristocracy, Iberians, and Semites—and he shares Baroja's hatred for rhetoric and hyberbole. ". . . I am a rootless vagabond. My tendency has always been to flee and to destroy."[1] Arcelu's destructive tendencies are at variance with his enfeebled will, and from this contradiction is born his nostalgia for immorality and violence. Such theoretical Neitzscheanism ill befits this timid, retiring, and disillusioned journalist whose habitual assumption of a cheerful mien cannot conceal his melancholy. His unexpressed love for Sacha evokes no response, and when she abruptly leaves Spain after her break with Velasco, he too escapes to another country. The pattern of flight is entirely familiar.

Juan Velasco is the Spaniard as described by Ganivet in his *Idearium español*: his one desire is to receive a personal charter according to which he is granted the right to behave exactly as he pleases. Velasco recognizes no obligations and no responsibilities; his only law is his caprice. Ernesto Klein is Baroja's shrewd Semite, self-seeking, avaricious, superficially clever, lacking in moral qualities. Both are stock characters with a disconcerting perfunctoriness about their presentation. Vera Petrovna, one of Sacha's classmates, is also categorized and classified, to be displayed in a case above the label, "Female of the Species." All three seem invented in obedience to a mechanical formula, and nowhere is there evidence of Baroja's usual enthusiasm for his secondary characters.

Observed and experienced rather than invented, however, are the anarchists' meetings, the excursions along Lac Leman, and the visit to the house of Madame de Staël which occupy the Swiss section of the novel. In the *Memoirs* Baroja mentions that all the excursions he had taken in Geneva left a lasting memory; the

May Day demonstration he witnessed in the same city evidently impressed him similarly, for it was on that occasion, according to Pío Caro Baroja, that the author met a Russian girl to whom he spoke several times.[2]

The marriage of Sacha and Juan Velasco in Biarritz, with which the novel opens, is the account of the wedding ceremony of Paul Schmitz and his Russian bride attended by Baroja in 1909, and the wedding trip à trois, recounted in the novel, is also briefly described in the Memoirs.[3] The section on Florence, which resembles nothing so much as a chapter in a guidebook, is a raw recollection of the author's previous visit, untransformed by distance or by art.[4] Baroja's sometimes indiscriminate utilization of experience infuses The Way of the World with a random quality that strongly suggests a lack of purpose and concentration. The author is not so much recapturing the past as casting about for stray memories. A case in point is the account of the maniacal laughter of the Russian Afsaguin over the innocuous phrase par la gendarmerie ("by the police"), a performance that is completely unintelligible unless the reader discovers the parallel episode in the past life of the author.[5]

The title of the novel derives from a legend on a shield which represents three daggers plunged into three hearts, and it is this image of the hunter and his prey, of the executioner and his victim, that prevails in the novel. The feeling of bleak despair extends beyond individuals to envelop abstract ideas as well; the initial view of Russia as an idealistic, young, and vigorous country is transformed by the end of the novel, with Russian idealism and enthusiasm depicted as having given way to cynicism and immorality.

César Barja has called this work una sinfonía en gris ("a symphony in grey").[6] The greyness, which is incontestable, may well be a symptom of the author's lack of genuine interest, for the novel seems to have been written while Baroja's attention was fixed elsewhere. He is in alien territory, surrounded by strangers, with only Arcelu to give him an anchor in his own reality. Sacha is not the appropriate alter ego, for too many aspects of her life had to be invented and the gap between Baroja and his heroine becomes too wide. Miscellaneous memories of recent experiences do little to bring the author into the center of his creation; he remains on the periphery. It is not enough for Baroja to write of what he knows; he must also write of what he feels. Baroja's previously quoted affirmation to the effect that his entire emotional background was formed by the time he reached twenty-six at the latest, may have some relevance in this context. If the author's testimony is to be believed, his period of maximum receptivity ended in 1898, after which his feelings became blunted.[7] In *The Tree of Knowledge,* Baroja relived the period up to 1898, and in the *Adventures . . .* and *The Restlessness of Shanti Andía* an even earlier time is recreated. The episodes included in *The Way of the World* belong to a somewhat older Baroja, the man in his thirties who was less affected by what he saw and what he did. The author remarks significantly in *Solitary Hours:* "It is strange that although I had an insignificant childhood, I spend all my life thinking about it. The rest of life seems grey to me . . ."[8] The greyness of *The Way of the World* is the greyness of emotional distance, for contrary to Flaubert's aesthetic principle, Baroja was usually at his best when he was everywhere present and everywhere visible.

If this particular novel does not appear to have fully engaged either Baroja's mind or sentiments, a further cause may be sought in his involvement with the figure of Aviraneta. It was in 1911 that the novelist became interested in the somewhat shadowy figure of this distant relative and began to do some research with a view to devoting a chapter to him. This short piece ultimately expanded into the twenty-two volumes that make up the Aviraneta series.

II *Aviraneta:* Las memorias de un hombre de acción (Memoirs of a Man of Action)

Eugenio Aviraneta Ibargoyen Echegaray y Alzate, whose full name is all "old iron," was born in 1792 and died in 1872. To Baroja he was both the embodiment of the heroic idea—the last of the individualistic lonely fighters—and the symbol of the ingratitude of history. Ortega has said that Aviraneta fought so that his deeds could be sung by Baroja, an observation that can scarcely be faulted, since the obscure adventurer's exploits filled a significant part of Baroja's time, occupying his mind during a lengthy period extending from 1911 to 1935.

Aviraneta, for all his activity, was a very minor figure in the long chain of wars and political upheavals that characterized Spain in the nineteenth century, and one may well conjecture why the novelist was attracted to him. In an article written in 1933, Baroja mentions that his father used to see Aviraneta strolling about a square in San Sebastián in the company of the Carlist general, Nazario Eguía; after their walk, they would go to the printer's shop belonging to the writer's grandfather, Don Pío Baroja, to talk about the past.[9] Baroja's mother also knew Aviraneta, having seen him quite often in the home of Don Antonio

María de Goñi. Both Angel Pirala, son of the historian, and Don Nicolás Estévanez, Baroja's informant in other matters, spoke to the novelist of Aviraneta on various occasions.[10] The fact that Baroja's great-great-grandfather, Don Sebastián Ignacio de Alzate y Emparan, was Aviraneta's uncle undoubtedly contributed further to drawing the author's attention to this enigmatic relative.[11]

Baroja's interest in history and in the possibilities of the historical novel was shared by many of his contemporaries, most notably by Galdós and Valle-Inclán, whose *Episodios nacionales* and *Ruedo ibérico,* respectively, are interesting documents of nineteenth-century history. Baroja also chose that same century as his field of investigation for the specific reason that it was near enough in time to be recreated imaginatively; a more remote period is beyond his capacity to imagine.[12] The ubiquitous Aviraneta, by virtue of a long life that stretched from the War of Independence to within a year of the establishment of the First Republic, and by virtue of his blood relationship to Baroja, was admirably suited to the author's needs. In keeping with his generation's preference for infrahistory and small or insignificant events, Baroja disclaims all interest in the brilliant epochs of Spain's erratic past: ". . . in historic events I have been intrigued more by enterprise than by success, more by merit than by good fortune."[13] Aviraneta's career was certainly far from brilliant. Unappreciated and unsung, he was the ideal receptacle for Baroja's personal sense of frustration and failure, another alter ego to whom he could transfer his attitudes if not his life.

Baroja's novels in the Aviraneta series constitute "imaginary reportage" rather than completely accurate history, hence the freedom of the novelist to invent and to reinvent. Baroja's insistence on the rôle of the imagination should not, however, lead the reader to false conclusions. He consulted whatever historical documents were available to him as is evident from his accounts in the prologue to *Aviraneta, o la vida de un conspirador* (*Aviraneta, or the Life of a Conspirator*) and in the *Memoirs.*[14] Characteristically, Baroja visited such places as Bailén, San Marcial, and Hontoria del Pinar, the better to understand the battles that took place there; the willingness of Galdós to write of places he had never seen was truly shocking to the conscientious Basque.

Aviraneta's career embraced the War of Independence, the constitutional movement of 1820-23 which culminated with the intervention of France, the first Carlist wars, the struggles during the reign of Isabel II between moderates and progressives. Whether in the foreground or in the background, Aviraneta is

surrounded by vast numbers of characters, caught up in a mael-
strom of historical events and fictional episodes defying enumera-
tion. The author's prose throughout the series reveals the brio
and dynamism that he associated with the period, and nowhere
in his collected works are his formidable talents as a chronicler
more in evidence. Although the order of the novels is not strictly
chronological, since the first five volumes were conceived as a
long prologue designed to synthesize the protagonist's deeds and
to justify the length of the series, the total effect is of a compre-
hensive and moderately coherent summary of the main historical currents of the period.

El aprendiz de conspirador (*The Apprentice Conspirator*), the
first novel of the series, makes patent the spiritual resemblance
between Aviraneta and Baroja. When discoursing on the political needs of Spain in the period after 1830, the adventurer
espouses a dictatorship of justice, intelligence, and liberty. He is
antireligious, believing only in natural forces; he is anti-Christian,
for Christianity permits massacres; he considers himself unlucky,
a conviction reinforced by Martín Zurbano who informs him that
he will never be a leader or a success.[15] At the age of forty,
Aviraneta is bald and rheumatic, and at twenty-eight he looks
older than his years; he is also a bachelor until 1852, by which
time he is sixty.

In *The Apprentice Conspirator* Baroja's walking trip from
Laguardia to Peñacerrada, undertaken in 1912, is fully described,
and in the second volume of the series the guerrilla fighters who
take part in the war against the French are modelled on the
archaic types the novelist had seen in the province of Burgos
in 1914.[16] The author discards the possibility of anachronism,
affirming that the rustic inhabiting a backward province in Old
Castile in 1914 would be little different from his ancestors in
1809. The utilization of his trip to Tangier of 1903 for some of
the material in *Los contrastes de la vida* (*The Contrasts of Fortune*) is similarly justified.

Aviraneta complains in *El escuadrón del Brigante* (*The Bri-
and's Squadron*) of a lack of recognition; while others are being
promoted to the rank of captain or colonel, his efforts go unrewarded. The paranoia that Aviraneta reveals at the beginning of
the series reappears periodically in the course of the remaining
twenty volumes and constitutes one of the few distinguishable
traits of his ambiguous character; he is in the habit of complain-
ing not only of his enemies, but of his friends as well. Aviraneta
proclaims his love for action, movement, and danger, his desire
to "do for the sake of doing."[17] He seeks out difficult enterprises

and feeds on conspiracy and intrigue, but yet is hardly a reckless hero. His first skirmish with Napoleon's troops leaves him "paralyzed, without will," and he is terrified of the danger in which he finds himself in the disorders of 1854.[18] On innumerable occasions he classifies himself as a disciple of Machiavelli, yet he is the self-proclaimed enemy of lies and hypocrisy. While Leguía insists that Aviraneta was always the same, from youth to old age, the subject himself declares as his creed the necessity of change, of inconstancy in one's allegiance to ideas and to people. When in the course of his multifarious conspiratorial activities he is betrayed, Aviraneta at first serenely accepts his fate, only to make a complete about-face shortly thereafter to swear vengeance on his enemies. The statement, "I was sustained by my stoicism and lack of needs," is followed immediately by, "I did not have the character or the temperament for resignation."[19] The confusion in the presentation of Aviraneta is almost inevitable, given the premises according to which Baroja writes. If a character casts a double image, both of himself and of his creator, consistency is not to be expected; César Moncada immediately springs to mind.

In Aviraneta there is more restlessness than striving, less will to power than indiscriminate political dabbling. Aviraneta, like his presumed opposite José Larrañaga, goes out with more of a whimper than a bang. Maravall has called Baroja a novelist of the *élan vital*,[20] but this élan belongs to virtually every aspect of the *Memoirs of a Man of Action* with the exception of Aviraneta. The interference of the author's temperament and, to a lesser degree, his experiences, makes of the archadventurer a figure smaller than life.

Almost two decades after the appearance of the last Aviraneta novel, José Luis Castillo Puche published the *Memorias íntimas de Aviraneta* (*Intimate Memoirs of Aviraneta*), subtitled "Réplica a Baroja" ("Reply to Baroja"). Castillo Puche considers Baroja's version of Aviraneta more folklore than history, and attributes the novelist's lack of proportion and judgment to the fact that he was *enfermo de aviranetismo* ("smitten with Aviranetism").[21] Castillo Puche's attitude toward the adventurer throughout the work is extraordinarily unsympathetic, not to say hostile. Using the *Intimate Memoirs* as a basis for his study, Castillo Puche concludes that Aviraneta was pathologically egocentric, a paranoiac with dreams of glory, who boasted of great adventures and terrible secrets which were neither terrible nor secrets.[22] In a particularly apt statement, however, Castillo Puche remarks of the author that *su propio yo flota en toda la obra*

... ("his own personality pervades the entire work").[23] Baroja's critic takes him to task for following Antonio Pirala's encomiastic *Historia de la guerra civil* and *Historia del convenio de Vergara*, for which Aviraneta himself supplied some of the material, but perhaps the most damaging remark made against Baroja by his quondam opponent was that he did not succeed in delineating his hero clearly, a criticism that is all too just. Baroja's defense, surely questionable, is that no other literary character is clearly delineated either.[24]

Pío Caro Baroja, in a "Réplica a la réplica" ("Reply to the Reply"), speaks disparagingly of Castillo Puche's estimate of Aviraneta and defends his uncle on the ground that he succeeded in recreating the violence and vitality of a past era with the same skill that Goya brought to his paintings.[25] *The Brigand's Squadron*, with its vigorous vignettes of guerrilla fighters and its picture of the barbarism of the War of Independence is an excellent illustration of Caro Baroja's contention.

Con la pluma y con el sable (*With Pen and Sword*) is of interest as a chronicle of the period from 1820 to 1823. Aviraneta's attempts to bring about progress and change in Aranda are rewarded in the same way that the opposing faction in Castro Duro rewarded César Moncada; an attempt is made on his life. *Los recursos de la astucia* (*The Resources of Cunning*) is a series of episodes and skirmishes associated with the French intervention, a picture of the deteriorating morale of the supporters of General Riego as against the reactionary fervor of the Royalist supporters of the Duke of Angoulême and the autocratic Ferdinand VII. Aviraneta emerges as a practical man of action in this novel, calculating, and far from scrupulous.

In *La ruta del aventurero* (*The Route of the Adventurer*), published in 1916, Aviraneta is subordinated to the figure of Juan Hipólito Thompson, a taxidermist's son who spent his childhood surrounded by stuffed crocodiles and snakes. Thompson is an Englishman who has read Kant and Berkeley, whose religious beliefs are confined to faith in "Our Lord the ego and Our Lady the thing-in-itself."[26] More a spectator than an actor, Thompson is slow to decide and slow to move in any one direction. He defines himself as an optimist without too much confidence in either men or events, whose greatest strength is in perseverance and stoical resignation. In his table of "moral and intellectual aptitudes," Thompson gives himself five percent for "liking for work" but fifteen percent for wanderlust;[27] his kinship to Silvestre Paradox requires no elaboration.

Thompson's all-too-numerous adventures take him from England to Greece via France and Spain, and his occupations include working in a pharmacy, drawing caricatures, concocting false genealogies under the supervision of the sometime counterfeiter Abraham Tick, making wax figures for a fair. He is successively a taxidermist, a medical orderly in the national militia in 1823, a prisoner of the Royalists. After his escape from prison he sets sail for Greece where, presumably, he joins Lord Byron in Missolonghi. In the prologue which functions as an epilogue, Baroja provides the information that Thompson finally married in Andalusia and forgot his artistic efforts along with Kant and Berkeley. To Baroja, marriage rather than death is the great leveler.

Thompson is a melancholy lover of nature, a sentimental rheumatic who composes odes in the manner of the O'Neil of *The Labyrinth of the Sirens* and of the Baroja of *Somber Lives* and *Paradox, King*. On the occasion of the suicide of his friend Burton, Thompson delivers a panegyric to life, to vitality, and to nature, the refrain of which is, "What a mistake to kill oneself!"; and this despite his realization that life has no purpose. In an apostrophe to the Sea of Serenity, Thompson asks for complete tranquillity "without anger and without humility, limited in the face of nature and content with my limitation,"[28] a request that is close to Hurtado's search for *ataraxia* and equally close to Iturrioz' advice on the necessity for limitation.

The Spain that Thompson sees as a foreigner is the nation the author has sketched many times before; the Church, the French Royalists, Spanish aristocrats, regionalism, fanaticism, the Spanish hatred for work, are all treated with corrosive contempt, for he speaks with the voice of his master. For the rest, Thompson is unlike most of Baroja's major protagonists in that he thinks but is not weakened by thought; he feels, but is not dissolved by feeling. Thompson is an attractive adventurer, an amalgam of the fey eccentricity of Silvestre Paradox and the sentimental effusiveness of Roberto O'Neil, with an overlay of Barojian satire and humor. Were he more clearly drawn and somewhat more metaphysically inclined, Thompson might have been one of the heroes whose existence had been heralded by Andrés Hurtado, the "precursor," for only he actively celebrates life while aware at the same time of its futility. But the pattern is set, and Thompson is condemned to go on to lesser rather than to greater things.

La veleta de Gastizar (*The Weathervane of Gastizar*) provides an animated picture of the Spanish émigrés in France in 1830, and is undoubtedly of greater interest as an historical document than as a novelistic entertainment. The fictional figure of Miguel

Aristy stands out in relief against the succession of characters and events both in *The Weathervane of Gastizar* and its accompanying *Los caudillos de 1830* (*The Chieftains of 1830*). Miguel Aristy is a bachelor, unencumbered by ambition, skeptical, uncommitted. He is a sedentary philosopher who consoles himself with books and music and is little given to the social amenities. Although he is not insensitive to the charms of women, he considers himself too imperfect to marry. At forty, he declares, *Va uno siendo viejo* ("I'm getting old"). It is not without interest that Miguel has a brother León who is weak, vain, and egotistical. He is, predictably, a painter. The author's shadow hangs equally over Pepe Carmona, whose journal forms part of *Las furias* (*The Furies*), as in the course of the narration he reveals himself as a melancholy, frustrated poet, timid with women, convinced that he is unlucky.

Aviraneta's view of the massacre of the Carlist prisoners in the Barcelona Citadel in 1836, his rôle in the proclamation of the Constitution of 1837, his unjust imprisonments and subsequent releases are all placed in their historical context in *The Furies*, and such figures as Generals Mina and Narváez share the stage with the inveterate conspirator. Pepe Carmona and Miguel Aristy occupy modest positions in the chronicles in which they appear, and one is inclined to be indulgent with Baroja's recurrent forays into self-portrayal. The case of López del Castillo in *Los confidentes audaces* (*The Daring Secret Agents*) is, however, of a somewhat different order. López del Castillo is one of the secret agents of the title, and he announces himself as a man without principles, a realist who accepts whatever is natural. Ingratitude and injustice leave him unmoved, but mendacity fills him with horror. This latter scruple would seem inconvenient for an effective secret agent, but the detail is passed over by the author. López del Castillo finds politics full of vulgarity and commonplaces, delights in reading Diogenes Laertius, and aspires to live idyllically in a pretty house in the country surrounded by flowers. If the Barojian overtones need further comment, it can be noted that the secret agent suffers from neuralgic pains. López del Castillo shares with Aviraneta certain aspects of personality that strike a dissonant note in the otherwise harmonious composition; for men supposedly dedicated to action, they are too sensitive, too vulnerable. A secret agent who insists on honesty is an anomaly, and a follower of Juan Martín *el Empecinado* who considers war absurd is equally so.

Jorge Stratford Grain, the idealized young Englishman who plays a minor role in *El amor, el dandismo y la intriga* (*Love,*

Dandyism and Intrigue), is yet another spokesman for the author's opinions. Aviraneta is a marginal figure in this account of dissension within the Carlist ranks, since the narrator is Pello Leguía and the work purports to be a continuation of the story that Leguía had begun, twelve volumes before, in *The Apprentice Conspirator.* Stratford Grain disappears fairly early in the course of the novel, but not before revealing his particular way of looking at the world. Like Tarrou in Camus' *The Plague,* the Englishman detests all principles which lead to violence and brutality, and can conceive of nothing more abhorrent than to kill in the name of an idea. Stratford Grain, who maintains that the primary obligation of a moral individual is to be a gentleman and to live in a pure and reasonable fashion, is Baroja's example of "spiritual dandyism," of a puritanical spirit at odds with all forms of corruption and duplicity, from the cult of Don Juan to the perfidy and treachery of the Carlists.

If some of the characters in the series are "Barojian," so too are some of the episodes. The wax figures at the fair in Pamplona, among the author's most vivid childhood memories, serve as partial inspiration for *Las figuras de cera* (*The Wax Figures*).[29] The dual plot swings irregularly from the wax figures of the ragdealer Chipiteguy to Aviraneta's political maneuvers in 1838. Aviraneta acts as *agent provocateur* sowing discord among the Carlists by circulating false proclamations and by producing a spurious document designated as "el Simancas," but his activities are virtually overshadowed by the somber gruesomeness of the wax museum. Baroja's mock ode to the art of ceroplastics is less a flight of the imagination than a nostalgic celebration of purity; the chief merit of the wax figures lies in their ability to duplicate only the human exterior to the exclusion of the tortuous interior.[30] Figures from the carnival and circus world are assimilated to the world of the wax museum, and descendants of Silvestre Paradox' employer Mr. Macbeth multiply in rich profusion. Equally numerous, and almost as vivid, are the Carlist *marotistas* (moderates) and absolutists who cluster about Aviraneta and his agents.[31]

La nave de los locos (*The Ship of Fools*) is a continuation of *The Wax Figures,* and is undoubtedly best known for its prologue on the art of the novel. In practice if not in theory, Baroja appears to have conceived of some of the novels in the Aviraneta series as a variety of circus sideshow or *grand guignol.* The exhibits in *The Ship of Fools* include a mad priest, a guerrilla fighter turned medicine man, a rustic novice who obligingly recites whole chapters from an edifying book distinguished for its academic style, and one Don Jerónimo who has discovered the key to the mysteries of the universe. Alvarito Sánchez de Mendoza and Manón, granddaughter of Chipiteguy, both of whom were introduced in *The Wax Figures*, continue to play a prominent role in *The Ship of Fools*. Alvarito is the scion of a supposedly noble Carlist family, but prefers actors and puppeteers to aristocrats and army generals. In his dreams he is haunted by the figures in the museum, and the tableau of three assassins brandishing their daggers becomes almost an obsession.[32] Corresponding to the wax murderers are the three flesh-and-blood thieves and murderers called *Martín Trampa, Malhombre,* and Perico Beltza, who resemble a tiger, a wolf, and a sheepdog respectively. The spirit of Hieronymus Bosch pervades these macabre passages, making manifest once again the grisly side of Baroja's imagination.

The preliminaries for the Vergara Pact which signalized the end of the Carlist wars in 1839 constitute the starting point for *Las mascaradas sangrientas* (*Blood-Stained Masquerades*). Alvarito's dreams continue to function as a counterpoint to the more highly colored portions of the narrative, and the effect is sometimes Goyesque. One of the dream masquerades is a world's fair, where the worst from everywhere is sold: ". . . bloody bandages from the battlefield, poverty, parasites, monsters, scabies, disease."[33] The members of the Black Band, a gang of Carlist marauders, are figures from the subterranean world of the nightmare: Bartolo, with his rat's eyes and tigerish fangs, the despotic and rapacious priest Macorra, the Frenchman Campagnac, a former innkeeper who disposes of his wealthy guests in mysterious ways, the escaped convict *el Galonero*. Baroja's huge *Narrenschiff* takes on more and more passengers with each succeeding novel, and what might be designated as the Alvarito trilogy is finally a gigantic canvas with figures in constant movement. Alvarito alone supplies a note of thoughtfulness and quietude; one of the author's spiritual aristocrats, Alvarito is not entirely successful in his sentimental life, and memories of his love for Manón accompany him even when all youth is gone.

The Basque background of *Blood-Stained Masquerades* inspires Baroja to make a series of observations on Basque ethnography and serves as an excuse to introduce an occasional song into the narrative. The songs continue to appear in *Humano enigma* (*A Human Enigma*), which was published one year later, in 1928. The "human enigma" of the title refers to the ferocious Conde de España, "the tiger of Catalonia," former

Captain General of Barcelona and Carlist chief in Berga in the last years of the Carlist war. The novel, despite side excursions involving the prototypical Englishman Hugo Riversdale, belongs to the General, and his despotism, cruelty, black humor, and at times seeming madness are recorded in a surprisingly neutral tone. The General is an object of curiosity, similar perhaps to an extinct monster; only the clinical examination interests Baroja at this juncture, and moral judgment is suspended.[34]

La senda dolorosa (*The Thorny Path*) continues the chronicle of the Conde de España up to his betrayal by the priests and Carlists of Berga and his subsequent murder. Baroja's now clearly sympathetic attitude toward "the tiger of Catalonia" may well be a manifestation of his tendency to ally himself with victims, even if this victim was once an executioner. Baroja's interest in phrenology, not yet extinguished, is transferred to a Dr. Alegret who decapitates the General's corpse in order to examine the skull. The severed head maintains a sprightly dialogue with the phrenologist Cubí y Soler in the Cathedral of Cervera, and the novel ends as the two are joined by other spectres who obligingly tie up whatever loose historical ends are still about.

Aviraneta weaves in and out of the novels in his long series, sometimes all but forgotten in the mass of details on battles, conspiracies, Freemasonry, and royal scandals. Secondary plots abound, and hundreds of characters sail briefly into the reader's field of vision, soon to disappear without a trace. At the end of the last volume, *Desde el principio hasta el fin* (*From the Beginning to the End*), Baroja takes leave of Aviraneta as his fellow countryman and "coreligionist in liberalism, individualism, and in a somewhat unfortunate life." The violence that underlies the series proceeds from the events themselves and the collision of opposing forces, with Aviraneta's voice often drowned by the clashing cymbals and thunderous drum rolls of this heroic symphony.[35]

III *Reprise: Essays 1917-1919*

Between 1917, by which time six volumes of the Aviraneta series had appeared, and 1919, when three more had been written, Baroja published several collections of essays: *Juventud, egolatría* (*Youth, Egolatry*) and *Nuevo tablado de Arlequín* (*New Harlequinade*), both in 1917, *Las horas solitarias* (*Solitary Hours*) in 1918, and *Momentum catastrophicum* (*Time of Crisis*) and *La caverna del humorismo* (*The Grotto of Humor*) in 1919. The shift from the personal narrative to the form of the essay is, in reality, scarcely perceptible. Baroja's fictions often resemble essays and vice versa; a case in point is the dialogued story, "Caídos" ("Failures"), which was first included in *Somber Lives*. Originally a two-page dialogue between a painter and his former mistress, it is expanded in the *New Harlequinade* into a sentimentalized, nostalgic farewell to the bohemian life.[36]

A. Juventud, egolatría (Youth, Egolatry)

Youth, Egolatry is a recapitulation of Baroja's ideas on politics, religion, sex, morality, literature, a parade of preferences and phobias, a regal bestowal of approbation and condemnation. The autobiographical details, already provided in some of the novels, are at last presented directly, without the interposition of a semi-fictional protagonist; San Sebastián, Pamplona, Madrid, Valencia, and Cestona are once again relived. Historians, philosophers, *littérateurs* past and present are given the benefit of Baroja's acerbic or benevolent commentary. The style is sometimes discursive, sometimes fragmented, but always assertive. The attitudes and opinions previously scattered throughout the novels are synthesized in this highly personal work, a collection the author himself later characterized as "sharp and violent" although adding immediately, "but perhaps with some good things in it."[37] To deny value to his work was to deny value to himself, a sacrifice for which Baroja was never fully prepared.

The portrait that emerges is refreshingly free from self-deception. Baroja's former insistence on his Dionysian tendencies is now recognized as exaggerated, and the author even admits that he is, despite his seeming espousal of non-conformity and extravagant behavior, simply a well brought up bourgeois, a *señorito. Youth, Egolatry* conveys the essential Baroja—the patriot, the biological entity destroyed by the sexual mores of his day, the careless but inveterate reader, the enemy of cruelty and injustice. Baroja recognizes that his former advocacy of action as a solution to life's ills has no more validity than any other prescription: the capacity to act, he now maintains, depends on inherited vitality and is therefore not optional.[38]

In the epilogue Baroja is at first radiant with comfort and satisfaction, pointing with pride to his house in Vera, his library, his economic independence, his friends. Now no longer young, and a bit melancholy and rheumatic, he is content to cultivate his garden and to meditate. This Apollonian air is soon dissipated, however, and on the last page of the epilogue the more familiar rumblings are heard: upon rereading the essay the author does not find it sufficiently strident, and wishes it were more violent, more antibourgeois. The reader feels somehow reassured.

B. Nuevo tablado de Arlequín (New Harlequinade)

Approximately one quarter of the *New Harlequinade* is devoted to the section "Alrededor de la guerra" ("Thoughts about the war"), Baroja's apology for his Germanophilia. His major contentions are already familiar and need not be repeated,[39] but the rhetorical outburst on the last page of the collection requires some commentary. It is in the five remarkably intemperate paragraphs with which the collection ends that the exacerbated tone of the *New Harlequinade* reaches a climax. The mission of Germany, declaims Baroja, is to crush the Catholic Church, to destroy Jehovah and his hook-nosed prophets, to eliminate vulgar, dirty friars and simple-minded pedantic priests. Parliamentarianism, "the old rhetoric," and the outworn and revolting Spanish traditionalism will be swept away with the plague of Semitic and Latin thinking, to be replaced by science, order, and technology. If Baroja later lost his faith in Germany's capacity to act in a constructive way, he never lost the conviction that the Judeo-Christian myths were inimical to the free development of the conscience of mankind.

The war may have engaged the author's interest for part of the time, but his Itzea refuge provided another and more agreeable focus of attention. The brief history of Vera del Bidasoa which occupies one chapter in the *New Harlequinade*[40] is of interest for the light it sheds on Baroja's attitude towards his ancestry. More or less as an introduction Baroja the antitraditionalist admits that the past necessarily weighs on the individual no matter how antihistorical he may try to be. In *Youth, Egolatry* the author had dedicated a brief study to three branches of his family—the Goñi, the Zornoza, and the Alzate. He does not fail to mention the "more or less authentic" coats of arms which represented "wolves passing by, wolves rampant, wolves biting."[41] The humorous tone does not conceal the author's family pride, even if it is only a question of "myths." By way of apology for his genealogical excursions, Baroja mentions that his investigations into the life of Aviraneta, who was of the noble and illustrious Alzate line, initiated him into this branch of studies. In the *New Harlequinade* Baroja's slight guilt and uneasiness at his evident delight in being an Alzate is excused on the following grounds: he was, he declared, tired of being called a baker.[42]

C. Las horas solitarias (Solitary Hours)

Solitary Hours are the notes of an "apprentice psychologist" whose solitude is more enforced than voluntary. It is out of necessity that Baroja lives a life of retirement: "I live in retirement not because I like solitude but because I cannot find an acceptable social life."[43] Like Kafka's Gregor Samsa, Baroja does not cease to eat because he is no longer hungry, but because he is not offered anything that he likes. If the novelist is now somewhat of a solitary *faute de mieux,* his solitude has at least the advantage of providing an opportunity to gain perspective on memories and ideas.

The miscellaneous character of *Solitary Hours* is evident from even the most cursory examination of the chapter headings; commentaries on Kierkegaard, Bergson, and Feuerbach are counterbalanced by descriptions of visits to Córdoba, Málaga, and San Sebastián. Still a capricious reader, Baroja continues to like Dickens and to admire Goethe, but finds the German author's equanimity and antimetaphysical tendencies disagreeable. In any case, art, when compared to philosophy, is a children's game.[44]

One of the most interesting portions of this collection is the section devoted to the novelist's account of his abortive election campaign of 1918, the result of which was to confirm the author's worst fears about the corruption and inefficiency of Spanish politics and to prompt him to conclude wryly that his kingdom was not of this world.[45] The war which Baroja tried unsuccessfully to eliminate from his consciousness intensified his xenophobia and augmented an already strong inclination to destroy reality by the expedient of turning away from it: "I like the French, the Germans, and the English less and less and want more and more to be in ignorance of what they are doing."[46] It is instructive to note the degree to which this desire to block out reality is at odds with the content of an essay published the year before in *New Harlequinade,* in which Baroja assails Spaniards in general for their refusal to take reality into account.[47]

In *Solitary Hours* Baroja once again reveals his longing for tranquillity, for a state of *ataraxia,* a paradise that constantly eludes him. Repose, however, is never far from restlessness and the inevitable palliative is literary creation, an activity rendered all the more indispensable given the author's image of himself as an exhausted horse constantly pulling a carriage; if he is ever unharnessed, he will collapse.[48]

D. La caverna del humorismo (The Grotto of Humor)

The notes of the subversive Dr. Guezurtegui are collected together to constitute *The Grotto of Humor,* a work which, the author tells us, was brought forth thanks to the zeal of a publisher dedicated to the propagation of completely useless literary and scientific works. Dr. Guezurtegui had taken part in an expedition to the North Pole and had visited a grotto-museum at Humor-Point; it was this grotto that subsequently served as a basis for a report to his University. The doctor's companions on the expedition are at least as picturesque as Paradox' associates in Fortunate House. Aboard the vessel "The Flying Fish" there is Savage, the Scottish misanthrope, Lady Bashfulness, Professor Werden, Miss Mitgefühl, Madame Weltschmerz, the Madrilenian Paco Luna, and another Basque doctor. The last named, Ignacio Illumbe, is a physician in an insane asylum and is, be it said in passing, a Basque nationalist.[49]

The Grotto of Humor is an attempt to analyze the ingredients of humor, to catalogue the diverse types, to give examples among novelists and essayists, and to characterize their particular brand of comedy. Baroja affirms that England, Spain, and Russia have produced the highest forms of humor in literature by utilizing the true stuff of comedy: the failure of the individual and his ensuing discomfiture. The lonely individualist accepts adversity and frustration up to a point and then suddenly takes decisive but badly-calculated action; soon defeated, he returns to his corner to laugh bitterly at his ill-timed manifestation of energy and decision. Baroja is describing, without acknowledgment, Dostoyevsky's Underground Man.

The rôle of various ailments in producing humor is elaborated in Chapter XX and it is here that Baroja's remarks on the effects of arthritis are concentrated. Humor and politics, humor and science, humor and painting all receive individual chapters, and black humor is illustrated with appropriately macabre anecdotes. The author periodically abandons the discursive tone of the essay to materialize behind the stove, as it were, in the person of Dr. Guezurtegui. Guezurtegui feels old, and has all but abandoned his former hopes of being a man of action. He is a jovial pessimist who suffers from both gout and insomnia; he is weak-willed but opinionated, sharing Baroja's negative views of socialism, religion, aestheticism. Guezurtegui, the violent anticlerical antiseparatist, expects to be appreciated by his fellow Basques in 1980, but in the meantime his life plan is to have no plan, to walk a path and never reach the end. To begin with, the path leads to Canada.

The novel and the essay overlap in *The Grotto of Humor* even more than is usual with Baroja, with the familiar assignment of discourses to a chorus composed of different members of the expedition alternating with Dr. Guezurtegui's heterogeneous pronouncements.

IV *The Sentimental Autobiography*: La sensualidad pervertida (Sublimated Sensuality)

Arcelu, Aviraneta, Miguel Aristy, J. H. Thompson, and Dr. Guezurtegui are reminders, souvenirs of Baroja's personality and preoccupations, but in the period between 1911 and 1920 there are no full-scale self-portraits. The ever introspective novelist now glances back at Andrés Hurtado, and perhaps aware that the portrait lacked one dimension, undertakes the journey back in time to reconstruct his sentimental history. Less intellectual than *The Tree of Knowledge*, less picturesque than *The Adventures* . . ., these memoirs of Luis Murguía are an attempt to shed light on the dual problems of frustrated sexuality and wounded sensibility.

Murguía is uncompromisingly honest and rabidly antitraditionalist, unable and unwilling to adapt himself to a society dominated by hypocrisy and deception. Sensitive and sentimental, his spirit is damaged by every disagreeable contact, and every sign of malevolence makes him retreat further into himself. His habits of rumination and self-criticism check his spontaneous impulses, and the indecision that is his outstanding quality is transformed into a rule of behavior: "do not act."[50] Murguía aspires to independence, nonclassification, freedom, while at the same time trying to find an outlet for his sexual tensions. The knowledge that the solution to his problem implies a negation of these aspirations drives him to seek a balance in indifference; by placing himself above the reach of material desires, Murguía hopes to find peace and tranquillity. Like Andrés Hurtado, he is an aristocratic spirit, an Epicurean.

Murguía, who is Basque through the paternal line,[51] spends his childhood in Arnazábal and Villazar. He is an undistinguished student with few social graces and meagre academic aptitudes: physics, mathematics, grammar, and languages are hopelessly alien, and no career attracts him. His friendship with Enrique Lozano and Ricardo Zumento, founded as much on hostility as on need, is a clear echo of the relationship between Hurtado and his two friends, between Baroja and Venero and Riudavets. Baroja's childhood in Pamplona is relived by Murguía in Arnazábal and Villazar, the author's early readings of serialized

novels are transferred to this new protagonist, the activities and
the attitudes are the same. Murguía is anticlerical, antimilitary,
antiseparatist, anti-Jesuit, fond of delivering inappropriate
opinions that are guaranteed to *épater*, to evoke indignant and
shocked responses. As Murguía progresses with his education—
he studies Law at the University of Valladolid—his readings
resemble Baroja's in every detail: Goethe, Schopenhauer, the
mystics, Kant, Huarte de San Juan, Nietzsche,[52] Gobineau, and
Vacher de Lapouge. Nor is he different in appearance and tastes
from his creator.[53] Murguía is arthritic and bald, at twenty-three
he looks forty or fifty, he dislikes gambling, hunting, the diversions of the casino. He is, as Machado has so correctly commented, an anti-intellectual intellectual who ultimately fails
because of his propensity for reflection.[54] The failure in Murguía's
case is sentimental, for he is uncommitted to worldly ambition.
His ideal has been to live decorously, ". . . to do the least possible
harm to others and to derive the greatest possible satisfaction. . . .
To live and to contemplate. That has been my ideal."[55]

Murguía is presented by Baroja as a man beset by erotic
thoughts and feelings, a biological entity who is more often
frustrated than satisfied because of his own ethics, fastidiousness,[56] and habits of caution. There are more women in *Sublimated Sensuality* than is so far customary in the Barojian novel,
and each one proves ultimately to constitute a missed opportunity, a failure of will on the part of the protagonist. The offer
of the young servant Anthoni to go away with the still-callow
Murguía is rejected because the young man stops to consider;
his vital energies dissipated by thought, his solution is to go
away. The Anthoni episode resembles in outline Baroja's brief
idyll with the girl from Azcoitia. Monetary considerations are
rarely far from either Murguía or Baroja and lack of funds is
the excuse most frequently put forth for remaining sentimentally
uncommitted.[57]

La Filo, the modiste who had had an affair with Murguía's
friend Lozano is no longer desirable because she had had a
child by the latter. Murguía's rancor is tenacious and unyielding:
her initial preference for Lozano cannot be forgiven. "My chief
sins were undoubtedly pride and rancor," Murguía later admits.
The seamstress Teresa is of unsuitable mentality and disposition,
the heiress selected for him by an actress looks domineering and
ill-tempered and is therefore likewise unsuitable. The story of
the heiress is retold in the *Memoirs* as one of the less successful
matchmaking efforts in the author's behalf.[58] The most deeply
felt of Murguía's skirmishes with love is centered in the figure of

Ana Lomonosoff, the Russian lady he had met first in San Sebastián and then in Paris. She is, unfortunately, married and there is no hope for a nonaggressive suitor. The Ana episode is retold as an "Intermedio sentimental" ("Sentimental Intermezzo") in the *Memoirs.*[59] Murguía sadly concludes that since she is married and he lacks money and energy, all is lost.

Murguía's last attempt at marriage coincides with the end of the novel. Bebé, whom he had known before, is now a reasonably accessible widow and Murguía considers marrying her. The project is frustrated when she marries a Count, and Murguía is left to consider as dispassionately as possible his many failures. Had he been more disdainful and had he grown a black beard, he asserts, his affairs might have gone otherwise. If a state of complete equilibrium is not reached, there is at least the refuge of irony.

Murguía, like many of Baroja's protagonists, is rootless and given to a genteel sort of vagabondage. In Valladolid, Madrid, Bibao, Paris, and again in Madrid, Murguía undertakes a variety of occupations from copying documents to inventing genealogies. He is one of Baroja's drifters, a man who is unemployed by profession and by vocation and who works only under duress. His usual state is one of penury, a state for which he feels no disdain but which he takes every opportunity to remedy; he easily overcomes his scruples and invests money belonging to his patron Don Bernabé in order to make a personal profit. Murguía is otherwise an ethical non-Christian, a would-be ascetic who aspires to live with the minimum of necessities. His judgment upon himself, from the vantage point of middle age, is unfavorable. He considers himself a sad failure, an unsuccessful rebel, a man who has been frustrated by society. His wounded sensibility and unsatisfied sensuality have metamorphosed into indifference and irony, the response of a too-vulnerable, too-candid spirit to the callousness of others. He can bear anything except other people.

Like Andrés Hurtado, Murguía seeks to calm the beast within by suppressing meat and wine—vegetarianism is accepted as a partial cure for erotic cravings. Huarte de San Juan, following Hippocrates and Galen, had affirmed that lust could be transformed into a voluntary state of chastity via the consumption of appropriate foods, and Baroja apparently shared this belief.[60] In a chapter in *The Tree of Knowledge* entitled "El dilema" ("The Dilemma"), Baroja posits the possible alternatives to Hurtado's sexual problems: either marriage or the brothel. The latter offends his pride and the former means submission and the

abandonment of his spiritual independence. Murguía is in much
the same situation, except that in his case the tension is constant
and intense rather than sporadic, and there is no long-lasting
solution.

Murguía attributes his indecisiveness and sentimentality to the
frustration of his instincts, for as the author makes plain in this
novel and in many of the essays, the awakening to puberty
in the narrow-minded and rigid atmosphere of a small Spanish
town is devastating. Interest and desire are awakened early by
innuendoes and salacious gossip only to be crushed later by
prohibitions and taboos. Unable to accept either brothel or
marriage, Baroja and Murguía accepted the resultant lack of
emotional balance as a necessary consequence. In *Youth, Egolatry*
the author suggests in the plainest language possible that if he
had been able to follow his instincts when he was young, he
would not have turned out to be so violent in his mature years.
His lack of equilibrium is a product of the unyielding morality
of Spanish society, and his intemperate criticisms are the natural
reflection of his resentment against this society.[61] Murguía's
sometimes misogynistic remarks have no other basis and his
occasional mockery ". . . is simply love and disguised enthusiasm
. . . and pain at my failure."[62] Murguía characterizes himself as
a rheumatic faun who has read a bit of Kant, a description
borrowed from an exchange many years before between
Maximiano Limeses and Baroja occasioned by the contemplation of a Greek amphora in a museum.[63] The reader has only to
glance at the reproduction of a bust of Baroja executed by
Sebastián Miranda for evidence of this faun-like appearance.[64]

The chronology of Murguía's life coincides with the author's:
in 1920, when Baroja was forty-eight, Murguía was nearing fifty.
The novelist's trip to Paris after the disaster of 1898 is reflected in
the fifth part of the novel in which Murguía laments the lack of
prestige which surrounded every Spaniard then travelling abroad.
Murguía's friend Mas y Gómez corresponds to Campos, the
author's companion in Paris, and the absurd incident in the café
described in *Sublimated Sensuality* is again narrated in the
Memoirs.[65] The homosexual Alfredito, whose disastrous life inspires Murguía with more pity than revulsion, is identified in
the *Memoirs* as the spurious Marqués de Montenegro; there is
also a section on this *poseur* in the *Intermezzi*.[66] The death of
Adelita, a young relative of Murguía, has no relevance to the plot
but serves once again to reveal the obsessive quality of Baroja's
memories; like Darío Baroja, Juan Alcázar in *Red Dawn*, and

Luisito Hurtado in *The Tree of Knowledge,* she dies of tuberculosis.

Murguía may be a sentimental idealist, a dissatisfied dreamer who might have been in another age a mystical friar, a painter of miniatures, or an organist in a monastery,[67] but he is by no means a suitable candidate for a tragic fate. By the time he reaches full maturity he has also accepted the necessity for limitation: "No grandiose projects, no great hopes; no close ties."[68] If he still experiences no feeling of solidarity with his era, his isolation is nonetheless confortable; if perfect tranquillity still eludes him, he still prefers his own life to that of the majority of his friends. Cat-like, he quietly curls up in a chair and stays close to the fire.

The Tree of Knowledge and *Sublimated Sensuality* together provide Baroja's intellectual and sentimental biography up to 1920. That Baroja had finally reached a *modus vivendi* with himself is evident in the shift from Hurtado's anguished rejection of life to Murguía's half-willing acceptance. He lacks, to use Machado's phrase, "physiological joy," but his self-characterization as "a rotted fruit on the tree of life"[69] is too highly colored. Murguía is not a brilliant social success, surely, yet he is less a failure than he would like to believe. There is a disparity between Murguía's behavior, which is not particularly striking for its outlandishness, and his theorizing about himself. He is not quite the misfit he declares he is. In comparison with Andrés Hurtado, he is almost a social butterfly, and Hurtado did not become a semi-hermit until the latter part of his life. Baroja surrounds Murguía with his now-familiar philosophical ideas, but this protagonist is not easily drowned in literature. The faun, the satyr, still peers out from the side of the vase.

V *Fantasy and Adventure*

Baroja's oscillation between the novel of ideas and the novel of adventure continues throughout his creative life, indicating the remarkably tenacious hold of his boyhood readings as well as his desire to escape the grip of circumstance and history. *The Labyrinth of the Sirens,* published in 1923 when the author was fifty-one years old, is a romantic fantasy involving a vast inheritance by Roberto O'Neil, a remarkable Calabrian villa and its grotto, various deaths by drowning, shooting, and poisoning. The sea apparently never failed to evoke childhood memories and to revive the author's early dreams of adventure, for the plot is hardly of the sort normally associated with a serious novelist of mature years.

The prologue to the novel is narrated by Shanti Andía, now so far removed from his former element that he becomes seasick on his journey to Genoa. His notes on Naples, which he visits in the company of Dr. Recalde, contain a combination of touristic and anthropological observations both of which serve to introduce the story of the Basque Juan Galardi. Shanti Andía acquires the first part of Galardi's story from the Countess of Roccanera and discovers that the continuation is in the possession of one Procopio Lanzetta; once he purchases Lanzetta's papers Andía has Galardi's story translated from the Basque and with this the novel begins. Baroja may not have read Homer and Dante, but he was obviously quite familiar with Cervantes.

Galardi's life is closely associated with the O'Neils, the owners of the "labyrinth" of the title, and it is the contrast between Roberto O'Neil and Galardi that occupies the author's attention. O'Neil is Irish-American and nominally a Protestant, but he is in no way different from Baroja's Spaniards. He is poetic and melancholy, has neither energy nor constancy, is imaginative and compassionate.[70] O'Neil's frequent flights of fancy are translated into odes of the type included many years before in *Paradox, King*, with the rhapsodic note now prevailing over the critical.[71] Roberto O'Neil is given to travelling to far-off places, but whether he is in Calabria or in Corfu, his is a shadowy presence, almost a non-presence.

Juan Galardi, Baroja's *vasco decidido y valiente* ("decisive and brave Basque") is an ex-seminarian and ex-sailor who serves as steward to the O'Neil estate. Galardi is extremely orderly and disciplined, if not imaginative, and possesses the expected virtues of vigor, simplicity, honesty, and perseverance. He is a solitary who has already found serenity, an active rather than a contemplative man. Yet this strong and calm Basque is easily dominated by a series of women. He has an affair with Laura Roccanera after she is separated from O'Neil, marries the devout Santa, and then allows himself to fall under the influence of the awesome Valkyrie Odilia. After the author dispatches O'Neil, Odilia, and Santa to the other world, Galardi turns to the priesthood. The destruction of the villa in an earthquake completes the unlikely chain of events.

The Labyrinth of the Sirens is a purely visual book, a work of the imagination rather than of the intellect. The sea, the weather, the changing light are painted with the delicacy of the artist's brush, and the author's facility for detailed description is given the freest possible rein. Baroja's artistic sensibility, often submerged under a wealth of ideological digressions in so many of the other works, here holds sway, and is perhaps the only *raison d'être* of the novel. *The Labyrinth of the Sirens* apparently did not displease Baroja entirely, for in "Ciudades de Italia" ("Cities of Italy") he diffidently suggests that some aspects of the novel may not be "entirely bad."[72] It seems ungrateful to disagree with so modest a judgment.

The Celestial Navigators and *Captain Chimista's Star* are somewhat related in spirit to *The Labyrinth of the Sirens*. Published in 1929 and 1930 respectively, they are representative of the author's adventurous vein and do not differ significantly in outline from, for example, large portions of *The Restlessness of Shanti Andía*. In respect to novels of this type, chronology is of no real importance; a juvenile fantasy written by Baroja at the age of forty or sixty is still exactly what it is. In these works the men move mechanically from one episode to another and the women, as Henry James had said of R. L. Stevenson's fictions, are like "so many superfluous girls in a boy's game." Deep exploration of character is entirely absent, a lack that is all the more evident when one compares these romances with the densely complex inventions of Joseph Conrad. In both novels, the principal characters are José Chimista and Ignacio Embil. After *The Celestial Navigators* opens, unpromisingly enough, with an account of an execution, the adventures soon pile up with the force of an avalanche. New Orleans, Charleston, Cuba, the Philippines, Rio de Janeiro, and Sierra Leone are the destinations of one ship after another; a succession of slavers are outfitted and then captured by the English; there are storms at sea, pirate ships, mutiny, and shipwreck. There is even an earthquake and an epidemic of cholera. The plots of both novels obviously require no further elaboration.

For *Captain Chimista's Star* Baroja utilized some of the stories he had heard from Francisco Iriberri, a former captain of a slave ship.[73] The novelist's fascination with slavers went beyond these stories, however, and in *The Celestial Navigators* there is a brief history of the slave trade, one of the purposes of which is to point out the cruelty of the Portuguese, the Brazilians, and the French. Baroja's humanitarian impulses led him to deplore the brutal practices of the captains and crews of the slave ships, but it was his curiosity more than his charity that drove him to write at such length about what was, after all, a remote subject. The history of the Conde de España in the Aviraneta series is of the same order.

Captain Chimista is, in one sense, a seagoing Roberto Hasting. "The important thing in life is to have a strong will," Chimista declares.[74] Life is not so much a series of obstacles as a string of opportunities, and one must believe in success and say yes to everything—*jasagen zum Leben* in Nietzschean language. Chimista loves danger and adventure and lives only for the present moment. He has the calm decisiveness of Juan Galardi, the fantastic imagination of O'Neil, and, surprisingly, a store of information that allows him to discourse as learnedly as Dr. Iturrioz.[75] Chimista is a skeptic, a non-believer, a relativist; at times it is impossible to distinguish his voice from Baroja's. Embil, perhaps because he was not born under the same star as Captain Chimista, more often fails than succeeds in his adventurous undertakings. It is he who is most often captured or shipwrecked, and while Captain Chimista finishes his days in an English castle with his wife Dolly Warden, it is Embil's melancholy fate to lead the lonely life of an elderly rheumatic. Chimista is one of Baroja's few completely idealized heroes; unscrupulous but never weak, he merits the tag line "a decisive and brave Basque" far more than his countryman Juan Galardi. It is rarely possible for Baroja to keep a suitable distance between himself and his creations, even in a work of fantasy or in a maritime picaresque novel. It is plain that the author stands just behind Roberto O'Neil and Ignacio Embil; he may lend his voice to Chimista, but his spirit resides in the others.

The nostalgia for a world where adventure replaces ratiocination and where unreality can be lavishly embroidered with rich detail holds Baroja in its iron grasp even during the years of the Spanish Civil War and the ensuing World War, as evidenced by a collection of four stories written between 1928 and 1941 and published under the general title of *Los impostores joviales* (*The Jovial Imposters*). The title story, as José Alberich has shown, is based on the case of Roger Charles Tichborne, as heard by the author in Le Havre.[76] Of significance is Baroja's attitude toward Lady Seymour, one of the principal characters in the story, for his description of her genealogy, servants, and estates reveals a high degree of interest in the ways of the aristocratic and the wealthy, an interest already more than adequately displayed in *The Labyrinth of the Sirens*. Such excursions into the higher social realms seem to suggest at least some basis for Ramón Sender's accusation that Baroja was in the habit of attributing all the virtues to the privileged and all the vices to the poor and the humble.[77] *El Tesoro del holandés* (*The Dutchman's Treasure, Yan-Si-Pao*, and *Los buscadores de tesoros* (*The Treasure Hunters*) are purely imaginative inventions, scarcely suitable for adults. The Chinese Yan-Si-Pao, Baroja admits, may be a

Basque in disguise, and the narrator of *The Treasure Hunters*
is a doctor who has read Claude Bernard, but the primary inspiration is Stevenson, and the literary devices are borrowed from
the serialized novels of the nineteenth century. It is sometimes
very difficult indeed to accept Baroja's self-characterization as
even a partial realist.

Back in Itzea, while the Second World War thundered across
Europe, Baroja resolutely continued to set his face toward the
past. With *D. Adrián de Erlaiz* the author retreats into the end
of the eighteenth century. Basque songs, geography, and folklore
adorn an otherwise thin novel, and sketches of gypsies and
picturesque Basques push the unreal Adrián Erlaiz into the
background. The superstitions of the Bidasoa region and the
cave of Zugarramurdi hark back to the story *The Lady of Urtubi,*
published in 1916, for as the author grew older he became less
and less inclined to abandon old themes and treasured memories.
As the purported hero of the novel, Adrián Erlaiz enjoys no
independence; whatever the reader knows about him is the
result of information supplied by the author. Baroja, as has
already been noted, was a great admirer of Stendhal, yet two
novelists could scarcely be further apart in their technique of
creating character. "For Stendhal's heroes are not predetermined. . . . They discover themselves existentially, through their
reactions; and they even discover their reactions as a surprise."[78]
The absence of this phenomenon of self-discovery in Baroja's
protagonists has by the last decades of his creative life the fixity
and immobility of long-consecrated custom.

VI *Twilight of the Idols:* Agonías de nuestro tiempo
(Agonies of our Time)

The fluctuations of Baroja's engagement with external reality
depended to a large extent on the frequency and nature of his
travels; for each important trip there is a corresponding novel.
In 1926 the author visited Germany, Holland, and Denmark in
the company of Paul Schmitz, and later in the same year went
to England and to France. The novelistic result of these visits
was the trilogy entitled *Agonies of our Time.* The first two works,
El gran torbellino del mundo (*The Great Whirlwind of Life*) and
Las veleidades de la fortuna (*The Caprices of Fortune*), appeared that same year, while *Los Amores Tardíos* (*Late Loves*)
was published in 1927. *Agonies of our Time* is a grey vision of
postwar Europe, an extended series of observations and divagations on philosophy, politics, religion, race, and nationality. Plot
and incident are subordinated to the sense of place and time,

and once again the Barojian novel is transformed into the diary of a meditative traveller.

Jose Larrañaga, the protagonist of the trilogy, belongs unmistakably to the continuing line of self-portraits. The sentimental episodes that befall him are his own, but his appearance, opinions, and personality belong to his creator. Larrañaga, an ex-seaman and ex-art student, is purportedly employed as a representative for a Basque shipping firm but is, in effect, a cicerone for his cousins Pepita and Soledad in their seemingly ceaseless travels. Rotterdam, Paris, Berlin, Hamburg, Copenhagen, and Vienna serve as background for the unfolding of a meagre plot that consists in the main of the record of Larrañaga's experiences with the young German girl Nelly Baur and with his cousin Pepita. Larrañaga, who sees himself as "old, sad, ugly,"[79] is a melancholy intellectual with a penchant for wandering and philosophizing. Without self-confidence and lacking in energy, arthritic and pessimistic, Larrañaga is predestined to failure.

The sickly and impressionable Nelly, for whom the protagonist entertains rather fraternal feelings, bears a resemblance to Lulú; her father is as indifferent to her well-being as was the mother of the Lulú Baroja had met. Nelly wishes to marry Larrañaga, but the latter checks her with the admonition to wait: "It is easy to follow your instincts, but then the catastrophe comes."[80] Larrañaga is an older Hurtado, unwilling to take risks. The death of Nelly obviates the necessity for a decision which Larrañaga would in any event have been incapable of making, but leaves him anguished and alone. Pepita, on the other hand, is one of Baroja's ebullient women; full of self-confidence, feminine charm, and deadly determination, it is she who takes the initiative in making Larrañaga her lover and she who terminates the affair with the decision to become reconciled with her husband Fernando. Once again abandoned, Larrañaga gives himself over to gloomy meditations on the devastating monotony of life. He desires tranquillity, a state of nirvana, but Pepita requires activity and emotional involvement. Her eruption into his placid life, "the life of an elderly cat,"[81] is an open window in an invalid's room, a gust of fresh and revivifying air, but Larrañaga sees the expulsion from paradise from the first moment he enters it, and the joy that should exhilarate him depresses him instead. The window opens on to the abyss, and the recognition of the emptiness just ahead makes the actual loss of happiness a mere repetition of the loss already experienced imaginatively, in advance.

Larrañaga believes no more in joy than in justice or in moral progress. His vision is of a world where mediocrity and opportunism triumph, where the virtues of work and decency go unrewarded, where all is disorder and blind chance. In the course of Larrañaga's interminable discussions with a wide variety of interlocutors, virtually every familiar Barojian topic is examined and expatiated upon: science and philosophy are held superior to the arts, painters and bohemians are considered neither spiritual nor clever, Wagnerianism is repellent. Nietzsche now is looked upon with a certain disfavor, and *Zarathustra* compared to an opera by Wagner. Larrañaga admits that Nietzsche's critical writings are valid, but concedes little else.[82] Goethe does not fare too well, for Larrañaga insists that he is too bourgeois, too much a respecter of accepted values.[83] Larrañaga had supported the cause of Germany in the war because he had had no personal experience of Germans and was therefore unaware of their defects, but now fully cognizant of their failings, his attitude is as much anti-German as it is anti-French. H. S. Chamberlain is characterized as "a little ariophile prophet" and his racial theories generally discredited.[84] Larrañaga affirms that he is an anarchist and a monarchist as well as an atheist and a Catholic.[85] His monarchical leanings are limited to an admiration for the Hapsburgs who kept Spain European by eliminating "Semitic and African elements," and his Catholicism emerges in the summertime when the cathedral offers blissful relief from a broiling sun.

Nelly's diary, the fourth part of *The Great Whirlwind of Life*, is both a recreation of the atmosphere of Europe at war and a sketch of the inner workings of Nelly's mind. In the former endeavor, Baroja is reasonably successful, for his historical imagination is vivid and dynamic, but the attempt to paint a portrait of Nelly is unfortunately another matter. Her ambition, she writes, is to surpass herself, to be more, to perfect and elevate herself. This unexpected echo of Nietzschean striving is in the nature of a cadenza and once stated, is forgotten, for shortly thereafter Nelly, now a governess, is shown—*mirabile dictu*—playing with her doll. Pepita is presented more coherently. Larrañaga considers his cousin a member of the master race, one of nature's successes. Egoistic and sensual, Pepita overcomes all obstacles to achieve her aim of the moment. Somewhat like Vera Petrovna in *The Way of the World*, Pepita is intuitive and intelligent albeit astoundingly ill-informed, for if Vera, a student in Geneva, never heard of either Calvin or Rousseau, Pepita does not seem to have heard of anybody.[86] Baroja has in no way retreated from his position vis-à-vis the dichotomy between knowledge and life.

Larrañaga meets citizens of Germany, Denmark, Holland, Russia, France, and Spain and there is an exchange of opinions at every turn. Paul Stolz, another incarnation of Paul Schmitz, appears in *The Caprices of Fortune* as an ex-socialist, an upholder of the superiority of the German people, an anti-Semite, and antirevolutionary. Larrañaga is similarly disapproving of the postwar revolutionary movements in Europe, failing to discover in the panorama before him the faintest prospect for progress and dismissing German and Russian revolutionaries as "unimaginative traditionalists."[87] Rasputin and Lenin appeal to the Spaniard's imagination, but the coupling of the two names is sufficient indication of the sort of hopes Baroja-Larrañaga entertained in respect to Russia.[88]

The three novels reveal a relentlessly garrulous protagonist surrounded by opinionated representatives of many nationalities, all speaking with the same voice. The result, of necessity, is of a stupefying monotony. Such flamboyant types as the Russian homosexual Igor are overshadowed by such pedants as the Norwegian seminarian who delivers a lecture, *ex tempore*, on Schelling. Larrañaga's identity is periodically submerged under the sea of words, but whenever he emerges it is to disclose his sense of ennui, of the tedium of life. To the right, there is emptiness and to the left, there is nothing.[89] The emblem *Los llenos de dolor y los vacíos de esperanza* ("The full [buckets] contain sorrow, the empty ones contain hope")[90] which serves to close the trilogy is the counterpart of Larrañaga's personal motto: "It is finished."

Larrañaga, like Luis Murguía, is essentially sensual despite appearances to the contrary: *Lo peor es que en el fondo uno es un hombre sensual . . . paralizado por la reflexión, por la cólera, por el despecho de no poder hacer . . .* ("The worst of it is that I am a sensual man, paralyzed by reflection, by anger, by the despair of not being capable of action").[91] Larrañaga speaks for Baroja, even to the extent of using the author's habitual *uno* in place of the first person pronoun.

Larrañaga is an idealist without hope, a conservative who is convinced of the inefficacy of change: "Life everywhere is practically the same."[92] This protagonist defines both himself, and Baroja, with disarming accuracy, as half-way in everything: "Somewhat misanthropic and solitary, somewhat sociable, somewhat good, somewhat bad, and always a disaster."[93] A circus performer without the courage to continue to turn somersaults, he is fearful of positive action, commitment, and responsibility, convinced that he is one of society's victims. Larrañaga resembles

Baroja in his mid-fifties; gone are the half-hopes, the compromises between a negative and an affirmative view; the descending note is incontestable.

With Luis Murguía and José Larrañaga the mold of the intellectual Barojian hero is firmly set. Unable to commit himself wholeheartedly to any cause, unwilling to sacrifice the known for the unknown, he plays the role of observer, dedicating himself largely to contemplation and commentary. This attitude of detached contemplation, according to Kierkegaard, is the attitude of the aesthete. The transformation from the aesthetic to the ethical stage is effectuated only when a decision of involvement is made, and it is this act of committing oneself to some decision, be it ethical or religious, that confers reality on the individual. In the Kierkegaardian sense, then, both Murguía and Larrañaga lack reality. They float uneasily on the waters of life, peering down continually in the hope of penetrating what is but dimly seen beneath the surface, but refusing to risk the danger of total immersion. In both cases a refined Epicureanism is preferable to the assumption of a fixed task or purpose, and living is reduced to running errands.[94]

VII   *The Failure of Religion*: El nocturno del hermano Beltrán (Friar Beltrán's Nocturne) *and* El cura de Monleón (The Curate of Monleón)

Baroja rather liked the idea of associating some of his *personae* either directly or indirectly with the priesthood. His periods of solitude, his sometimes ascetic life (pursued more out of necessity than out of desire), his conviction of the accuracy of his moral and personal judgments, suggested to him the lonely but human figure of the idealized priest. The artist Bagaría's caricature of Baroja as a Franciscan is not without interest in this connection.[95] Dr. Labarta of the *Adventures* . . . is described as a "spiritual but gluttonous friar," Juan Alcázar in *The Struggle for Life* trilogy is an ex-seminarian as is Fermín Acha in *The Dark Wood* series, and Joshé Mari, one of the characters in *Sublimated Sensuality*, remarks that Murguía might have been a friar or an organist in a monastery.

The protagonist of the dialogued novel *Friar Beltrán's Nocturne* (1929) is a friar who believes in prayer, charity, and music, but does not seem to believe in God. He is a mystic without expectations, a pantheist, more of a sentimental dreamer than a man of energy and determination. As in the case of Juan Galardi, his peaceful life in the monastery is at variance with a violent past that encompasses adventures at sea from New Zealand

to Alaska, brief periods as a ship's pilot, a miner, a journalist,
and a political agitator. The friar's account of his past, the
mystery surrounding his birth, his duel with a Marquis and subsequent flight to Paris are in the author's *folletín* or serialized
novel vein, but the conversations in a Parisian salon are vintage
Baroja. The *reunión intelectual* ("intellectual meeting") of Chapter XVIII centers in the figure of the pedantic Professor Grobenius
and the Danish diplomat Petersen. Grobenius is Frobenius, the
specialist in African ethnography whom Baroja had met in
Paris,[96] and Petersen represents the author. In his brief appearance, the Dane expresses his distrust of democracy and communism and his belief that nowhere is there any prospect for progress except in science.

The tendency to write dialogue of the question-answer type,
already evident in the *Agonies of our Time* trilogy, becomes increasingly marked in *Friar Beltrán's Nocturne*, as opinions are
requested and then rendered much in the manner of a journalistic
interview.[97] In response to a series of queries, Beltrán reveals
musical preferences that are, not surprisingly, Baroja's. Mozart
and Beethoven are supreme, Debussy, Richard Strauss and Stra-
vinsky are *poca cosa* ("unimportant").[98] In *Friar Beltrán's Nocturne* nothing happens because everything has already happened:
Beltrán has no psychological interior, no distinguishable personality. His death as he is playing his nocturne on the church organ
is an event of no dramatic consequence, for one form of non-
being is simply exchanged for another.

In 1936 Baroja returned to the theme of the priest without
faith, this time in a much more extended work. *The Curate of
Monleón*, for which the tale "Un justo" ("A Just Man") was a
preliminary sketch, is both the story of the priest Javier Olarán
and an historical survey of Christianity. In this novel Baroja's
extensive readings impinge on Javier's personality to the extent
that the priest's "notebooks" serve principally to convey the
author's views on religion from a socio-historical and ethical
standpoint. Javier's subsequent loss of faith is without drama,
for it is foreordained, already determined from the beginning
by his creator, the sometime Augustinian. The loss of faith or the
struggle to believe achieves the dimensions of tragedy in the
hands of Unamuno, but when Baroja takes up the theme he is
floundering in uncharted waters. The failure to give solidity to
either Beltrán or Javier is the measure of Baroja's radical incapacity to so much as imagine the agonies that doubt and
incredulity inflict on the truly religious; the dark night of the

soul is as alien to the author as a sustained period of exhila-
rating exuberance.

The descriptions of Javier's years in the Seminary in Vitoria
bear comparison with the pages written over three decades before on the Piarist school attended by Fernando Ossorio; the
skepticism is still present, but the harsh note is gone. Javier is
sensitive and lacking in ambition, unwilling to live in the
secular world, and without interest in advancing in the clerical
hierarchy. His is a pragmatic Christianity, an application of religious ideas to daily life.[99] Rome and Paris mean less to him
than his native Basque region, and music speaks more directly
to his spirit than any treatise on religion. Once Javier is ordained,
his life in Monleón is both sybaritic and ascetic; the delights of
a charming country home compensate for the non-alcoholic and
vegetarian diet he prescribes for himself much in the manner
of Luis Murguía. Javier's fastidious distaste for some of the
secrets of the confessional denotes a degree of erotic suscepti-
bility ill-befitting his station, and when a young servant girl is
allowed by his aunt to stay in his house he is fearful and
uneasy.[100] He is later greatly tempted by Mary, *la bella irlandesa*
("the beautiful Irish girl") but refrains from following her, not
so much through conviction as through dislike of uncertainty.

José María Basterreche, the village doctor of Monleón,
serves as a counterpoise to the young cleric. Dr. Basterreche is
anti-bourgeois, anti-Catholic, anti-Semitic. He is anticlerical
only in so far as the dignitaries of the church are concerned, for
his attitude toward the lower clergy is decidedly sympathetic—
a clear reflection of Baroja's sympathies after the establishment
of the Second Republic. Basterreche is an ex-supporter of the
Republic who is now convinced that all Socialists are egotistic
and pedantic, and looks upon himself as an agnostic, a relativist,
and a skeptic. The ideals of Basque nationalism would be acceptable to the Barojian doctor provided that it meant a revival
of the old Basque beliefs, superstitions, and customs: "Paganism,
individualism and anarchy in an orderly framework."[101] The
impracticality of such a prescription indicates beyond any
shadow of doubt that the doctor is merely indulging in fantasies.

Javier refuses to take sides in the political conflicts which erupt
after the establishment of the Republic, despite which fact he is
accused by his fellow clerics of holding Socialist sympathies. The
civil marriage of his sister Pepita to Dr. Basterreche, who had
once been divorced, completes Javier's downfall and he quickly
leaves Monleón. Once Javier is banished to Alava, in this case
the clerical equivalent of Siberia, he devotes himself almost

exclusively to study and meditation. The notebooks, which are
the product of his voracious readings, trace a course from doubt
to complete incredulity, and with the conclusion of the novel
he prepares to leave the priesthood. Javier applies to questions
of faith the methods of science; the heart in his case does not
have reasons which reason does not know. His announcement,
Creo que he perdido la fe ("I think I have lost my faith"), has
no more dramatic effect than the mislaying of a small household
object, and his decision to put aside the habit is reduced to in-
consequence.[102] Baroja's natural habitat was the bookstall, the
library, or the well-set table, but surely not the monastery or
the rectory.

VIII   *The Past Recaptured*: Las noches del Buen Retiro
        (Nights in the Gardens of the Retiro)

Nights in the Gardens of the Retiro was published in 1934,
the same year that Baroja was elected to membership in the
Royal Spanish Academy. Like Lot's wife, the aging writer obeys
the impulse to look back yet another time to survey what lay behind him, and the past is once more recaptured. Sections of the
novel have the atmosphere of a *zarzuela* (musical comedy) set in
turn-of-the-century Madrid; the aristocratics and the snobs, the
social climbers and the social castoffs do their turn on the large
and well-lit stage as the audience strolls and chats. The plot
concerns both Carlos Hermida and Jaime Thierry, but it is
only the latter who engages the reader's attention to any degree.

No sooner is Thierry introduced as a rabid individualist and
revolutionary dandy than his aggressive opinions on South
America, France, and the United States are quickly encapsu-
lated, to be followed by the information that he had read
Nietzsche, Dostoyevsky, Meredith, Stevenson, and Kipling.
Thierry springs full-blown from the brow of the author, and it
is only a matter of keeping the reader informed. Thierry pro-
fesses to be attracted by Nietzsche's admonition to live dangerously, but his courage and capacity for violence are subject to unpredictable variations. When the South American Peña Montalvo
maliciously circulates the rumor that Thierry had been expelled
from school for homosexual activities, his first reaction is of
abject fear: ". . . he felt cowardly, . . . in a state of perplexity,
vacillation and fear."[103] In a *volte face* however, he attacks his
maligner with such violence that a duel necessarily ensues. He
reacts similarly to the aggressive intentions of the caricaturist
Pipo who had the bad taste to draw him in an offensively feminine fashion. The scene in which the victim strikes Pipo over

the head with his cane is an adaptation of an episode involving Ramiro de Maeztu and a cartoonist named Poveda, but Maeztu, less fortunate than Thierry, was obliged to flee to England to escape the complications of a legal suit.[104]

Thierry is a writer of promise who devotes himself, much in the manner of Quintín Roelas of *The School for Rogues,* to scurrilous attacks against aristocrats and politicians in a satirical newspaper. The scandals that result are echoes of the hostility evoked in response to Maeztu's *El disloque* and Azorín's *Charivari.* The picture of Thierry that emerges from the data supplied by the author is curiously hybrid; he is a theoretical Nietzschean, a Baudelairian dandy, weak and sentimental, aggressive and violent, both a successful and a frustrated lover. His somewhat tearful affair with Concha, the Marquesa de Villacarrillo, ends on a note of despair when she decides to become reunited with her husband;[105] as in *Late Loves,* the conventionally puritanical Baroja prefers whenever possible to honor the sanctity of the home. Thierry's fate is, in any case, sufficiently adverse since he is stricken with tuberculosis and dies with Concha's portrait at his breast—an operatic touch Baroja was powerless to resist. Thierry is one more sensitive protagonist at odds with the vulgarity and bad faith that surround him; the death of his body merely makes tangible the death of his spirit.

Only the minor figures create an atmosphere of reality: Don Florestán del Rayo, with his memories of executions, the Marqués de Castelgirón, with his addiction to morphine, the lesbian Victoria Calatrava, the Marqués de Quiñones, Madrid's foremost expert on tailors, horses, wines, and oysters, Pepito Velarde of the pisciform face, the Marqués de la Piedad, nicknamed "the Divine Marquis." The Spanish novelists of Baroja's generation showed little inclination to take into serious account certain of the seamier aspects of urban life, for only Baroja appears to have noticed and to have recorded so many examples of homosexuality and drug addiction. Perhaps it is the doctor more than the novelist at work.

It is worthy of note that it is precisely in the period of the Second Republic that the author is moved to revive the political issues, the literary and musical discussions, the social life of aristocrats and bohemians of the Madrid between 1897 and the early years of the following century. Faced with the apparent triumph of a bourgeois society, Baroja turned his back as was his wont and sought refuge in the only world that was, ironically and for all his protestations to the contrary, truly his. The novelist's repeated insistence on destruction and change was no doubt sincere, but only the former truly attracted him. At every critical juncture Baroja reveals a deep dislike for novelty and a distrust of change, and it becomes increasingly evident that his uneasiness in the face of real transformations can be assuaged only by the reassurances of the past.

IX   *Reprise: Essays 1926-1936*

Baroja's address upon his reception into the Royal Spanish Academy, "La formación psicológica de un escritor" ("The Psychological Background of an Author"), continues the voyage back in time. Always the recidivist, Baroja supplies information on his childhood and education, his readings and philosophical orientation, his political opinions, the years as doctor and small businessman.[106] Somewhat uneasy at the prospect of charges of repetitiousness, the novelist maintains that he is offering the details of his life not for their inherent personal interest but as a specific example of the failure typical of many youths of his era, a defeat that is symptomatic of an age of decadence.

After discreetly holding up to view his former faith in the efficacy of action, his "agnostic, Schopenhauerian anarchism," and his love for truth, Baroja remarks that his youthful slogan might have been: "Believe nothing, affirm nothing."[107] One is inclined to take the author at his word, but such a slogan could never have been his once his early youth was past. Everything Baroja wrote constitutes a series of statements of belief, of affirmations, even if in the form of negations. "Truth . . . as the basis of life and science; fantasy and imagination in their proper place,"[108] for all its ambiguity, comes somewhat closer to summing up the novelist's lifelong creed.

Baroja characterizes himself, past and present, as an ineffectual huntsman; while he is making up his mind to shoot, the prey disappears.[109] Acceptance into the august body that is the Royal Spanish Academy might be considered by many authors to be the crowning achievement of a distinguished career, yet to Baroja it is simply another opportunity to reveal his intimate sense of failure. "You will never amount to anything" and sentimental frustration are ultimately more persuasive than public honor.

Aside from the acceptance speech, of particular interest among the collections of essays and lectures belonging to the period between 1926 and 1936 is the address entitled "Tres generaciones" ("Three Generations"), delivered in Madrid in May of 1926. The three generations which are analyzed incisively, despite the absence of "data and statistics," are the generations of 1840, 1870 and 1900.[110] Baroja inveighs against the pomposity, falseness, and materialism of the generation of 1840, the generation responsible for the revolution of 1868 and the restoration of the Bourbons after the First Republic. Anticlerical in public, the men of this generation are clerical in private; the life of the politician is fraught with immorality and the moral standards of the journalist are scarcely higher. They lived in mediocrity, the author continues, but thought they were living in glorious times.

The generation of 1870 is Baroja's designation for what is usually called the Generation of 1898, for the novelist consistently maintained that the latter generation never existed.[111] Languid and sad, the men of the generation of 1870 had to choose between the life of the intellect or a life of either shrewd calculation or abysmal ignorance. The path of public service was blocked to these young idealists without influence, thus driving them into the refuge of a private, bookish world. The desire for social justice, contempt for politics, cultivation of individualism and the ethical ideal, "hamletism, anarchism and mysticism," complete the profile of this tormented generation.[112] Baroja's analysis is brief yet complete, and is surely one of the best capsule introductions to the subject of the Generation of 1898 to be found. Baroja's talent for synthesis, so often a defect in his novels, is displayed to best advantage in these essays.

The men of the generation of 1900, according to the novelist, are far more vigorous and optimistic than their immediate predecessors. Essentially practical, they do not disperse their energies in tilting against windmills, nor do they fall into despair at the spectacle of the too-slow incorporation of Spain into the modern world. It is in this new, relatively happy generation that Baroja places his hopes for the salvation of the country, hopes that were shattered by the outbreak of the Civil War a decade later.

Intermezzi, published in 1931, provides excellent illustrations of the short sketch that was Baroja's specialty; bohemians, eccentrics, imposters, anarchists, and mystics pass in rapid succession, some receiving the benefit of only a short but vivid paragraph. Reminiscences, anecdotes, observations on literary topics, even playlets, round out the exceedingly heterogeneous collection. The author's old enemies Don Benito Hernando and Letamendi reappear to be castigated once more, and a sentimental interlude recalled from the days of Cestona materializes as a fragment entitled "El primer sueldo" ("The First Salary").[113]

The *Picturesque Showcase,* published in 1935, touches on a variety of topics including hangmen, beggars, Jesuits, Free-masons, and Jews; an essay on the rivers of Spain is followed by a "travellers' bestiary" as the concrete and the abstract, the past and the present, history and folklore occupy the author's restless attention. One essay, entitled "Epigrafía callejera" ("Street Signs"), represents Baroja at his humorous best, while the pieces on carnivals, fairs, and the old streets of Madrid once again reveal Baroja's love for the outlandish and the mysterious.[114]

The essay "Nuestra juventud" ("Our Youth") is a self-interview which casts an interesting light on the nature of the author's true tastes. Baroja declares that the irregular life of bohemians and vagabonds had always attracted him. Late nights, endless conversation, coffee, tobacco, and alcohol, all shared with aimless, deracinated types exercised an appeal which only a certain degree of self-imposed solitude could conquer. The novelist affirms his consistency as a thinker and as a writer: had he been possessed of a suitable philosophical background, he would have been a Kantian. In biological and social questions, he is a Darwinian. Literary style has been a definite preoccupation, but Baroja is convinced that he can go no further than he had already gone: "I have struggled with the language as best I could."[115]

Juan Uribe Echevarría uses the apt designation of *micro-ensayismo* ("microessayism") to describe the special nature of the Barojian essay.[116] This "microessay," with its opportunities for the quick rendition of impressions or the synthetic imparting of information, is Baroja's most authentic genre. What is chaos in a novel is diversity in the essay, and the movement and change that are so often unmotivated in the works of fiction are fully justified in collections that do not pretend to unity or harmony.

X *The Paris Novels*: Susana, Laura *and* El Hotel del Cisne
(Swan Hotel)

The Civil War which erupted in 1936 displaced Baroja in the physical sense and accentuated his melancholy but caused no significant shift in his literary themes. *Susana,* published in 1937, exemplifies what must finally be called the impermeability of the author, the radical inability to reflect the outer world without at the same time casting his own shadow. The badly articu-lated plot of *Susana* purportedly concerns the ill-fated love of Miguel Salazar for the Susana of the title, and the details need not detain the serious reader. Salazar is another semi-portrait of the author as a young man; pessimistic and rather old at twenty-eight, he is timid and usually unsuccessful with women. At the outbreak of the war he is in Paris, and presently finds work as a translator of scientific works. Poor and lonely, his image of life is the Santé prison: "boredom and sadness inside, and death outside."[117] Salazar, like Baroja, is an observer of the small detail and a chronicler of the fleeting moment; there is more art in the streets than in libraries or museums.

The archivist Susana is a greatly augmented version of Javier Olarán's Irish friend Mary. Her erudition is seemingly limitless and her learned discourses on history and poetry might easily put to flight a less intrepid spirit than Salazar. In the eighteenth poem of the *Songs from the Outskirts,* there is a reference to "Susana, soon to be an archivist," and both in the *Memoirs* and in the *Strolls of a Solitary Man,* Baroja mentions that almost all the characters in the novel are real, modelled on people he had met in Paris during the war. Pérez Ferrero quotes the novelist as having said that the novel was something of a joke, written just to pass the time of day,[118] but it might be more accurate to consider *Susana* less of a joke than the visible and concrete evidence of failing powers and flagging resources.

The acquaintances and friends of the same period in Paris appear in even greater profusion in *Laura* (1939). Laura is the shadowy heroine who is at first presented as a sensitive medical student, an intellectual who is fond of books but who derives little joy from either her studies or her pastimes. As the novel advances, her resemblance to Baroja increases: she is indecisive and melancholy, and the world around her seems grey and vapid. In what amounts to another of the author's self-interviews, Laura admits that she frequents neither museums nor the cinema, reads very little although previously she had liked Dickens, Tolstoy, Dostoyevsky, and serialized novels. All her reading was undertaken without order, chaotically. Juan Avendaño, one of Laura's relatives, also bears the Baroja family stamp in several respects. He is poorly dressed, indecisive, full of curiosity, antidemocratic; he has strange friends, some of them semianarchists. At fifty he likes to consider himself old and decrepit "... probably to avoid involvements and trouble";[119] he has never married, in part for lack of money.

Many of the secondary characters in *Laura* are women, and their stories occupy a fair portion of the novel.[120] Germans, Russians, Indians, and Jews, theosophists, and musicians create a cosmopolitan atmosphere and an air of miscellaneousness that are rarely absent from the later novels. The Russian mathematician and astronomer whom Laura eventually marries, "Saint Golowin," is a pallid Prince Myshkin whose tenuous personality barely leaves a trace. The spirit of Laura's melancholy, which the author admits is without foundation, casts dark shadows over the last pages of the novel, but it is clear that Laura's anguish and supposed loneliness reflect only the author's intense feelings of deracination. The aura of greyness which surrounds her comes not from within but from without, for although her experience in no way resembles that of Sacha Savarof, she is equally despairing.

In *Susana* the Civil War is almost entirely forgotten, for only at the conclusion does Miguel Salazar go back to Spain to engage in laboratory work at the front. There are summary references in *Laura* to military skirmishes involving Luis Monroy, the heroine's brother, and Laura's friend Mercedes is a victim of the violence of the early days of the war, but the conflict seems very remote. Switzerland and London are far more agreeable to contemplate, and it is there that Baroja sends his bloodless heroine. It is a measure of Baroja's lack of receptivity to the present moment that the war which was devastating his own country has less concrete reality than, for example, the Russian revolution. The past is more secure than the shifting ground of the present and has the added and inestimable advantage of requiring a less costly commitment.

Once again the scene is Paris and the time is the beginning of the Second World War. *Swan Hotel*, written in 1940 but not published until 1946, is devoted in part to the dreams of the seventy-two-year-old Procopio Pagani, in part to the opinions of the well-informed and ironical bookdealer Gentil. Pagani's disastrous physical, emotional, and economic state reflects the anxieties of the displaced and aging author, while Gentil's observations recall Baroja in his more halcyon days. It is Gentil who proposes that the ten inhabitants of the fifth floor of the hotel band together to form a syndicate. The ten residents, whose aggregate age totals almost six hundred years, are an international assortment vaguely reminiscent of Silvestre Paradox' crew, and Gentil's qualities of organization are, on a small scale, similar to his ancestor's. Pagani's dreams, which Baroja defines in advance as commonplace, resemble those of Alvarito Sánchez de Mendoza in that they are too manufactured, too literary, to resemble authentic dreams. The disorder is obviously ordered, the irrationality is clearly rational. On many occasions Baroja ridiculed both Freud's theories and those members of the avant-garde who attempted to write directly from the subconscious, yet it must be asserted that the novelist's approach to the hidden and the irrational is hardly an adequate substitute.[121] Once in a while, fortunately, the dreams are delightful caprices, involving such unheard-of artifacts as the "critiscope" and the "imaginoscope," or remarkable synthetic animals like the crocodile-vulture; there is a skyscraper-cemetery and obviously subversive loaves of bread marked with the sign of the Freemasons. Despite the numerous fancies, however, *Swan Hotel* is an old man's book, pervaded with ennui and thoughts of death.

Even in such a miscellany as *Los enigmáticos* (*Enigmas*), published in 1948, Baroja finds it necessary to reflect his Parisian period via the figure of the ex-professor Don Jesús Martín Elorza, a pessimist who is convinced of the accuracy of his adverse judgments on mankind and who even derives some amusement from seeing all his worst expectations fulfilled. Don Jesús, like Procopio Pagani, has been visited simultaneously by old age, poverty, and loneliness. The Paris period was by no means exhausted in the novels, for in the *Songs from the Outskirts, Yesterday and Today, Strolls of a Solitary Man,* and in a section of the *Memoirs* entitled "Nuevamente en París" ("In Paris Again"), the author goes over the same ground in the familiar fashion, with no change in either literary or political opinions.[122]

XI   *And there is nothing new under the sun*:
Canciones del Suburbio (Songs from the Outskirts)

Baroja's non-fictionalized autobiography took the form of the oft-mentioned *Memoirs,* the first volume of which appeared in 1944, and the collection of poems entitled *Songs from the Outskirts.* The poems were written in 1940 but not published until four years later, by which time the author was beset with grave doubts about their value. In the "Explanation" which precedes the poems Baroja characterizes his efforts as "faulty, the product of old age and neurasthenia." Pedro Salinas has likened the *Songs* to blind men's ballads and Ramón Sender has called the collection "horrible,"[123] but the work need not be judged from the aesthetic standpoint alone; as Emilio Carrere has so rightly pointed out, the collection would indeed be dreadful if judged by the standards one might apply to the poetry of Rubén Darío, but for Baroja, the prose writer, the standards must be different.[124]

The collection is an evocation of the author's childhood and student days, of the bohemian life, a gallimaufry of street vendors, pool sharks, bakers' apprentices, gamblers, pawnbrokers, and café habitués. The memory of the cloister of El Paular and the warm comforts of the Basque inn is preserved as if under glass, radiating the same freshness that it had possessed decades before. The satirical vein of Baroja's youth is still evident in the mordant poems dedicated to the aesthete and to the traditional, authentic Madrilenian, and the author's lifelong preoccupation with crime and death appears undiminished.[125] The section entitled "Recuerdos de vagabundo" ("Recollections of a Vagabond") contains notes on the villages of Spain which belong in spirit to the genre of travel literature already cultivated by the author in *The Wandering Lady*.

In the section entitled "Impresiones de París" ("Impressions of Paris"), the author's private view of himself as a failure floats once more to the surface in the poem "El hombre que falla" ("The Man who Misses"), in love and in books. The image of the marksman who never hits the target, already a familiar one, is joined to the concept of a rigidly determined fate; change is impossible. I would like to abandon my name, my physical identity, my profession, Baroja laments, along with my morality and style.[126] The question of change in Baroja's total outlook is, indeed, a crucial one. In the course of a lifetime of writing about himself, the author sometimes declares his desire to change, but more often either admits that he is incapable of this feat or implies that his consistency is a positive virtue.[127] Baroja's firmly held belief in the impossibility of progress in all but the sciences (and even here there are reservations about the limits of science) is fatally linked to his conviction that neither he nor anyone else ever really changes. The astonishing statement that the first pages of Dickens, Dostoyevsky, and Tolstoy are the same as the last[128] indicates the author's habitual failure to take into account any evidence that might contradict his seemingly *a priori* judgments. The progression from, for example, *A Raw Youth* to *The Brothers Karamazov* or the retrogression from *War and Peace* to the *Kreutzer Sonata* apparently go unnoticed. The notion that a writer can refine and polish his style by unremitting labor is alien to the novelist who once affirmed that "style cannot be acquired by work any more than an oyster can be opened by persuasion";[129] the development and maturing of literary technique that is so evident in the works of D. H. Lawrence or Henry James, for example, is not perceptible to Baroja.

Cela once told Baroja that the future in which he had so much interest was, in fact, in the past, a statement that seems to have

surprised the Basque novelist although it could never have surprised a student of his work.[130] There are no great figures after
Ibsen, Tolstoy, and Nietzsche, sculpture and architecture can
go nowhere, and in Le Corbusier's work "there is nothing new";
there are no more great doctors like Pasteur and Bernard, nor
are there great astronomers.[131] Writing in 1947, Baroja declares
that in the novel of the "last forty or fifty years" there is nothing
new in technique and psychology, an astounding statement from
an author who was not entirely unfamiliar with Proust, Joyce,
and Kafka. Nothing in modern art can compare with the art of
former centuries, and Picasso's work is not a solid contribution.
The novelist's hostility to "-isms," prevalent in his earlier works,
has already been sufficiently commented upon. Later, Existen-
tialism has its turn and the leaden verdict is "nothing new,"
"insignificant," "ridiculous," "absurd."[132] Moral progress, of
course, is out of the question. "Nobody is capable of self-renewal
and everything is a repetition";[133] at seventy, maintains the
author, he is as he was at twenty.

Nihil novum sub sole is Baroja's battle cry.[134] The admirer of
Heraclitus, the philosopher of change, annihilates the reality
of change and the possibility of progress by affirming that nothing
new is ever new. The flow of history is a constant return to the
source, and the entire panorama of man and society becomes
frozen in familiar attitudes. Baroja's paralytic view of art and
man is, certainly, reactionary, and the death sentence that he
passes on virtually every new artistic movement is equally so,
but there is the lurking suspicion that the author's bias is no
less personal than ideological. In the *Memoirs* the novelist states
that in forty years of writing novels he has learned nothing.
Ergo, he implies, nobody else has learned anything either.
This type of argument has been used before by Baroja, always
with a view to defending his own limitations.

The constant return to past experience, the recurrent projec-
tions of personality through a variety of heroes, heroines and
sub-heroes, the backward flow of time and memory produce a
novelistic world without a future. If the author returns constantly to what was or already is, with no concept of what may
become, the circle of his life is closed. If the world is but the
reflection of the author's subjectivity, then the world too is
closed. The future is the yet-to-be, the uncreated; if the subject
is not there to confer solidity and reality on the world and its
phenomena, then the world ceases to be and nothing can be

projected into the future. The death of Baroja's consciousness is the death of the world.

Nietzsche had said in his "Nachtgesang" ("Nightsong") that whoever is incapable of change will always be a stranger to him; Baroja would surely not have been his friend. Baroja begins to feel like a stranger to himself in "The Man who Misses," but it is, as his friend Azorín was fond of saying, too late. Self-transcendence is a belated and idle dream.

XII   *The Decline*

By 1949 the last volume of the *Memoirs* had been published. The well-trodden ground of Baroja's early life, travels, contemporaries, literary, racial, and political opinions was again gone over in what should have constituted a final catharsis for the author. Baroja projected his image from every angle in the *Memoirs,* quoting not only himself but the critics as well. Some of the material is new, but much has been inserted by the cut-and-paste method; there are anecdotes, jokes, vignettes, songs. Yet, despite the length of the *Memoirs,* the old demons are not completely exorcised, and in 1950 there is another return in the shape of Luis Carvajal y Evans, *El cantor vagabundo* (*The Wandering Singer*). Known as "the lynx," Luis Carvajal sings and plays the guitar in cafés and is generally successful with women, but for the rest he is of the purest Barojian lineage. He is in France at the time of the Dreyfus affair, he goes to London, Algiers, and finally to Spain after a vague indication that he had spent some years in America. Carvajal is an admirer of Kant, Schopenhauer, Gracián, Huarte de San Juan, Ibsen, and Verlaine; he dislikes Anatole France and D'Annunzio. He affirms that science will always be a source of progress although he now recognizes, along with Baroja, that science alone cannot solve the existential problem. Once abnormally melancholy and indecisive, Carvajal is now merely restless, generally pessimistic, and an avowed skeptic. In the course of the novel Carvajal produces numerous opinions; among them are the assertions that Catholics and Communists are alike, man is a cruel beast, war is useless and brutal. Carvajal has been successively a romantic and a realist, a Schopenhauerian and a Nietzschean. Although essentially apolitical, he does not disapprove of an enlightened despotism.

During the period of the Civil War, Carvajal runs a bookstore and also devotes some of his time to wandering about the countryside selling ballads and chapbooks. This somewhat extravagant activity not only satisfies Carvajal's love for vagabondage and helps to keep boredom at bay, but serves also to exemplify his philosophy of non-involvement. The Civil War fills him with revulsion, and his conclusion is that the only viable solution is to abstain from the struggle: *Vender romances, como vendo yo* ("Sell ballads, as I do").[135] His spirit of aloofness does not save him from a political arrest, but once he is released the time-honored pattern reemerges. When Carvajal is over sixty, the last hopes, the few remaining illusions vanish and reasons for living can no longer be invented. The "wandering singer" sets sail in a small craft and, in the words of the author *probablemente . . . desapareció en el mar* ("he probably disappeared into the sea").[136]

Carvajal, like the inmates of Swan Hotel, is an old man; the young Andrés Hurtado, the middle-aged José Larrañaga now give way to the protagonist with more past than future. Carvajal talks of his lack of good fortune and even says that people find him dull, although on a previous page Baroja had described him as a man blessed with good luck who had found favor with women.[137] His innate sadness, so much like Laura's, is no more intelligible. The major weakness of the novel lies in Baroja's conception of Carvajal. He is too respectable, too economically comfortable to be a persuasive vagabond; like his creator, he has all the earmarks of a *señorito*. More than a character, Carvajal is a wax figure in a museum that is becoming crowded. The purposelessness of Carvajal's life indicates as well the novelist's lack of direction; the heroes and heroines of the Barojian novel are becoming more and more mechanical, often endowed with contradictory characteristics. In the last decades of his life, Baroja was creating characters by rote, in obedience to a set of fixed formulae. The historical context is often changing and real, the minor types are still conceived with brio, but the principal figures are becoming petrified.

Las veladas del chalet gris (*Evenings in the Hotel Gris*) is, in part, a collection of commentaries and anecdotes, as its subtitle indicates, but complete disjointedness is avoided by the inclusion of one Javier Arias Bertrand, whose voice dominates whatever conversations there are. Arias Bertrand, a seventy-five-year-old bachelor at the time of the Civil War, no longer has any enthusiasms; modern literature and music do not appeal to him, everything is repetition, there is nothing new under the sun. The cinema, bullfights, the radio, the newspapers all displease him, and his only ideal is the Stendhalian "to see clearly

into reality." Bertrand remembers a variety of famous crimes,
among them the crime of Fuencarral Street; there are disquisitions on theosophy, hypnotism, witchcraft; numerous questions
are asked and Bertrand answers them, interview-fashion, setting
forth Baroja's ideas and sentiments. The date of the work is
1951 and the author is seventy-nine years old, but the only significant change is an intensification of his pessimism and
discouragement. The author donates most of his attitudes to
Bertrand, but distributes some leftover opinions to several other
characters: Dr. Arias Miranda maintains that familiarity with
the *Aphorisms* of Hippocrates and with the study on experimental
medicine of Claude Bernard is sufficient qualification for the
practice of medicine; Eduardo Arias is a medical student who
reflects Baroja's love for impressionist painting and the works of
the Arcipreste de Hita, Espronceda, Bécquer, and Verlaine.
Evenings in the Hotel Gris is a work striking only for its super-
fluousness, and it is evident that Baroja is writing only out of
habit or, to use his more vivid image, out of fear of collapsing
entirely if he is unharnessed.

Los amores de Antonio y Cristina (*The Loves of Antonio and
Cristina*) appeared in 1953, three years before the death of the
author. The failing energies and growing fatigue of the aged
Baroja are all too evident in this brief and sadly inept work.
Antonio Zabala is an unsuccessful student of pharmacy-turned-
painter, a Basque who lacks self-confidence, decisiveness, and
constancy. In 1936 he finds himself in sympathy with neither
side in the Spanish conflict, and goes to France. His artistic bias
is far clearer than his political preferences; he likes Regoyos,
dislikes Sorolla, and considers Picasso and Dalí far too extravagant to be taken seriously. His patron and protector, Doña
Dolores Ibarra de Garibay, characterizes him as "an insignificant man," and her judgment is eminently accurate. Zabala
feels inferior to the girl he loves, but in an unexpected return to
youthful romanticism Baroja allows them to marry and, presumably, to live happily ever after. In a faint echo of the conflicts
that added piquancy to the serialized novels, Baroja introduces
the heroine's ex-suitor René, whose function it is to take potshots
at Antonio while the latter is painting outdoors. A Communist
and a Jew, René is "capable of anything." Dolores Ibarra is
intended to be one of Baroja's eccentrics, but her only manifestation of eccentricity, which to be sure is sufficiently peculiar, is
her custom of wearing a false nose.

The Loves of Antonio and Cristina is still recognizably Baroja, but the bouquet is gone, the wine has been quaffed, and only the dregs remain in the goblet. Carlos Orlando Nallim has had access to the unpublished works of Pío Baroja, and affirms that . . . *reiteran los mismos rasgos novelísticos, estilísticos, críticos y morales que se observan en su anterior producción* ("They repeat the same novelistic, stylistic, critical and moral traits that are evident in his previous works").[138] It could not have been otherwise.

CHAPTER 7

Summation and Conclusion

BAROJA has been classified variously as a part-time Nietzschean, Schopenhauerian, Kantian, relativist, skeptic, Epicurean, and existentialist. In one respect or another, and at one time or another, all the labels bear some semblance of accuracy, but in the most rigorous sense the novelist adhered to no single school of thought. Baroja was a specialist in divagations, and speculation was his *forte,* but the discourses led to no discoveries, the open monologue that was his work uncovered no new philosophical possibilities. In his deification of the ego, Baroja was, if anything, a Kantian, and in his lifelong desire to avoid strong emotions, a latter-day Epicurean. Shunning involvement with its requirements of decision and its concomitant risks, Baroja practiced a philosophy of disengagement, renouncing the experience of great pleasure in order to be spared the experience of great pain.

Although the novelist produced opinions in massive quantities, he possessed few working convictions. More of a witness to his times than a novelist of social protest, more of a puritan than a true moralist, more a dissenter than a revolutionary, Baroja was an authentic *paseante de la vida*—a stroller through life, a philosophical tourist.[1] In the earlier part of his career, the author's slogan might have been José Arcelu's *huir y destruir* ("flee and destroy"), albeit in reverse order; in the latter part of his life he echoes the advice of Luis Carvajal y Evans: *vender romances, como vendo yo* ("sell ballads, as I do"). Baroja's incorrectly labelled Dionysian tendencies merely denote restlessness, a radical inability to be where he is. The frustrated desire for action that so many commentators have read into Baroja's works is more a tangible manifestation of external literary and philosophical influences than the expression of a deep and unfulfilled need for activity. It is probably not too much to say that the men of action in his novels led lives that would have been abhorrent to the comfort- and security-loving writer.[2]

The heroes who mirror Baroja's personality and preoccupations are, inevitably, as uncommitted as their creator. There are adventurers and reformers *manqués,* but only the drifters—

168

Paradox, Arcelu, Murguía, Larrañaga, Acha, Carvajal y Evans— truly reflect to a faithful degree the author's desire to stay free of all manner of encumbrances. Although they have seen the void, these heroes fail to sustain their vision of the futility of life, electing instead to continue along a path leading to nowhere; the existentialist hero prefigured by Andrés Hurtado fails entirely to materialize. Baroja's non-teleological novel illustrates, on a larger scale, the life of the individual protagonist: the open horizon may seem to have the advantage of freedom, but it is ineluctably inconclusive.

The Barojian hero and the Barojian novel together serve to exemplify life in the Orteguian sense of "what we do and what happens to us," but the indispensable ingredient of *werden* or "becoming" is, typically, lacking. With the exception of Andrés Hurtado, the protagonist of the author's only genuine *Bildungsroman*, the novelist's heroes do not make themselves, do not discover their own authentic possibilities. Malraux has said that man is what he does; Baroja's principal characters show in the main what is done *to* them. The train moves and the scenery changes, but the passengers remain the same. Fermín Acha had remarked in *The Cape of Storms* that a true hero needs courage, fanaticism, and character.[3] In the absence of all three, the Barojian alter ego says no to life in an anti-Nietzschean *neinsagen zum Leben*. The autobiographical novels are not a quest, not a search for identity, but rather the literary version of the haeckelian "ontogeny recapitulates philogeny": each protagonist virtually recapitulates the entire step-by-step history of his predecessor.

Baroja's obsession with the motto symbolizing the destruction wrought by time, *Vulnerant omnes, ultima necat*, (They [the hours] all wound, the last one kills), is evidence of his excessive sensitivity to the possibilities of pain, loss, and death, a sensitivity that is most appropriately expressed in a minor key. There are no convincing heroes of Byronic dimensions; instead of grandeur and passion there is only a vague anxiety and a pervasive melancholia. Andrés Hurtado alone escapes the reduction in size of the typical alter ego, and only he springs free of the author's constricting grasp to affirm, at least, his right to non-being.

Baroja's curiosity exceeded his creativity and, like Gide, the Spanish novelist was tormented by the problems of invention. The latter viewed novelistic action from within the fortress of his own ideas and sensibility, relegating the reader to an inferior plane. The tensions of drama and the aesthetic niceties might very well appeal to the reader, but the writer is little concerned for a public he is convinced is incapable of responding to him.

Events take precedence over character, and the casual and the
episodic reign in place of the coherent whole; there is no vast
plan such as in Balzac's *Comédie Humaine* or Zola's Rougon-
Macquart novels. What the Barojian novel loses in focus and
direction, however, it gains in eccentricity, vividness, and
dynamism. In the novels and essays, the writer has indeed caught
the color of life itself. Noah's Ark or Pandora's box, the human
and the non-human spill over to fill pages unexcelled in sheer
variety. If there are few memorable minor figures, the aggregate
is overwhelming in its prodigality. The so-called realism of the
Barojian novel is, however, often a deception; although the details
are authentic, the perspective is a product of an exceedingly subjective approach to man and society. Instead of facing reality—
the here and the now—the author persistently turns back to an
earlier and safer time. Lacking a "thou" to mirror his "I," Baroja
seeks to cast anchor in the sea of the past to prove to himself
that he exists; only the reassurances provided by the known past
can serve adequately to shore up the author's fragile identity.

The writer's fear of novelty led him to deny the possibility
of real change, obliging him to cling tenaciously to the belief
that there was nothing new under the sun. Huarte de San Juan,
one of the novelist's lesser idols, repeatedly inveighed against
the fallacy of declaring that *nada se dice que no esté dicho ya*
("nothing is said that has not already been said"),[4] but if Baroja
often showed an inclination to follow the sixteenth-century doctor
in some of his scientific formulations, he was unwilling to become
his disciple in questions of change and progress. Convinced that
the future already lay in the past, Baroja discarded all hope for
improvement except in the limited field of the sciences. Nor
was his abstract humanitarianism of the sort to be translated
into concrete political solutions; like Oscar Wilde, Baroja found
it easier to have sympathy with suffering than with thought.

An antidogmatic dogmatist, an antibourgeois bourgeois, and
a fanatical enemy of fanaticism, Baroja did battle against
principles he unconsciously accepted. For all his fulminations
against conformity and middle-class standards, the novelist's
dearest wish was to be applauded. appreciated, and ultimately
rewarded in the conventional manner with ostentatious fame and
showers of gold. The statement "I have lived in obscurity,"[5] with
its implications of poverty, is not supported by the testimony of
Julio Caro Baroja to the effect that his uncle accumulated
750,000 pesetas by the time of his death, a sum that scarcely
suggests the romantic indigence of the bohemian life.[6] Baroja's
election to the Royal Spanish Academy is equally indicative of

the mythical nature of the writer's conviction that he suffered a lack of appreciation bordering on outright neglect.

There is a large corpus of critical studies on many aspects of the novelist's work, but just and measured appreciations are not numerous. The greatest handicap to Barojian criticism is the interposition of the author's shadow between the work and the critic, and the temptation to take Baroja at his word is all but overwhelming. George Bernard Shaw once remarked that one should never believe what an author has to say about himself, a piece of advice that is often more honored in the breach than in the observance. To judge Baroja primarily by what he declares he is, and only secondarily according to how he reveals himself indirectly and often unconsciously in his works, is to risk the twin dangers of deception and naiveté. The Basque had insisted so repeatedly on his own absolute integrity and sincerity that until recently few have felt inclined to disagree with his own modestly flattering self-portrayal;[7] it is equally noteworthy that Baroja also considered himself a moralist, a designation that accords ill with a philosophy of disengagement and flight.

The question of the author's contributions to the art of the novel in Spain is undoubtedly less controversial than the author himself. Baroja was the most authentic and most prolific novelist of the Generation of 1898, and the only one to have followers. Unamuno's novels were *sui generis*, the art of Azorín anticipated the works of Nathalie Sarraute and Alain Robbe-Grillet far more than the later Spanish novel, and the delicate aestheticism of Valle-Inclán found a more fertile ground in poetry than in prose. Baroja expressed successively in the course of his literary lifetime both the nihilism and hopes of his generation, the dismay of the intellectual in the face of corruption and violence, and the intense melancholy of that characteristic twentieth-century phenomenon, the displaced person. The complete works of Baroja are a chronicle of the author's times, the concrete evidence of a talent that is primarily reportorial. That the sum is greater than the parts is beyond question, although the difficulty of reading the collected works is not to be underestimated. The sensation of *déjà vu* is at times overpowering, for the totality of Baroja's production is an outstanding example of literary overkill.

Camilo José Cela, one of Spain's most prominent contemporary literary figures, has affirmed that Baroja opened the doors to *una España novelesca*, revealing the infinite possibilities of the novelistic art: . . . *de Baroja sale toda la novela española a él posterior* ("the entire Spanish novel after Baroja stems from him").[8] The incisive, unaffected style of Baroja left its mark on the early Cela, on Zunzunegui, Delibes, Gironella, Aldecoa. Baroja helped to free prose style from the rhetoric often characteristic of the nineteenth century, and elevated the novel of ideas to a position of prominence in modern Spanish letters. The Barojian novel, as much a novel of objects as of abstractions, has also prepared the ground for the modern objective novel with its emphasis on *cosas*. The *náusea* experienced by so many of the author's protagonists clearly anticipates the anguished perspective of the existentialists of recent decades, even though the Spanish writer admittedly lacks the passionate constancy and fortitude necessary to sustain or to overcome the shattering vision of nothingness; there is no light at the end of the tunnel.

If Baroja managed to fall short of greatness, it is as much a product of his absence of dramatic sense as it is of his lack of passion. The drama inherent in the unfolding of a hero's life as it is shaped by historical circumstances is cancelled out by the author's relentlessly authoritarian approach to plot and character. If Baroja as a non-believer theoretically sees man, weak and alone, as the center of the universe, at the mercy of blind, mysterious life-forces, in practice the irrational and the chaotic lie almost purely in the realm of the abstract, for what actually happens is predetermined by an author functioning as surrogate deity, and only the accompanying details are left to chance. The Barojian novel illustrates vividly the polarity between practice and theory, between a virtually predestined order and capricious disorder.

Baroja's novels are situated at the crossroads of personal history and undifferentiated anecdote, and it is precisely at this juncture that the writer's work acquires its unmistakable flavor. "The content suggests the style," affirms the author, and it is undeniable that the style is perfectly adjusted to the content. One may more easily quarrel with what Baroja expresses than with the manner in which he expresses it. On balance, the weaknesses of the Barojian novel are a faithful reflection of the weaknesses of the novelist, and the degree to which a critic responds to these personal crotchets will determine the degree to which objective criticism may be possible. As in the case of that other archegoist, Miguel de Unamuno, a neutral reaction is too much, or possibly too little, to expect.

Notes and References

Chapter One

1. For a discussion of *krausismo* see Juan López Morillas, *El Krausismo español* (Mexico, 1956). For a general survey of the Generation of 1898, see Pedro Laín Entralgo, *La generación del 98* (Madrid, 1956).
2. Gonzalo Sobejano, *Nietzsche en España* (Madrid, 1967), pp. 74-75.
3. Pedro Laín Entralgo, *España como problema* (Madrid, 1957), p. 535. For text of the manifesto see Ramón Gómez de la Serna, *Azorín* (Buenos Aires, 1957), pp. 127 ff.
4. Azorín, *La Voluntad* (Madrid, n.d.), pp. 188 ff.
5. José García Mercadal, ed., *Baroja en el banquillo* (Zaragoza, 1947-1948), II, 276.
6. José Guimón Ugartechea, "Las ideas médicas de don Pío Baroja," *Revista de Occidente,* XXI (May, 1968), 225-43; for Baroja's views on science see E. H. Templin, "Pío Baroja and Science," *Hispanic Review,* XV (1947), 165-92. See also Carmen Iglesias, *El pensamiento de Pío Baroja* (Mexico, 1963), pp. 105-32.
7. Pío Baroja, *Obras completas* (Madrid, 1946-1951), VII, 529. Hereafter called *Obras*.
8. *Obras,* V, 194.
9. *Ibid.,* 723, 874, 1077; VII, 550, 1105; VIII, 981. This last is the first poem in the *Canciones del suburbio.*
10. *Obras,* V, 724, 878; VI, 31, 616; VII, 995, 1120; VIII, 1127.
11. *Ibid.,* V, 878; VII, 1110.
12. Antonio Elorza, "El realismo crítico de Pío Baroja," *Rev. de Occidente,* XXI (May, 1968), 164-65.
13. The other writers and artists with whom Baroja associated at this time are repeatedly recalled and described in *Obras,* V, 990 ff.; VII, 836 ff.; VIII, 1021.
14. On Unamuno, see *Obras,* VII, 860-66, 784, 859.
15. Baroja denies the accusation of having abandoned Ciro Bayo; see *Obras,* VII, 851.
16. Ricardo Baroja, *Gente del 98* (Barcelona, 1952), pp. 124-28.
17. See Fernando Baeza, ed., *Baroja y su mundo* (Madrid, 1961), I, for an excellent Baroja iconography.
18. César González-Ruano, *Mi medio siglo se confiesa a medias* (Barcelona, 1951), p. 128.
19. *Obras,* VII, 403.
20. Luis S. Granjel, *Retrato de Pío Baroja* (Barcelona, 1953), p. 20.

21. *Obras,* VII, 401-5; see Azorín, *La voluntad,* p. 188, for a description of Olaiz; see also Granjel, *op. cit.,* pp. 18-19.

22. *Obras,* V, 167-68. The reason for Baroja's animosity toward Don Benito is fully and repeatedly explained in V, 668-69, 879; VII, 589.

23. Baroja refers to his turbulence, dynamism, and love for action in the prologue to *La dama errante, Obras,* II, 231. Upon his reception into the Real Academia the author characterizes himself as more Dionysian than Apollonian; see V, 896.

24. The publication of *Camino de perfección* was the occasion for a banquet offered Baroja by his publisher Rodríguez Serra and attended by Azorín, Valle-Inclán, Maeztu, and Galdós, *inter alia.*

25. *Obras,* V, 1081.

26. Julián Marías recalls having seen Baroja quite often in a bookstore on the Calle San Bernardo.

27. José María Salaverría, *Retratos* (Madrid, 1926), p. 69.

28. Jean-Louis Schonberg, *Federico García Lorca* (México, 1959), pp. 39-40, reproduces the section of the Catalonian publicist's diary which evokes the Madrid of about 1920.

29. *Obras,* V, 1086; VII, 1282.

30. Baeza, *Baroja y su mundo,* I, 44.

31. *Obras,* V, 263-82.

32. Baroja admits that time was the one gift he never lacked.

33. Don Serafín died in 1912.

34. *Obras,* VII, 877.

35. See Miguel Pérez Ferrero, *Pío Baroja en su rincón* (San Sebastián, 1941), pp. 243 ff., and Pío Baroja, *Ayer y hoy* (Santiago de Chile, 1939), pp. 33-38, for a full account of this episode.

36. Pío Baroja, *Memorias* (Madrid, 1955), p. 1076. This one-volume edition of the author's memoirs will be referred to henceforth in the notes as *Memorias.*

37. Numbers 70 and 71 of the *Indice de artes y letras* (Jan.-Feb., 1954) were dedicated to Baroja; the British Institute in Madrid also paid the author homage at this time. Ernest Hemingway declared in 1956 that Baroja "should have received the Nobel Prize many times over." See José Luis Castillo Puche, *Hemingway, entre la vida y la muerte* (Barcelona, 1968), pp. 319-33 for an account of Hemingway's visit to Baroja.

38. Nietzsche declared that "a married philosopher belongs *in comedy* . . ." Quoted from Walter Kaufmann, *Nietzsche* (Cleveland, 1966), p. 346.

39. Pío Baroja, *Paseos de un solitario* (Madrid, 1955), p. 148.

40. *Obras,* VII, 579-80.

41. *Ibid.,* 613-14. Baroja went to Azcoitia some time later to inquire, in vain, for the girl.

42. *Ibid.,* V, 671 ff.; VII, 617-18.

43. See below our Chapter V, pp. 79-80.

44. *Obras*, VII, 651-52, provides an account of these efforts.

45. See, for example, *Obras*, V, 246-47.

46. *Ibid.*, VIII, 762.

47. *Ibid.*, VII, 939-46; II, 957-69.

48. *Ibid.*, VII, 1330 ff.

49. *Ibid.*, 1336 ff.

50. For Gabriela's letters, see *Obras*, VII, 1341-49. The last two poems of the *Canciones del suburbio* are apparently dedicated to her.

51. *Obras*, VII, 1349-50.

52. García Mercadal, *Baroja en el banquillo*, II, 104.

53. Baroja, *Memorias*, p. 1117.

54. In *Juventud, egolatría, Obras*, V, 170-71, on which this section is based, Baroja does not take exception to the more elegant establishments designed for the affluent.

55. *Obras*, V, 461-62.

56. In *La ruta del aventurero* the by no means weak J. H. Thompson makes no attempt to secure Dolores, the object of his desires.

57. Granjel is evidently not convinced by Freud's theories on the Oedipus complex; see *op. cit.*, p. 39. In *Rev. de Occidente*, XXI (May, 1968), 242, n. 5., there is mention of a forthcoming work by José Guimón Ugartechea, *Baroja y la medicina*. Dr. Ugartechea is a psychiatrist, but the title suggests an entirely different sort of study. Ramón Sender, *Los noventayochos* (New York, 1961), p. 143, hints darkly at anomalies in Baroja's attitudes.

Chapter Two

1. The prologue to *La nave de los locos* is Baroja's answer to Ortega's essay *Ideas sobre la novela*. In the prologue to *La dama errante* Baroja takes up the topic of his supposed literary influences.

2. *Obras*, VI, 12.

3. *Ibid.*, IV, 321-42; VII, 1057.

4. *Ibid.*, IV, 320; VIII, 970.

5. *Ibid.*, VII, 1032; in *ibid.*, 1053, Baroja remarks that he could not write about a secondary character without knowing him to some extent.

6. *Ibid.*, 754.

7. *Ibid.*, 430.

8. *Ibid.*, VIII, 11.

9. See, for example, *La ciudad de la niebla* in *Obras*, II, 395 ff.

10. *Obras*, V, 850. Juan A. de Zunzunegui, *En torno a D. Pío Baroja y su obra* (Bilbao, 1960), p. 23, refers to the *novela paralítica* of Proust.

11. *Obras*, II, 982.

12. José Ortega y Gasset, *Obras completas* (Madrid, 1963), II, 78.

13. *Obras*, VIII, 957; VII, 400.

14. Baeza, *Baroja y su mundo*, I, 38.

15. *Obras,* IV, 325; VII, 1058; VIII, 972.

16. *Ibid.,* VII, 1305.

17. *Ibid.,* 991, 1307. Spengler, particularly, antagonized Baroja. See *ibid.,* V, 945, wherein Spengler is designated as a Fascist.

18. *Obras,* VII, 986; see also *ibid.,* VII, 153, VIII, 10.

19. In the *Canciones del suburbio* Baroja reaffirms his love for the showy singing of Italian opera and refers despectively to the *tribu vagneriana.* See *Obras,* VIII, 986.

20. The Spanish version, *hay que ver en lo que es,* appears four times in one section alone of the *Memoirs,* for which see *Obras,* VII, 419, 420, 430, 453.

21. *Obras,* V, 1065.

22 *Ibid.,* 230.

23. *Ibid.,* VII, 425. For a study on Baroja and the early Gorki, see Hildegard Burfeindt-Moral, *Pío Baroja und der frühe Maksim Gor'kij* (diss., Hamburg, 1964).

24. *Obras,* II, 966. In *El amor, el dandismo y la intriga,* Leguía calls Dostoyevsky *un loco genial.* See *Obras,* IV, 133; for references to Gogol and Turgenev see *ibid.,* V, 431.

25. *Ibid.,* VII, 820; VI, 888.

26. *Ibid.,* VII, 1048, 1078. José Alberich, *Los ingleses y otros temas de Pío Baroja* (Madrid, 1966), p. 46, states that there are only two volumes of Proust in Baroja's library.

27. *Obras,* VII, 745; IV, 212; VII, 738, 1001, 1083.

28. Alberich, pp. 39-63, provides a convenient summation. See *Obras,* III, 1203; V, 710, 728, 1034, 429-32; VII, 567-68, 576 ff.; VIII, 875, 902, 917.

29. *Obras.,* VII, 576.

30. *Ibid.,* V, 292.

31. *Ibid.* VII, 414-15.

32. Thompson in *Los contrastes de la vida* and O'Neil in *El laberinto de las sirenas* both read Goethe. For Heine, see below, Chapter 3, n. 101.

33. Baroja mentions in *Obras,* V, 1050, that Schopenhauer was responsible for the revival of interest in Gracián and Huarte de San Juan.

34. Baroja grants that there is much in the Romantic literature of the nineteenth century that is ridiculous and exaggerated, but adds that it is the only literature still capable of moving the man of today; see *Obras,* IV, 52.

35. *Obras,* VII, 1307; V, 582; VII, 1055.

36. Alberich, pp. 42-43.

37. Carlos Orlando Nallim, *El problema de la novela en Pío Baroja* (México, 1964), p. 260; Baroja, *Paseos de un solitario,* p. 64.

38. See *Obras,* III, 541-46; VIII, 11; V, 1040-46, 1052-56.

39. For a survey on imposters, see *ibid.,* VIII, 923-33, V, 719 ff.

40. See for example, *Obras,* V, 1342 ff.; II, 1338 ff.; III, 363 ff.; IV, 640 ff. Antonio Regalado García, "Verdugos y ejecutados en las

novelas de Pío Baroja," *Papeles de Son Armadans,* XLI (1966), 9-29, considers Baroja's preoccupation with executions a humanitarian protest against capital punishment.

41. *Obras,* VIII, 231.
42. *Ibid.,* VII, 1253, 775, are examples.
43. See *ibid.,* VI, 1255 for the text of the farce.
44. *Obras,* IV, 828. A story by Zunzunegui, "La vida y sus sorpresas," is a variation and amplification of this bizarre anecdote.
45. *Obras,* III, 549.
46. Diogenes Laertius, *Lives of the Eminent Philosophers* (London, 1925), II, 413.
47. *Obras,* VII, 1088.
48. *Ibid.,* V, 1063.
49. Baroja attributes his dislike for rhetoric to the fact that his ancestors did not speak Castilian; see *Obras,* II, 231; III, 10.
50. Gabriel Celaya, "De Norte a Sur," *Poesía* (Madrid, 1962), p. 480.
51. García Mercadal, *Baroja en el banquillo,* I, 80.
52. Leo Tolstoy, *What is Art* (London, 1959), pp. 165-66.
53. *Obras,* V, 1050.
54. *Ibid.,* I, 1048; Baroja notes in V, 661, that the perverse artists of Wilde, D'Annunzio, Huysmans, and Benavente are conceited *farceurs.*
55. See below, Chapter V, p. 89.
56. William Hubben, *Four Prophets of our Destiny* (New York, 1952), p. 59.
57. *Obras,* V, 162; see also *ibid.,* I, 1082, 1307.
58. *Ibid.,* I, 381-83; cf. Ricardo Baroja, *Gente del 98,* pp. 175-80.
59. The short story is part of *Vidas sombrías.* See *Obras,* VI, 1044 ff.
60. Sender, *Los noventayochos,* pp. 146-52, defends Picasso against Baroja's attacks.

Chapter Three

1. Alberich, *El tema de los ingleses,* p. 163, n. 9; see Templin, "Pío Baroja and Science," pp. 179-82, for Baroja's anthropological observations.
2. *Obras,* VIII, 1040.
3. *Ibid.,* V, 998.
4. *Ibid.,* VII, 525.
5. *Ibid.,* II, 1004.
6. *Ibid.,* VIII, 737-38.
7. *Ibid.,* V, 373; 514-16.
8. *Ibid.,* I, 1116.
9. See *ibid.,* 1260, 1272.
10. See *ibid.,* VI, 133-34; V, 1145, 1238; IV, 1341.
11. *Ibid.,* V, 947.
12. *Ibid.,* 996 ff.

13. *Ibid.*, VIII, 942.

14. *Ibid.*, I, 1119, 1126.

15. *Ibid.*, V, 517.

16. *Ibid.*, I, 901.

17. García Mercadal, *Baroja en el banquillo*, II, 198.

18. *Obras*, IV, 720.

19. Miguel de Unamuno, "La envidia hispánica," in *Mi religión y otros ensayos breves* (Buenos Aires, 1955), p. 48.

20. *Obras*, II, 255. See *ibid.*, I, 1126, wherein Julieta Nord, a Northerner who hates the North, is informed by Larrañaga that if she wants to meet showy, frivolous men, the South is their natural habitat.

21. *Ibid.*, VII, 485.

22. See, for example, *La ciudad de la niebla, ibid.*, II, 349 ff, and *Laura, ibid.*, VII, 222 ff.

23. For a more detailed treatment, see Alberich, pp. 123-42.

24. See below, Chapter 6, pp. 131-32.

25. *Obras*, II, 87 ff. Mr. Philf delivers himself from the hands of Indian fanatics by removing and reinserting his false teeth, thereby surrounding himself with a sacred aura.

26. *Ibid.*, VI, 499.

27. *Ibid.*, II, 170; cf. Miss Douglas in *La dama errante*, II, 235-36, Miss Clark in *La ciudad de la niebla*, II, 340, and Miss Dawson in *César o nada*, II, 616.

28. *Obras*, II, 337, 345, 366, 370, 400.

29. *Ibid.*, II, 595, 623.

30. *Ibid.*, III, 310.

31. *Ibid.*, 703.

32. *Ibid.*, II, 932; see the essay, "Lo individual y lo anónimo," *ibid*, VIII, 960.

33. *Ibid.*, V, 905.

34. *Ibid.*, VII, 404, 821, 982.

35. See *ibid.*, V, 148.

36. *Ibid.*, 138 ff.

37. *Ibid.*, I, 1271.

38. *Ibid.*, 1247.

39. *Ibid.*, 1317.

40. *Ibid.*, VII, 1030, 1309, 1326, *et passim*.

41. *Ibid.*, VIII, 225.

42. *Ibid.*, II, 1265.

43. *Ibid.*, I, 1202.

44. *Ibid.*, 1164.

45. *Ibid.*, 1202-4.

46. *Ibid.*, 1324.

47. *Ibid.*, V, 29.

48. See *ibid.*, VII, 687-725, "París fin de siglo," for the author's recreation of his early visits to Paris.

49. *Ibid.*, V, 48.

50. See *ibid.*, V, 974, 902.

51. In *El amor, el dandismo y la intriga, Obras*, IV, 133, the Abbot Girovanna maintains that the French lack spontaneous geniuses; there are no Titians, no Goyas, no Dantes.

52. *Obras*, II, 616, 642.

53. *Ibid.*, 1089.

54. *Ibid.*, III, 183-85.

55. See *ibid.*, III, 439, 1208, 735; as late as 1943, in *El caballero de Erlaiz*, there is a reference to the vanity and conceit of French soldiers.

56. *Obras*, V, 133-52.

57. Baroja is referring to the ill-fated Moroccan venture; in 1904 Spain and France had agreed, by secret treaty, to partition Morocco. At the Algeçiras conference in 1906, it was agreed that both countries would police the territory, but France began annexation under the pretext of pacification, occupying Fez in 1911. While not objecting to the German expedition to Morocco, France took exception to the Spanish occupation of Ifni. See Rhea Marsh Smith, *Spain, a Modern History* (Ann Arbor, 1965), pp. 391 ff.

58. *Obras*, V, 255 ff.

59. *Ibid.*, IV, 542.

60. See *ibid.*, I, 1056, 1227, 1317.

61. *Ibid.*, II, 1404, 1357.

62. *Ibid.*, VII, 403.

63. *Ibid.*, 692.

64. *Ibid.*, 864-65.

65. *Ibid.*, VIII, 414.

66. *Memorias*, pp. 1115-16.

67. *Obras*, II, 967.

68. Baroja, *El país vasco* (Barcelona, 1953), p. 41, gives as variants Urci and Urzia; Thor's Day in Basque is Urci's Day or Ortzeguna.

69. *Obras*, IV, 517-18.

70. Walter Kaufmann, *The Portable Nietzsche* (New York, 1954), p. 500.

71. *El país vasco*, pp. 127, 130, contains the comment that San Sebastián is an excellent example of the lack of social life in Spain.

72. *Obras*, VI, 134.

73. See *ibid.*, V, 383, 498, 685; VI, 1132.

74. *Ibid.*, VI, 1000 ff.

75. "La venta" reappears in the *Tablado de Arlequín* (V, 59-61) in identical form, and in *El país vasco*, pp. 476 ff.

76. "Elizabide" was published in the *Obras*, VIII, 623 ff. See *ibid.*, VII, 634, for Baroja's comment on the festival.

77. *Obras*, VIII, 601-23.

78. *Ibid.*, VI, 1172.

79. *Ibid.*

80. For a detailed study of this work, see Iglesias, *El pensamiento de Pío Baroja*, pp. 95-97.

81. *Obras*, IV, 334-39; III, 744.

82. See "El guerrillero vasco," *Obras*, V, 539-41; III, 968; VIII, 904.

83. *El país vasco*, p. 7.

84. *Ibid.*, p. 8.

85. *Obras*, VII, 1170-75, 1295.

86. *Ibid.*, V, 237.

87. See *ibid.*, IV, 689, 750; V, 703, 940, 1359; VIII, 243.

88. See also *ibid.*, V, 141, 1016; VI, 868; VII, 1037; *Memorias*, p. 1085.

89. *Obras*, VIII, 1100.

90. *Ibid.*, I, 1239-40; VII, 811, 923, 1310, 1312; see also V, 493, 652, 934; VII, 272, 434.

91. *Ibid.*, VI, 787, 766; in *Ayer y hoy*, p. 89, Baroja maintains that psychoanalysis has not clarified any human problems.

92. *Obras*, II, 462, 830.

93. *Ibid.*, III, 809 ff., 949.

94. Baeza, *Baroja y su mundo*, I, 55.

95. See the description of Manesés León in *Obras*, IV, 241; see also *ibid.*, II, 966, for a description of Lubecki; II, 632, for Pereyra; and also II, 402.

96. *Obras*, III, 805; IV, 1448-49.

97. *Ibid.*, V, 356.

98. *Ibid.*, 450; VII, 1081. In *La nave de los locos*, IV, 312, Baroja refers sardonically to the need of the *pequeños judíos de París* to invent literary forms every three or four years.

99. *Obras*, V, 593.

100. *Ibid.*, VII, 1312. Baroja describes this *algo* as . . . *una novela en que un hombre cree que se convierte en una araña.*

101. *Ibid.*, 922. Baroja's views on Heine are variable; cf. *ibid.*, V, 243; VII, 989, 1309, wherein Baroja finds him more Jewish than German, and V, 373, where Heine exemplifies German humor.

102. *Obras*, II, 461; I, 1236, 1261, 1235; VII, 409. Pérez del Corral in the *Aventuras* . . ., II, 112, an obvious transformation of Valle-Inclán, has a "Jewish nose."

103. *Ibid.*, V, 1017; in the prologue to *La dama errante*, II, 229, Baroja had said that the ethnic element is of prime importance in the formation of individual character.

104. *Ibid.*, VIII, 962.

105. *Ibid.*, I, 1325; II, 632.

106. *Ibid.*, I, 1239. Baroja had seen Bergson at the home of Ana Lomonosoff, and considered him very intelligent and spiritual.

107. *Ibid.*, VII, 704.

108. *Ibid.*, 1321-22; *Memorias*, p. 1033. In *Obras*, VII, 672, n. 1, Baroja expresses horror at the death of Max Jacob in a concentration camp.

109. *Memorias*, p. 1034.

110. *Obras*, II, 405; V, 1294, 213, 843.

111. See, for example, General Pompilio García, Señora Rinaldi in

ibid., II, 335, 374; Aníbal, Angel Mellado, and Rita in I, 931, 932; see also V, 331, 339; III, 372-73, 508, 511, 1260; VI, 135, 136, 178, 607.

112. *Obras,* IV, 87, 79. Cf. Nietzsche's statement, "Where races are mixed, there is the source of great cultures," Kaufmann, *Nietzsche,* p. 131.

113. *Obras,* I, 1048, 1065.

114. *Ibid.,* 1290. Larrañaga states that no European has ever been able to say that he has understood the Chinese.

115. See *ibid.,* II, 634, 1228, 1245; I, 1290; *Memorias,* pp. 997, 1014.

116. *Obras,* V, 388.

117. *Ibid.,* II, 542.

Chapter Four

1. *Obras,* V, 168.

2. *Ibid.,* 14, 49.

3. *Ibid.,* III, 82-83, 393.

4. *Ibid.,* IV, 442.

5. Azorín, *Las confesiones de un pequeño filósofo* (Buenos Aires, 1950), p. 51, quotes this characterization of Yécora (or Yecla) by Baroja. In the prologue to *El mayorazgo de Labraz,* Baroja describes Labraz similarly as *un pueblo terrible.* Both authors consider the Holy Week procession in Yécora the symbol of the triumph of death over life; cf. *Obras.* VI, 100 and Azorín, pp. 51-52.

6. *Obras,* VI, 86.

7. *Ibid.,* V, 48-49.

8. See also *ibid.,* 29-34, 19-23.

9. *Ibid.,* II, 450.

10. *Ibid.,* 678.

11. In support of this charge of regionalism and also to indulge his love for folk sayings and popular poetry, Baroja dedicates two pages of *Vitrina pintoresca* to a catalogue of insulting regional quips. See *Obras,* V, 832-33; IV, 634-35; VIII, 1014.

12. Huarte de San Juan and H. S. Chamberlain make similar assertions. See also *Obras,* I, 567; III, 739.

13. *Obras,* II, 548, 697; III, 744.

14. Velasco in *El mundo es ansí* and Aracil in *El árbol de la ciencia,* are illustrations.

15. Andrés Hurtado's brother Alejandro has a similar position; see *Obras,* II, 452.

16. *Obras,* VII, 580; V, 198-99. In *El árbol de la ciencia,* Andrés Hurtado and his brother Pedro pass courses by the same method, and in *Mala hierba* Manuel Alcázar is excused from military service through influence; see *Obras,* II, 452, 456; I, 475.

17. Unamuno, *op. cit.,* pp. 43-51; Antonio Machado, "Por tierras de España," *Obras completas* (Madrid, 1962), pp. 737-38.

18. *Obras,* I, 741, 830-31.

19. *Ibid.*, VIII, 813.

20. *Ibid.*, II, 396; VIII, 856.

21. *Ibid.*, IV, 59.

22. *Ibid.*, II, 518.

23. *Ibid.*, I, 1257.

24. Azorín, *La voluntad*, p. 194. Arthur Schopenhauer, *On Human Nature* (Aberdeen, 1957), p. 18, states categorically that "man is at bottom a savage, horrible beast," later fortifying his judgment by quoting Gobineau's description of man as *l'animal méchant par excellence*.

25. Baroja, *Ayer y hoy*, p. 144.

26. Elorza, p. 164. *Rev. de Occidente*, XXI (May 1968) is devoted exclusively to a homage to Baroja.

27. Fernando Martínez Laínez, "El sentimiento político de Pío Baroja," *Rev. de Occidente*, XXI (May, 1968), 192.

28. *Obras*, I, 599, 632; V, 217-18, 836, 921, 964; VIII, 880; *Paseos de un solitario*, p. 142. It has already been noted that Baroja did not advance very far in his reading of Marx.

29. *Obras*, VI, 515-16.

30. The number of members in the Spanish UGT or General Union of Workers, which had been organized in 1888, was to reach about 85,000 by 1910.

31. For an excellent account of the attitude of the Generation of 1898 toward the middle class, see Gonzalo Sobejano, *Forma literaria y sensibilidad social* (Madrid, 1967), pp. 199 ff.

32. *Obras*, V, 56.

33. See *ibid.*, 992, wherein Baroja accuses the Communists and Fascists as well of hating whatever is distinguished. For specific references to democracy, see I, 1270; IV, 762; V, 24, 32, 705; *Memorias*, p. 1007.

34. Philip Wheelwright, *Heraclitus* (Princeton, 1959), p. 11.

35. Quoted from Harry Levin, *The Gates of Horn* (New York, 1963), p. 287.

36. *Obras*, II, 252.

37. Pío Baroja, *Páginas escogidas* (Madrid, 1918), p. 168, writes that he considers *Aurora roja* one of his best works: . . . *puse en ella una retórica más apasionada*. The concluding eulogy of the novel is a rare example of the pompous style usually so detested by Baroja.

38. *Obras*, I, 610. *El mundo es ansí*, II, 783 ff., contains a description of a meeting of anarchists in Geneva.

39. *Obras*, V, 524-37.

40. *Ibid.*, VII, 780.

41. Bomb-throwing incidents and political assassination had already become associated with Spanish anarchists by the end of the nineteenth century. During the premiership of Sagasta, two bombs were thrown in a theatre, killing eighteen persons; in 1897 Cánovas was assassinated; in Paris, in May of 1905, an attempt was made on the life of King Alfonso XIII when bombs exploded near his carriage;

just one year later the Mateo Morral episode took place. Canalejas was assassinated by an anarchist in 1912 as was Premier Dato in 1921.

42. *Obras*, II, 252-54.

43. For a version in English of Baroja's views, see "The Mistakes of the Spanish Republic," *The Living Age*, CCCLI (1937), 422-27; see also John T. Reid, *Modern Spain and Liberalism* (Stanford, 1937), pp. 60-138.

44. *Obras*, V, 921.

45. Baroja, *Ayer y hoy*, pp. 83-84; *Memorias*, pp. 1022, 1042.

46. *Obras*, VI, 384.

47. *Ibid.*, 297-99, 400.

48. *Ibid.*, 458-72.

49. *Ibid.*, 513. Acha, Baroja informs us, was born in 1873. We recall that Baroja was born in 1872.

50. Baroja, *Ayer y hoy*, pp. 78, 85; *Memorias*, p. 976.

51. *Obras*, I, 567; V, 31; VI, 441.

52. *Ibid.*, II, 660; Giménez Caballero, "Pio Baroja, precursor español del fascismo," Baeza, *op. cit.*, II, 226 ff., maintains that the complete passage in *César o nada* is an anticipation of fascism. Baroja has denied the imputation of fascist thinking in *Obras*, VII, 1070.

53. Arthur Schopenhauer, *On Human Nature*, p. 132, had said ". . . every constitution should be a nearer approach to a despotism than to anarchy."

54. *Ayer y hoy*, p. 44.

55. *Memorias*, p. 1105.

56. *Ayer y hoy*, p. 144; *Memorias*, p. 1021.

57. *Obras*, V, 1122.

58. *Memorias*, p. 1036.

59. Sobejano, *Forma literaria*, p. 209.

60. *Obras*, V, 937.

61. *Ibid.*, VII, 835, 984.

62. *Ibid.*, V, 214. The one exception was Baroja's support of the lower clergy against the Second Republic.

63. *Ibid.*, 194-95.

64. *Ibid.*, 311.

65. In *ibid.*, 321, Baroja blames the clergy for discouraging their parishioners from reading; truth, the priests maintain, is to be found in prayer, not in books.

66. The text is intact in *Camino de perfección* (New York, 1952), pp. 149-50.

67. Schopenhauer, *Essays of Schopenhauer* (London, n.d.), p. 101.

68. *Obras*, II, 555, 646, 724, 741, 832; III, 552; VII, 647-48.

69. *Ibid.*, V, 927; VIII, 538.

70. *Ibid.*, III, 740.

71. *Ibid.*, V, 251; Kaufmann, *The Portable Nietzsche*, p. 589.

72. *Obras*, II, 607; V, 855.

73. *Obras*, I, 1115-16; see V, 237-38, 1120, for a negative view of

Kierkegaard; in VII, 816, Baroja criticizes Kierkegaard for his positing of anguish at the root of human existence.

74. *Ibid.*, V, 295 and II, 1444-47.

75. *Ibid.*, II, 40, 212.

76. *Ibid.*, III, 616, 536; VI, 376.

77. *Ibid.*, V, 327-28.

78. *Ibid.*, II, 826-64.

79. *Ibid.*, V, 739-43; see also I, 1098, 1359.

80. *Ibid.*, IV, 416.

81. *Ibid.*, III, 556 ff; II, 585-87, 691; VI, 352-53 *et passim.*

82. *Obras*, I, 116-17.

83. The vicar in Anarzábal is also a great gourmand; see *Obras*, II, 857.

84. *Ibid.*, VIII, 763-64.

85. *Ibid.*, II, 693; III, 1123; VI, 207; VII, 291 ff., 319; III, 547 ff., esp. 554-55.

86. *Ibid.*, V, 319.

87. *Ibid.*, I, 1375.

88. *Ibid.*, V, 340.

89. *Ibid.*, VI, 785.

90. *Ayer y hoy*, pp. 83, 136; see too "The Mistakes of the Spanish Republic."

91. *Obras*, VI, 847.

92. *Ibid.*, III, 1031.

Chapter Five

1. Zunzunegui, *En torno a D. Pío Baroja y su obra*, pp. 26-27.

2. *Ibid.*, p. 20.

3. There are also at least two uncompleted novels, belonging to his student days.

4. See Baeza, *Baroja y su mundo*, I, 381 ff., for a listing of Baroja's journalistic contributions.

5. "La venta," the ode to Basque inns, had already appeared in *El País* in 1899 and subsequently reappeared in various collections.

6. *Obras*, VI, 990.

7. *Ibid.*, 994.

8. Baroja, *Páginas escogidas*, p. 28.

9. Baeza, II, 11-12.

10. *Obras*, VII, 602.

11. *Ibid.*, 633.

12. *El país vasco*, p. 8.

13. *Obras*, VIII, 285-86.

14. *Ibid.*, VII, 615; VI, 1037.

15. Laín Entralgo, *La generación*, pp. 145 ff.

16. *Obras*, VII, 1032.

17. Miguel Pérez Ferrero, *Vida de Pío Baroja* (Barcelona, 1960), p. 178, states that Baroja was reading a good deal of Ibsen about 1900.

18. *Obras,* I, 53; Baroja does not specify the nature of these romantic illusions, but a quick survey of the feminine inspirations for "Bondad oculta" and this novel, as well as the accounts of frustrated meetings with women during his medical and bakery periods, suggests that part of his melancholy was caused by sentimental failure. It is no doubt equally possible that Baroja is referring to the general atmosphere of hopelessness that prevailed in Spain at that time—a hopelessness to which he had fallen victim.

19. See Pérez Ferrero, *Vida,* p. 94, for an account of the circumstances of this trip.

20. The model for Mister Bothwell is identified by Ricardo Baroja, *Gente del 98,* pp. 156-74, as José Sttatford [*sic*] Gibson, an English watercolorist he had met in Aragón. The local inhabitants considered Gibson quite mad, a quality that could not fail to capture the imagination of the Barojas.

21. *Obras,* I, 119 ff.

22. *Ibid.,* 118.

23. *Ibid.,* 155.

24. To be referred to henceforth as *Adventures.* . . . The author indicates in *Obras,* VII, 587, that during his student days he had started, but soon abandoned, a novel entitled *Las buhardillas de Madrid,* a work that bore some resemblance to the Paradox novel.

25. *Obras,* VII, 651.

26. Baeza, I, 47-48; see also Manuel Durán, "Silverio Lanza y Silvestre Paradox," *Papeles de Son Armadans,* XXXIV (July, 1964), 57-72.

27. *Obras,* V, 888; VII, 649-50. For Paradox' inventions, see II, 51; Ricardo Baroja, *Gente del 98,* p. 140, has called Silvestre Paradox *símbolo y arquetipo fantástico* of all these inventors.

28. *Obras,* II, 48-49. This procedure was followed by an acquaintance of Baroja's; see VII, 651, 1251.

29. *Ibid.,* II, 144.

30. *Ibid.,* 57.

31. *Ibid.,* 58.

32. *Ibid.,* 76.

33. *Ibid.,* 148.

34. See *ibid.,* V, 210, for a description of the beginning of their friendship.

35. The duel in the painter's studio described in II, 82 ff. is a recreation of the mock duel in the studio of the painter Vivó. See VII, 946, and Ricardo Baroja, *Gente del 98,* pp. 97-113.

36. Baroja, *Páginas escogidas,* prologue to *Camino de perfección.*

37. *Obras,* II, 125 ff.

38. *Ibid.,* 128.

39. Iglesias, *El pensamiento de Pío Baroja,* p. 75, states, for example, that Fernando Ossorio is . . . *en muchos aspectos el propio Baroja.* Azorín may have started the trend of identifying Ossorio with Baroja, for which see Francisco J. Flores Arroyuelo, *Las primeras*

novelas de Pío Baroja (Murcia, 1967), pp. 53-54.

40. *Obras*, VII, 730-31. Flores Arroyuelo, p. 49, mentions the model for Ossorio, but does not draw any conclusions.

41. *Obras*, VII, 587.

42. See above, n. 24.

43. Sobejano, *Nietzsche en España*, p. 49, n. 19.

44. *Obras*, VIII, 853-54.

45. George Bernard Shaw, "The Sanity of Art," *Major Critical Essays* (London, 1948), p. 331.

46. *Obras*, VI, 10 ff., cf. above, Chapter 4, p. 72.

47. Max Nordau, *Degeneration* (New York, 1895), p. 35. A more accessible edition is that of London, 1913. Both English versions are translated from the second German edition of *Entartung*, and the pagination in both cases is the same.

48. Nordau, pp. 18-22.

49. *Obras*, VI, 58.

50. Nietzsche, *Twilight of the Idols*, considers it a sign of decadence to think that "nothing is worth anything, life is not worth anything." See Kaufmann, *The Portable Nietzsche*, p. 536.

51. Nordau, p. 121.

52. *Ibid.*, p. 46.

53. *Obras*, VI, 10.

54. Laín Entralgo, *La generación*, p. 66.

55. The visit to Illescas and the Church of Santo Tomé had previously been described in an essay "Tierra castellana—en Santo Tomé," *Obras*, VIII, 829-33. The nightmarish scene of the white coffin, VI, 79 ff., appears also in Azorín, *La voluntad*, p. 163.

56. *Obras*, VI, 40-47.

57. Baroja gives various accounts of these excursions: V, 793, 891; VIII, 803 ff., 1001.

58. Pérez Ferrero, *Vida*, p. 96.

59. Sobejano, *Nietzsche en España*, pp. 103-4.

60. *Obras*, V, 18-19.

61. *Ibid.*, VI, 111; the music of the *jota*, which had offended Ossorio with its brutality and vulgarity in the early part of the novel suddenly seems a healthy expression of natural and barbaric instincts. Cf. VI, 51 and 125.

62. *Obras*, VI, 128.

63. In *The Antichrist*, Nietzsche maintains that Christianity hates the spirit, hates freedom and the senses, hates joy itself. See Kaufmann, *The Portable Nietzsche*, pp. 589, 627.

64. Ortega, *Obras completas*, II, 124.

65. I have given the customary English translation, which, however, fails to convey the connotations of illicit trafficking and soliciting which is suggested by the Spanish.

66. *Obras*, VII, 753.

67. Martínez Laínez, "El sentimiento político de Pío Baroja," p. 196.

68. *Obras*, I, 373.

69. *Ibid.*, 384. See Alberich, *El tema de los ingleses*, p. 135, n. 22, for the possible model for Roberto Hasting.

70. *Obras*, I, 633.

71. *Ibid.*, 635.

72. Cf. *ibid.*, 287; VII, 1129.

73. *Obras*, I, 279; V, 810; see also VII, 1128-29.

74. *Ibid.*, V, 816-17; VII, 842, 1226. Monzón is a double of the sculptor Juan Mani, to whom Ricardo Baroja, *Gente del 98*, devotes a chapter.

75. Summaries are available in Nallim, *El problema de la novela*, pp. 235-44, and Flores Arroyuelo, *Las primeras novelas*, pp. 62-78.

76. *Obras*, I, 457.

77. *Ibid.*, 723.

78. *Ibid.*, 798.

79. *Ibid.*, 743.

80. *Ibid.*, V, 462.

81. *Ibid.*, II, 154.

82. *Ibid.*, 214.

83. *Ibid.*, 212.

84. *Ibid.*, 203-4. For the others, see 169-70, 215-16.

85. *Ibid.*, V, 84.

86. *Ibid.*, 989-92; VII, 949-50.

87. *Ibid.*, VII, 955.

88. Baroja, *Páginas escogidas*, p. 208.

89. *Obras*, V, 462.

90. *Ibid.*, VII, 791; *Ayer y hoy*, p. 185.

91. *Obras*, I, 937.

92. *Ibid.*, II, 590.

93. *Ibid.*, I, 931, 934.

94. *Ibid.*, 952.

95. *Ibid.*, VII, 791-92.

96. *Ibid.*, I, 1037.

97. *Ibid.*, VII, 847-48.

98. In *Ayer y hoy*, p. 178, Baroja states that he once knew an anarchist named José Aracil. It is sometimes said that Aracil is based on the figure of José Nákens. See Eduardo Gómez de Baquero, *Novelas y novelistas* (Madrid, 1918), p. 148.

99. *Obras*, II, 301. In *La ciudad de la niebla* the Scot Mr. Roch describes himself as vague and indecisive, possessing neither will nor character.

100. *Obras*, VII, 765 ff.

101. *Ibid.*, II, 440. Margarita Tilly, in the Aviraneta series, traces the same trajectory from freedom to stolidity, as does Margot in *La selva oscura*.

102. *Obras*, II, 243.

103. *Ibid.*, 250 ff.

104. To be referred to henceforth as *Zalacáin*.

105. *Obras*, I, 196.

106. Sobejano, *Nietzsche en España*, p. 365, refers to . . . *ese fracaso que el hombre de acción barojiano encuentra siempre al final de sus afanes;* Alberich, p. 141, writes: *Casi todos los héroes barojianos (Zalacaín, César Moncada, Quintín, el mismo Aviraneta) ven coronadas sus hazañas por el fracaso, la pobreza o el olvido.* Granjel, *Retrato*, pp. 188 ff., 200 ff., distinguishes between Nietzscheans (Hasting, Quintín, Yarza, Moncada, Thierry) and adventurers (Zalacaín, Shanti Andía, Galardi, O'Neil) and connects failure only with the former group.

107. *Obras*, I, 179.

108. See *ibid.*, 222, wherein a foreigner sums up Spain as "gambling, bells, Carlism, and the *jota.*"

109. Sherman Eoff, *The Modern Spanish Novel* (New York, 1961), pp. 172-85, studies the novel in Bergsonian terms.

110. *Obras*, VII, 795.

111. See *ibid.*, II, 622-23, 632, 649, 673, for some of Moncada's derogatory statements.

112. *Ibid.*, 653.

113. *Ibid.*, V, 524-37.

114. In one of many dialogues with his vivacious sister Laura, César remarks that since life is hard, the individual must be equally hard in order to succeed. In response to Laura's question as to whether or not he considers himself so qualified, César replies in the negative. See *Obras*, II, 581.

115. *Ibid.*, 737-38.

116. *Ibid.*, 751. The first edition of *César o nada* (Madrid, 1910), contains another chapter, more properly an epilogue, entitled "Finis Gloriae Mundi." Moncada, now living in a fine house in Castro Duro, is depicted as a collector of objets d'art. "I am nothing, nothing," he declares.

117. See, for example, *Obras*, II, 624, 651, 733, 739.

118. *Ibid.*, 748.

119. Sobejano, *Nietzsche en España*, p. 371.

120. Eoff, p. 184, n. 47.

121. Granjel, *Retrato*, p. 194.

122. Nallim, *El problema de la novela*, pp. 214-28.

123. *Obras*, VII, 799.

124. Pío Caro Baroja, *La soledad de Pío Baroja* (México, 1953), p. 98.

125. Baeza, *Baroja y su mundo*, I, 48, reproduces the painting and is the source of this information.

126. *Obras*, II, 999.

127. *Ibid.*, 1056.

128. *Ibid.*, VII, 801.

129. *Ibid.*, 651. Baroja frequented the Retiro Gardens when he was a medical student and then later when he managed the bakery.

130. Schopenhauer, *Essays*, p. 163. This theme is introduced by the bandit Melitón in *El mayorazgo de Labraz*.

131.. *Obras*, II, 491-94; in *Los últimos románticos*, I, 854, the advice appears as: *Limitarse es hacerse feliz.*

132. Cf. Schopenhauer, "Metaphysics of Love," *Essays*, pp. 171-90 and *Obras*, II, 558-59.

133. Baroja, *Familia, infancia y juventud, Obras*, VII, 520, writes about his exhausted family line, enumerating three relatives who died insane and two who died of tuberculosis. *La mayoría de la gente de mi familia no creo que fuera de una gran vitalidad.*

134. It was Baroja's practice to take soporifics; insomnia was one of his most persistent problems.

135. *Obras*, II, 561.

136. The chapters on the struggle for life and the selection of the species invite comparison with Thomas Hardy's *Jude the Obscure*. Hardy's work is Darwinian in the same sense; nature's law is "mutual butchery," and Sue and Jude believe they have no right to have children because of their hereditary taint.

137. *Obras*, VII, 731.

138. Arthur Schopenhauer, *The World as Will and Idea* (New York, 1961), p. 408, declares: "Far from being denial of the will, suicide is a phenomenon of strong assertion of will. . . ." In suicide, Schopenhauer continues, it is not life that is rejected, but only ". . . the conditions under which it has presented itself."

139. *Obras*, II, 508.

140. Albert Camus, *The Myth of Sisyphus* (New York, 1959), p. 4.

141. The story in *Obras*, II, 497, of the frivolous and callous woman who, upon being informed of her son's death when she was about to go to a ball, instructs her servant Venancia to keep the news to herself, recalls a scene in *Jude the Obscure* wherein Arabella, when faced at an inconvenient moment with Jude's death, behaves similarly. A later and undoubtedly better-known version of this tale is told by Proust of the Duke and Duchess de Guermantes.

142. *Obras*, V, 669-70, 880; VII, 578-79; II, 450-51.

143. *Ibid.*, V, 670, 879; VII, 587; *El árbol de la ciencia*, II, 463-65. In *Aventuras* . . ., II, 115, Pérez del Corral accuses the interns assisting him of speaking an incomprehensible jargon which they had learned from a book by Letamendi.

144. *Obras*, V, 880; VII, 596-97; II, 469-70. The story of Paca Dávalos in *El sabor de la venganza*, III, 1161, is a schematic recollection of San Juan de Dios.

145. *Obras*, II, 449, 463; VII, 583-84. See Sebastián Juan Arbó, *Pío Baroja y su tiempo* (Barcelona, 1963), pp. 92-94. Riudavets had participated in the fantastic inventions and projects of Pío and Ricardo Baroja.

146. See *Obras*, II, 467; VII, 648-49, where only Maximiano's first name is given; Pérez Ferrero, *Vida*, p. 77, identifies him as Maximiano Limeses. It was Limeses who compared Baroja to a faun on a Greek amphora; cf. below, *La sensualidad pervertida.*

147. *Obras*, II, 473-74; V, 659-60, 880; VII, 594-96, 1126.

148. *Ibid.*, V, 661.

149. See the description by Ricardo Baroja, *Gente del 98*, pp. 151-55.

150. *Obras*, VI, 593.

151. Cf. *ibid.*, II, 475-76; VII, 1324-25.

152. *Ibid.*, VII, 1325.

153. Cf. *ibid.*, II, 496-98; VII, 608-10. In *Camino de perfección*, VI, 120, the brief description of the house belonging to Ossorio's relatives in the province of Valencia is a preliminary sketch for the two above-noted extended descriptions.

154. *Obras*, II, 517-42; see also V, 886-88; VII, 613-34.

Chapter Six

1. *Obras*, II, 828. Carlos Yarza wanted to sack Paris and Hurtado dreamt of gunning down all the spectators at a bullfight as they left the ring.

2. *Ibid.*, VII, 793; Pío Caro Baroja, *La soledad de Pío Baroja*, p. 111.

3. *Obras*, VII, 391.

4. *Ibid.*, 792; VIII, 704. The description of *Lo scoppio del carro* in II, 798-99 is repeated in VIII, 720-21.

5. Cf. *ibid.*, II, 790-91; VII, 889-90.

6. César Barja, *Libros y autores contemporáneos* (New York, 1935), p. 324.

7. *Obras*, VII, 1058; IV, 325; VIII, 972.

8. *Ibid.*, V, 233.

9. *Ibid.*, 1155-56.

10. *Ibid.*, IV, 1173.

11. *Ibid.*, VII, 519.

12. *Ibid.*, V, 499.

13. *Ibid.*, 895. Speaking of Valle-Inclán and Baroja, Laín Entralgo, *La generación del 98*, p. 167, states . . . *evocan la historia instalados en la intrahistoria.*

14. *Obras*, VII, 1072-75; in the *Paseos*, p. 198, Baroja recalls that during his stay in Paris in 1913 he was in the habit of frequenting the bookstalls along the Seine in search of documentation.

15. *Obras*, III, 67, 71, 79.

16. *Ibid.*, VII, 506, 1075.

17. *Ibid.*, III, 296.

18. *Ibid.*, 154, 1152. See Antonio Ballesteros Beretta, *Síntesis de historia de España* (Barcelona, 1936), p. 499, for data on these upheavals.

19. *Obras*, IV, 1116.

20. See José Antonio Maravall, "Historia y novela," in Baeza, *Baroja y su mundo*, I, 177.

21. José Luis Castillo Puche, *Memorias íntimas de Aviraneta* (Madrid, 1952), p. 66.

22. *Ibid.*, p. 50.
23. *Ibid.*, p. 84.
24. *Obras*, IV, 316.
25. Pío Caro Baroja, *La soledad de Pío Baroja*, pp. 119-24.
26. *Obras*, III, 731.
27. *Ibid.*, 709.
28. *Ibid.*, 762.
29. Baroja had also visited Madame Tussaud's wax museum and chamber of horrors in London;; see *Obras*, V, 813; VII, 770, 1109.
30. *Obras*, IV, 239-41. The ode is the work of the imaginary poet Julius Petrus Guzenhausen of Aschaffenburg.
31. For *Las figuras de cera* alone, Corpus Barga has estimated the number of characters at 135. See Baeza, II, 140.
32. See *Obras*, IV, 233, for a hallucinatory description of the group.
33. *Ibid.*, 565.
34. Regalado García, "Verdugos y ejecutados," sees the Conde de España novels as an indictment of brutality, a point of view I find difficult to share.
35. In 1931 Baroja published his biography of Aviraneta, *Aviraneta o la vida de un conspirador;* two years later he wrote another biography entitled *Juan Van Halen, el oficial aventurero.*
36. Cf. *Obras*, VI, 1026-27; V, 101-6.
37. *Obras*, VII, 673.
38. *Ibid.*, V, 173.
39. See above, Chapter 3.
40. *Obras*, V, 116-20.
41. *Ibid.*, 189.
42. *Ibid.*, 117.
43. *Ibid.*, 231.
44. *Ibid.*, 293
45. *Ibid.*, 263-82.
46. *Ibid.*, 259.
47. "El español no se entera," *Obras*, V, 100-101.
48. *Obras*, V, 366.
49. *Momentum Catastrophicum* is, for the most part, an anti-separatist tract.
50. *Obras*, II, 882.
51. He was born *por casualidad* in Cádiz.
52. He reads Nietzsche as a diversion, to lift his spirits. See *Obras*, II, 947.
53. *Ibid.*, 888-89.
54. Antonio Machado, *Los complementarios* (Buenos Aires, 1957), p. 53.
55. *Obras*, II, 894.
56. When La Sátur offers herself to him, he notes her physical defects and refuses her invitation. See *Obras*, II, 952 ff.
57. *Ibid.*, 918-19. Murguía cannot consider marrying one María

Nájera; she is rich and he is not.

58. *Ibid.*, VII, 652.

59. *Ibid.*, 939 ff.; II, 960 ff. Baroja gives the year of this meeting as 1913.

60. Juan Huarte de San Juan, *Examen de ingenios para las ciencias* (Buenos Aires, 1946), pp. 111, 126.

61. *Obras,* V, 170-71.

62. *Ibid.*, II, 994.

63. Cf. *ibid.*, 848; VII, 411.

64. Baeza, *Baroja y su mundo,* I, Plate 116. In *La caverna del humorismo, Obras,* V, 462, Baroja points out the baldness of many of the fauns and satyrs on Greek vases.

65. Cf. *Obras,* II, 932-33; VII, 708-9. In VII, 724, Baroja rebuts the charge that the Paris he described in *La sensualidad pervertida* was the Paris of Eugene Sue. It was, he maintains, simply the city as seen by a man with neither money nor influence.

66. *Obras,* VII, 964, 1250; V, 661-62. In the *Paseos,* p. 199, Baroja refers to him again, this time as Alfredito.

67. *Obras,* II, 956. The suggestion is made by Murguía's practical cousin Joshé Mari.

68. *Ibid.*, 989.

69. *Ibid.*, 858.

70. It may be noted in passing that O'Neil suffers from neuralgic pains and insomnia.

71. See, for example, "El gran Pan ha muerto," *Obras,* II, 1281; "La canción de los hijos de Aitor," II, 1302.

72. *Obras,* VIII, 742.

73. *Ibid.*, VII, 1273.

74. *Ibid.*, II, 1363.

75. At one point in *La estrella del capitán Chimista,* Chimista practices homeopathic medicine in Cuba under the name of Dr. Temple. See *Obras,* VI, 146.

76. Alberich, *El tema de los ingleses,* pp. 175 ff.

77. Sender, *Los noventayochos,* p. 128.

78. Victor Brombert, *Stendhal: Fiction and the Themes of Freedom* (New York, 1968), p. 95.

79. *Obras,* I, 1053.

80. *Ibid.*, 1182.

81. *Ibid.*, 1085.

82. *Ibid.*, 1260.

83. *Ibid.*, 1149.

84. *Ibid.*, 1262.

85. *Ibid.*, 1215; on p. 1261 he classifies himself as an agnostic.

86. The lacunae include, for example, Tristan and Isolde.

87. *Obras,* I, 1151.

88. In *El nocturno del hermano Beltrán,* VI, 1213, Petersen refers to Lenin as a "wise gnome" who would have ultimately turned against Communism.

89. *Obras*, I, 1372.

90. The shield above this emblem represents a *noria* or chain pump, with water buckets alternately empty and full. See I, 1376, epigraph to Chapter IX.

91. *Obras*, I, 1364. Emilia Pardo Bazán had once commented that Baroja was sensual rather than intellectual. See V, 48.

92. *Obras*, I, 1057.

93. *Ibid.*, 1331.

94. Søren Kierkegaard, *Fear and Trembling* (New York, 1954), p. 54, asserts that without a single act of consciousness, without concentration, one "will be constantly running errands in life."

95. Baeza, I, Plate 131; *Memorias*, p. 1335.

96. Cf. *Obras*, VI, 1210-11; VII, 936-38.

97. Isidoro de Fagoaga, *Unamuno a orillas del Bidasoa y otros ensayos* (San Sebastián, 1964), p. 106, notes that Baroja was in the habit of interrogating his interlocutor with an endless string of questions.

98. *Obras*, VI, 1208-9.

99. *Ibid.*, 750.

100. When Olarán begins to lose his hair, his diagnosis is sexual abstinence; the ghost of Andrés Hurtado hovers near.

101. *Obras*, VI, 804.

102. Elena Soriano accepts at face value the reasons given by Baroja for Javier's loss of faith. These same reasons, however, could just as well have strengthened his faith. For Soriano's views, see Baeza, I, 220.

103. *Obras*, VI, 637.

104. *Ibid.*, VII, 775-76. Aside from such reworkings of real episodes, there are disconcerting tag lines included in *Las noches del Buen Retiro* left over, as it were, from such novels as *Camino de perfección* and *El árbol de la ciencia*. Cf. the anecdotes in VI, 662-63 and VI, 19; Dr. Guevara, who warns Thierry of the dangers of *un ambiente demasiado oxigenado* is quoting Don Ramón Torres Muñoz de Luna. Cf. II, 450; VI, 634.

105. This pair bears a striking resemblance to Larrañaga and Pepita; as she flourishes, her lover wanes.

106. *Obras*, V, 863 ff.; included in *Rapsodias* (1936) along with thirteen other essays.

107. *Obras*, V, 881.

108. *Ibid.*, 868. Baroja accepts a materialistic, deterministic approach to science but considers such philosophies of no value in understanding history. See V, 884.

109. The image of the huntsman appears first in *Camino de perfección, Obras*, VI, 44.

110. *Obras*, V, 567-84.

111. See *Vitrina pintoresca, Obras*, V, 842, in which Baroja wonders why everyone talks so much about the Generation of 1898 which he is convinced never existed. Cf. too V, 898; VII, 445 ff.

112. *Obras*, V, 575.

113. *Ibid.*, 671-74.

114. In "Los demonios del carnaval," *Obras*, V, 819-23, Baroja recalls an episode going back thirty-five years, in which he and a friend, upon seeing a man lying on the pavement in the early hours of the morning, ran away without stopping to investigate if they could be of help. The pattern of flight is persistent, if not incomprehensible, for Baroja was, after all, a doctor.

115. *Obras*, V, 844.

116. *Camino de perfección*, ed. Juan Uribe Echevarría (Santiago de Chile, 1963), p. 33.

117. *Obras*, VII, 16.

118. García Mercadal, *Baroja en el banquillo*, II, 113.

119. *Obras*, VII, 179.

120. Baroja identifies many of them in *Obras*, VII, 827, 1336-39. See Pérez Ferrero, *Vida*, p. 265.

121. For a different view of these dreams, see Luis Granjel, *Baroja y otras figuras del 98* (Madrid, 1960), pp. 57-83. This section is subtitled "Retrato onírico de Pío Baroja."

122. Not included in *Obras;* see *Memorias*, pp. 965 ff.

123. Sender, p. 124.

124. Baeza, II, 250.

125. See *Obras*, VIII, 998, 996, 981, 988, 991, 999, 1028-31.

126. *Ibid.*, 1042.

127. See *ibid.*, V, 176; VII, 1039; IV, 308, 309 for the first view, and V, 844; VII, 452, 1061, 1063, 1084, 812, 880, 881 for the latter two.

128. *Ibid.*, VII, 452.

129. *Ibid.*, 1093.

130. Camilo José Cela, *Cuatro figuras del 98* (Barcelona, 1961), p. 33.

131. *Obras*, VII, 1310, 1124, 277.

132. *Ibid.*, 1051, 1307; VIII, 435, 1114; *Memorias*, p. 1006.

133. *Obras*, VII, 801.

134. The statement in V, 416, that *todo fluye, todo cambia* can be counterbalanced by Thierry's statement, VI, 631, to the effect that *Siempre es lo mismo; no se cambia nada.*

135. *Obras*, VIII, 482.

136. *Ibid.*, 596.

137. Cf. *ibid.*, 568, 535.

138. Nallim, *El problema de la novela*, p. 252; six works are listed on pp. 251-52, including *Ayer y hoy*.

Chapter Seven

1. Sender, *Los noventayochos*, p. 130, has said of the author: *Va a todas partes y sin embargo no entra.*

2. Cela, *Cuatro figuras*, p. 32, has seen this clearly.

3. *Obras,* VI, 395.

4. Huarte de San Juan, *Examen,* p. 68.

5. Baroja, *Ayer y hoy,* p. 149.

6. Baeza, *Baroja y su mundo,* I, 66.

7. See the articles by Elorza and Martínez Laínez in *Rev. de Occidente,* XXI (May, 1968), for example, for a closer approach to the realities.

8. Cela, p. 55.

Selected Bibliography

PRIMARY SOURCES

A Partial Listing of Baroja's Works, in Order of Publication:

Vidas sombrías (Madrid: Miguel de Pereda, 1900).
La casa de Aizgorri (Bilbao: Fermín Herrán, 1900).
Aventuras, inventos y mixtificaciones de Silvestre Paradox (Madrid: Rodríguez Serra, 1901).
Camino de perfección (Madrid: Rodríguez Serra, 1902).
El mayorazgo de Labraz (Barcelona: Heinrich y Cía., 1903).
La busca (Madrid: Fernando Fe, 1904).
Mala hierba (Madrid: Fernando Fe, 1904).
El tablado de Arlequín (Valencia: Sempere, 1904).
Aurora roja (Madrid: Fernando Fe, 1904).
La feria de los discretos (Madrid: Fernando Fe, 1905).
Paradox, Rey (Madrid: Hernando, 1906).
Los últimos románticos (Madrid: Hernando, 1906).
Las tragedias grotescas (Madrid: Hernando, 1907).
La dama errante (Madrid: Hernando, 1908).
La ciudad de la niebla (Madrid: Hernando, 1909).
Zalacaín el aventurero (Barcelona: Domenech, 1909).
César o nada (Madrid: Renacimiento, 1910).
Las inquietudes de Shanti Andía (Madrid: Renacimiento, 1911).
El árbol de la ciencia (Madrid: Renacimiento, 1911).
El mundo es ansí (Madrid: Renacimiento, 1912).
El aprendiz de conspirador (Madrid: Renacimiento, 1913).
El escuadrón del Brigante (Madrid: Renacimiento, 1913).
Los caminos del mundo (Madrid: Renacimiento, 1914).
Con la pluma y con el sable (Madrid: Renacimiento, 1915).
Los recursos de la astucia (Madrid: Renacimiento, 1915).
La ruta del aventurero (Madrid: Renacimiento, 1916).
Nuevo tablado de Arlequín (Madrid: Caro Raggio, 1917).
Juventud, egolatría (Madrid: Caro Raggio, 1917).
La veleta de Gastizar (Madrid: Caro Raggio, 1918).
Los caudillos de 1830 (Madrid: Caro Raggio, 1918).
Idilios y fantasías (Madrid: Caro Raggio, 1918).
Las horas solitarias (Madrid: Caro Raggio, 1918).
Páginas escogidas (Madrid: Editorial Calleja, 1918): For Baroja's prologues to his own works (Not all of these prologues were later included in the *Obras completas*).
Momentum catastrophicum (Madrid: Caro Raggio, 1919).

196

La caverna del humorismo (Madrid: Caro Raggio, 1919).
La Isabelina (Madrid: Caro Raggio, 1919).
Divagaciones sobre la cultura (Madrid: Caro Raggio, 1920).
Los contrastes de la vida (Madrid: Caro Raggio, 1920).
La sensualidad pervertida (Madrid: Caro Raggio, 1920).
El sabor de la venganza (Madrid: Caro Raggio, 1921).
Las furias (Madrid: Caro Raggio, 1921).
La leyenda de Jaun de Alzate (Madrid: Caro Raggio, 1922).
El amor, el dandismo y la intriga (Madrid: Caro Raggio, 1922).
El laberinto de las sirenas (Madrid: Caro Raggio, 1923).
Divagaciones apasionadas (Madrid: Caro Raggio, 1924).
Las figuras de cera (Madrid: Caro Raggio, 1924).
La nave de los locos (Madrid: Caro Raggio, 1925).
Las veleidades de la fortuna (Madrid: Caro Raggio, 1926).
El gran torbellino del mundo (Madrid: Caro Raggio, 1926).
Los amores tardíos (Madrid: Caro Raggio, 1927).
Las mascaradas sangrientas (Madrid: Caro Raggio, 1927).
Humano enigma (Madrid: Caro Raggio, 1928).
La senda dolorosa (Madrid: Caro Raggio, 1928).
Los pilotos de altura (Madrid: Caro Raggio, 1929).
La estrella del Capitán Chimista (Madrid: Caro Raggio, 1930).
Los confidentes audaces (Madrid: Espasa-Calpe, 1930).
Intermedios (Madrid: Espasa-Calpe, 1931).
Aviraneta o la vida de un conspirador (Madrid: Espasa-Calpe, 1931).
La familia de Errotacho (Madrid: Espasa-Calpe, 1932).
El cabo de las tormentas (Madrid: Espasa-Calpe, 1932).
Los visionarios (Madrid: Espasa-Calpe, 1932).
Juan Van Halen, el oficial aventurero (Madrid: Espasa-Calpe, 1933).
Las noches del Buen Retiro (Madrid: Espasa-Calpe, 1934).
Siluetas románticas y otras historias de pillos y extravagantes (Madrid: Espasa-Calpe, 1934).
Vitrina pintoresca (Madrid: Espasa-Calpe, 1935).
Crónica escandalosa (Madrid: Espasa-Calpe, 1935).
Desde el principio hasta el fin (Madrid: Espasa-Calpe, 1935).
El cura de Monleón (Madrid: Espasa-Calpe, 1936).
Rapsodias (Madrid: Espasa-Calpe, 1936).
Locuras de carnaval (Madrid: Espasa-Calpe, 1937).
Ayer y hoy (Santiago de Chile: Ediciones Ercilla, 1939).
Laura o la soledad sin remedio (Buenos Aires: Editorial Sudamericana, 1939).
Historias lejanas (Santiago de Chile: Ercilla, 1939).
Los impostores joviales (Madrid: Hesperia, 1941).
El caballero de Erlaiz (Madrid: La Nave, 1943).
Pequeños ensayos (Buenos Aires: Sudamericana, 1943).
Canciones del suburbio (Madrid: Biblioteca Nueva, 1944).
El escritor según él y según los críticos (Madrid: Biblioteca Nueva, 1944).
Familia, infancia y juventud (Madrid: Biblioteca Nueva, 1944).

Final del siglo XIX y principios del XX (Madrid: Biblioteca Nueva, 1945).

El puente de las ánimas (Madrid: La Nave, 1945).

El Hotel del Cisne (Madrid: Biblioteca Nueva, 1946).

Galería de tipos de la época (Madrid: Biblioteca Nueva, 1947).

La intuición y el estilo (Madrid: Biblioteca Nueva, 1948).

Los enigmáticos (Madrid: Biblioteca Nueva, 1948).

Reportajes (Madrid: Biblioteca Nueva, 1948).

Bagatelas de otoño (Madrid: Biblioteca Nueva, 1949).

Ciudades de Italia (Madrid: Biblioteca Nueva, 1949).

El cantor vagabundo (Madrid: Biblioteca Nueva, 1950).

Obras completas. 8 vols. (Madrid: Biblioteca Nueva, 1946-1951). Contains the important novels, theatre, poetry, and essays up to 1951. Vol. VII contains the *Memorias* "Desde la última vuelta del camino," which comprises *El escritor según él y según los críticos, Familia, infancia y juventud, Final del siglo XIX y principios del XX, Galería de tipos de la época, La intuición y el estilo, Reportajes,* and *Bagatelas de otoño.*

Los amores de Antonio y Cristina (Madrid: Col. "La novela del sábado," año 1, núm. 5, 1953).

El país vasco (Barcelona: Destino, 1953).

Los contrabandistas vascos (Madrid: Biblioteca Nueva, 1954).

Memorias (Madrid: Minotauro, 1955). Contains *Infancia, adolescencia, juventud, Final del siglo XIX y principios del XX, Galería de tipos de la época, Conversaciones en París el año 39, Nuevamente en París, El escritor según él y según los críticos.*

Paseos de un solitario (Madrid: Biblioteca Nueva, 1955).

Aquí, París (Madrid: Grifon, 1955).

La obra de Pablo Yarza y algunas otras cosas (Madrid: Espasa-Calpe, 1956).

SECONDARY SOURCES

1. Books

ALBERICH, JOSÉ. *Los ingleses y otros temas de Pío Baroja* (Madrid: Alfaguara, 1966). A good collection of essays on diverse aspects of Baroja and his art.

ARBÓ, SEBASTIÁN JUAN. *Pío Baroja y su tiempo* (Barcelona: Planeta, 1963). A mammoth work marred by a discursive, anecdotal approach.

AZORÍN (JOSÉ MARTÍNEZ RUIZ). *Ante Baroja* (Zaragoza: Librería General, 1946). Essays on individual works, more lyrical than critical.

————. *La voluntad* (Madrid: Biblioteca Nueva, n.d.). For a portrayal of Baroja as the fictional Enrique Olaiz.

BAEZA, FERNANDO, ed. *Baroja y su mundo.* 2 vols. plus supplement (Madrid: Arion, 1961). I, 325-89, contains an extensive bibliography compiled by Jorge Campos, as follows: Primary Sources,

325-30; Translations, 330-33; Secondary Sources, 334-77; Contributions to Periodicals, 381-89. This same volume contains also valuable iconography and biography. Both I and II include articles and essays of unequal merit on the author and his works. The supplement, "Apéndices a *Baroja y su mundo*," provides an index of characters (incomplete but useful) and a thematic index.

BALSEIRO, JOSÉ AGUSTÍN. *Blasco Ibáñez, Unamuno, Valle-Inclán y Baroja, cuatro individualistas de España* (Chapel Hill: University of North Carolina Press, 1949). Interesting sidelights on Baroja vis-à-vis Unamuno and Valle-Inclán.

BALLESTEROS BERETTA, ANTONIO. *Síntesis de historia de España* (Barcelona: Salvat, 1936). Relatively brief and very useful handbook of Spanish history.

BARJA, CÉSAR. *Libros y autores contemporáneos* (New York: G. E. Stechert and Company, 1935). The section on Baroja, pp. 299-359, is still one of the finest and most perceptive studies to date.

BAROJA, RICARDO. *Gente del 98* (Barcelona: Juventud, 1952). Impressionistic descriptions of the artist's contemporaries.

CARO BAROJA, JULIO. *La soledad de Pío Baroja* (México: Ed. Pío Caro Baroja, 1953). On the declining years of the novelist.

CASTILLO PUCHE, JOSÉ LUIS. *Memorias íntimas de Aviraneta* (Madrid: Biblioteca Nueva, 1952). Aviraneta as seen by an unsympathetic observer.

CELA, CAMILO JOSÉ. *Cuatro figuras del 98* (Barcelona: Aedos, 1961). A brief but penetrating appreciation of Baroja.

DEVLIN, JOHN. *Spanish Anticlericalism* (New York: Las Américas, 1966). The section devoted to Baroja, pp. 123-33, is a not entirely accurate summary of the novelist's anticlerical views.

EOFF, SHERMAN H. *The Modern Spanish Novel* (New York: New York University Press, 1961). Contains a suggestive study of *Zalacaín el aventurero* in Bergsonian terms.

FAGOAGA, ISIDORO DE. *Unamuno a orillas del Bidasoa y otros ensayos* (San Sebastián: Auñamendi, 1964). Some personal reminiscences plus notes on Baroja as reader and critic, pp. 103-83.

FLORES ARROYUELO, FRANCISCO J. *Las primeras novelas de Pío Baroja* (Espinardo-Murcia: La torre de los vientos, 1967). Uncritical study of the novels through 1912.

GAOS, VICENTE. *Temas y problemas de literatura española* (Madrid: Guadarrama, 1959). Excellent study of Baroja as an essayist and as a Kantian, pp. 237-51.

GARCÍA MERCADAL, JOSÉ, ed. *Baroja en el banquillo*: Antología crítica. 2 vols. (Zaragoza: Librería General, [1947-1948]). Vol. I contains articles on Baroja written by Spaniards, Vol. II consists of articles by foreigners. The pieces are of varying quality.

GOBINEAU, ARTHUR DE. *The Inequality of Human Races*, trans. by Adrian Collins (London: William Heinemann, 1915). For the genesis of some of Baroja's ideas on race.

GONZÁLEZ-RUANO, CÉSAR. *Mi medio siglo se confiesa a medias* (Barcelona: Noguer, 1951). Useful for providing a general, if subjective, view of Baroja's period.

GRANJEL, LUIS S. *Retrato de Pío Baroja* (Barcelona: Barna, 1953). Well-balanced study of Baroja from virtually all important aspects.

————. *Panorama de la generación del 98* (Madrid: Guadarrama, 1959). Background on the Generation plus selections from Baroja, Azorín, *et al.*, and from various critics.

————. *Baroja y otras figuras del 98* (Madrid: Guadarrama, 1960). Of particular interest for a section entitled "La personalidad médica de Pío Baroja," pp. 17-51.

IGLESIAS, CARMEN. *El pensamiento de Pío Baroja* (México: Antigua Librería Robredo, 1963). Sympathetic, sensitive analysis of Baroja's ideology.

KAUFMANN, WALTER. *The Portable Nietzsche* (New York: Viking Press, 1954).

————. *Nietzsche* (Cleveland: The World Publishing Company, 1966). Helpful towards a study of the influence of Nietzsche on Baroja.

LAÍN ENTRALGO, PEDRO. *La generación del 98* (Madrid: Espasa-Calpe, 1956). Indispensable for background of the Generation of 1898.

————. *España como problema* (Madrid: Aguilar, 1957). A classic. *La generación del 98* is included as part of this work.

LÓPEZ MORILLAS, JUAN. *El krausismo español* (México: Fondo de cultura económica, 1956). For some philosophical antecedents of the Generation of 1898.

NALLIM, CARLOS ORLANDO. *El problema de la novela en Pío Baroja* (México: Ateneo, 1964). Very detailed studies of some of the major novels, including extensive summaries.

NORA, EUGENIO G. DE. *La novela española contemporánea.* 3 vols. (Madrid: Gredos, 1963). I, 97-229, contains summaries and critical comments on Baroja's novels. Not adulatory.

NORDAU, MAX. *Degeneration,* trans. from the second edition of *Entartung* (New York: Appleton and Company, 1895). Bible of fin-de-siècle "degeneracy."

ORTEGA Y GASSET, JOSÉ. *Obras completas* (Madrid: Revista de Occidente, 1963). Vol. II contains the extremely influential "Ideas sobre Pío Baroja" and "Una primera vista sobre Baroja."

————. *Meditaciones del Quijote* (Madrid: Espasa-Calpe, 1964). Contains *Ideas sobre la novela,* pp. 159-214, an anti-Barojian view of the novelistic art.

PELAY OROZCO, MIGUEL. *La ruta de Baroja* (Bilbao: Sendo, 1962). Some personal reminiscences, but no critical apparatus. Interesting mostly for emphasis on Baroja as a Basque.

PÉREZ FERRERO, MIGUEL. *Pío Baroja en su rincón* (San Sebastián: Internacional, 1941).

————. *Vida de Pío Baroja* (Barcelona: Destino, 1960). Biographies by Baroja's Boswell.

REID, JOHN T. *Modern Spain and Liberalism* (Stanford: Stanford University Press, 1937). Baroja's political attitudes are well summarized on pp. 60-138.

SCHOPENHAUER, ARTHUR. *On Human Nature*, trans. by Thomas Bailey Saunders (Aberdeen: The University Press, 1957).

————. *Essays of Schopenhauer*, ed. Mrs. Rudolf Dircks (London: Walter Scott Publishing Company, n.d.).

————. *The World as Will and Idea*, trans. by R. B. Haldane and J. Kemp (New York: Doubleday and Company, 1961). The last three volumes named are helpful in determining Baroja's borrowings from Schopenhauer.

SENDER, RAMÓN J. *Los noventayochos* (New York: Las Américas, 1961). Acute, highly critical analysis of certain aspects of Baroja's psychology.

SERRANO PONCELA, SEGUNDO. *El secreto de Melibea y otros ensayos* (Madrid: Taurus, 1959). The essay "Eros y tres misóginos," pp. 139-67, is, in part, a contribution to the myth of Baroja's misogyny.

SMITH, RHEA MARSH. *Spain, a Modern History* (Ann Arbor: University of Michigan Press, 1965). A valuable reference work

SOBEJANO, GONZALO. *Forma literaria y sensibilidad social* (Madrid: Gredos, 1967). Excellent observations on the sensibility and attitudes of the members of the Generation of 1898.

————. *Nietzsche en España* (Madrid: Gredos, 1967). An indispensable study, with an important section on Baroja, pp. 347-95.

TOLSTOY, LEO. *What is Art*, trans. by Aylmer Maude (London: Oxford University Press, 1959). An anti-aesthetic tract.

ZUNZUNEGUI, JUAN ANTONIO. *En torno a D. Pío Baroja y su obra* (Bilbao: Publicaciones de la Excma. Diputación de Vizcaya, 1960). Zunzunegui's address on the occasion of his reception into the Royal Spanish Academy. Highly encomiastic remarks on Baroja's art.

2. Articles

(A minimal listing. The reader is referred to the collections of essays and articles in Baeza, *Baroja y su mundo*, García Mercadal, *Baroja en el banquillo*, as well as to the extensive bibliography listed in Baeza, I, 339-77. Articles of particular interest reproduced in *Baroja y su mundo* or in *Baroja en el banquillo* are noted below).

BATAILLON, MARCEL. "Para la biografía de un héroe de novela," *Baroja en el banquillo*, II, 149-52. On the denunciation of Aviraneta to the Inquisition by a nun.

CARO BAROJA, JULIO. "Recuerdos," *Baroja y su mundo*, I, 35-73. An intimate memoir of the novelist by his nephew.

CORRALES EGEA, JOSÉ. "De *La sensualidad pervertida* a *La estrella del Capitán Chimista*," *Baroja y su mundo*, I, 183-206. A critical, rather hostile, study.

DÍAZ DE LEÓN DE RECASÉNS, MARTHA. "Dos ensayos sobre Pío

Baroja," *Cuadernos Americanos*, XCI (enero-febrero, 1957), 71-106. Contains some interesting observations on the mixed ethnic origins of Baroja's men of action.

DUNN, PETER N. "Baroja y Valle-Inclán: la razón de un plagio," *Revista Hispánica Moderna*, XXXIII (1967), 30-37. Some of Valle-Inclán's borrowings from his contemporary.

DURÁN, MANUEL. "Silverio Lanza y Silvestre Paradox," *Papeles de Son Armadans*, XXXIV (julio, 1964), 57-72. Silverio Lanza as a model for Paradox.

ELORZA, ANTONIO. "El realismo crítico de Pío Baroja," *Revista de Occidente*, XXI (mayo, 1968), 151-73. A measured appraisal of Baroja's political views.

FERNÁNDEZ ALMAGRO, MELCHOR. "Pío Baroja," *Baroja y su mundo*, II, 316-21. In praise of the novelistic art of Baroja.

FOX, E. INMAN. "Baroja and Schopenhauer," *Revue de littérature comparée*, XXXVII (1963), 350-59. Brief analysis of Baroja in Schopenhauerian terms, with emphasis on *El árbol de la ciencia*.

GARCÍA-LUENGO, EUSEBIO. "El alma de Baroja," *Baroja y su mundo*, II, 333-38. On the egolatry and fanaticism of Baroja.

LLORIS, MANUEL. "Baroja, presunto escritor misógino," *Revista Hispánica Moderna*, XXXIII (1967), 293-98. The author offers a refutation of the popular view of Baroja as a misogynist.

MARAÑÓN, GREGORIO. "Contestación al discurso de ingreso de Don Pío Baroja en la Academia Española," *Baroja y su mundo*, II, 213-22. A defense of Baroja's much-maligned style.

MARAVALL, JOSÉ ANTONIO. "Historia y novela," *Baroja y su mundo*, I, 162-82. An excellent study of Baroja and his historical novels.

MARTÍNEZ LAÍNEZ, FERNANDO. "El sentimiento político de Pío Baroja," *Revista de Occidente*, XXI (mayo, 1968), 185-203. Baroja as a conservative.

REGALADO GARCÍA, ANTONIO. "Verdugos y ejecutados en las novelas de Pío Baroja," *Papeles de Son Armadans*, XLI (abril, 1966), 9-29. Baroja as a humanitarian opponent of capital punishment.

TEMPLIN, E. H. "Pío Baroja: Three Pivotal Concepts," *Hispanic Review*, XII (1944), 306-29. On the novelist as a collector and a classifier.

———. "Pío Baroja and Science," *Hispanic Review*, XV (1947), 165-92. Baroja on medicine, anthropology, psychology, and other branches of science.

VAZ DE SOTO, JOSÉ MARÍA. "El ejemplo de Baroja," *Revista de Occidente*, XXI (mayo, 1968), 174-83. Traditional view of the novelist as a simple, honest man.

VÁZQUEZ ZAMORA, RAFAEL. "Cuentos y novelas cortas," *Baroja y su mundo*, I, 77-91. Appreciation of Baroja's style from *Vidas sombrías* to *Los amores de Antonio y Cristina*. Not overly critical.

Index

(The works of Baroja are listed under his name)

8 2 5 6 7

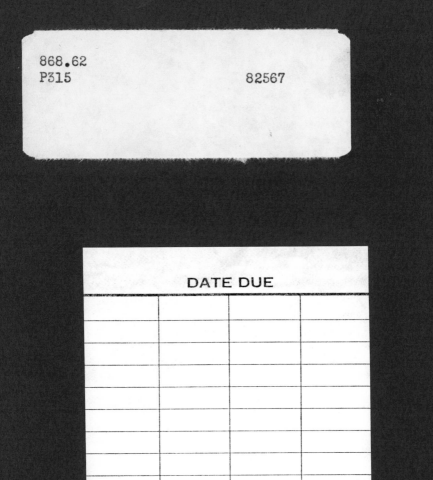

DATE DUE